Regional Cases in U.S. Foreign Policy

Second Edition

Donald M. Snow
Emeritus, University of Alabama

ROWMAN & LITTLEFIELD

Lanham • Boulder • New York • London

Executive Editor: Traci Crowell
Assistant Editor: Mary Malley
Marketing Manager: Deborah Hudson
Cover Designer: Neil D. Cotterill

Credits and acknowledgments borrowed from other sources and reproduced, with permission, in this textbook appear on appropriate page within the text.

Published by Rowman & Littlefield
A wholly owned subsidiary of The Rowman & Littlefield Publishing Group, Inc.
4501 Forbes Boulevard, Suite 200, Lanham, Maryland 20706
www.rowman.com

Unit A, Whitacre Mews, 26-34 Stannary Street, London SE11 4AB

British Library Cataloguing in Publication Information Available

Library of Congress Cataloging-in-Publication Data Available

ISBN 978-1-4422-6819-7 (cloth : alk. paper)
ISBN 978-1-4422-6820-3 (pbk. : alk. paper)
ISBN 978-1-4422-6821-0 (electronic)

∞™ The paper used in this publication meets the minimum requirements of American National Standard for Information Sciences—Permanence of Paper for Printed Library Materials, ANSI/NISO Z39.48-1992.

Printed in the United States of America

Contents

Introduction

The Case for Cases

The conduct of foreign policy occurs at different levels, and so does its study. The levels are arranged roughly hierarchically, from the broadest and necessarily most general level to the application in specific instances in particular places. One can approach understanding foreign policy from any level, but that understanding is incomplete if one does not look at each level and at the relationship between them.

This hierarchy can be thought of as having three levels that are more distinct analytically than they often are in practice. At the broadest, most macro level, it is possible to talk about general, overarching principles on which a country's policy is based. This level, sometimes known as grand national strategy, articulates the broadest view of how a country views itself in the world, and which of its national values it most wants to promote or protect in a world that is not uniformly amenable to those values. For the United States, for instance, the most basic values include the protection of its soil from hostile outsiders, the promotion of American values such as democracy and self-determination for itself and others (at least those who share American basic orientations), and the ability of Americans to interact with and prosper in the world environment. These values come into play as a guide to policy when someone challenges American ideals and attempts to thwart their realization generally or in specific places and instances.

At the level of grand strategy, there is consensus about their content. Virtually no Americans disagree that American safety must be ensured in the world, and when the country faces a clear, pervasive challenge to American values, the country will normally respond with virtual unanimity. The Cold War challenge of communism was such a challenge, and the response, the national strategy of containment, was consensually agreed as the appropriate national response. The same is largely true of the challenge currently posed by radical Islamic terrorism.

Foreign policy becomes more complicated and often more controversial as one moves from broad principles to their application in the world environment, which occurs at the other two levels of policy. The intermediary level attempts to apply basic principles to various parts of the world. Because different parts of the world have different values and interests, the basic complication is how to confront challenges to American proclivities and preferences in those states and areas where American interests and those in the region may not coincide or may even collide. In these instances, there is often disagreement about policy, some of which can become rancorous within both the domestic political context and with regional actors.

Controversy arises from different sources. One is that there is honest disagreement on the basic orientation the country should take to different crises in different situations. In contemporary American terms, these are often divided into military and nonmilitary options; differences about how to deal with Middle Eastern terrorism are a prime example. At the same time, no geographic region is monolithic, and this means that a regional application of a policy preference to one place may be inappropriate or counterproductive in another situation. Sometimes the disagreements at this level can become very animated and be informed by very different perspectives and even levels of knowledge and expertise. There has been, for instance, a great deal of political disagreement about how the United States should deal with the threat posed by the Islamic State in Syria and Iraq and spreading elsewhere (some of which I discuss in the pages that follow). The arguments are often based on different understandings of the threat and the situation, and thus on appropriate ways to confront it. In these kinds of circumstances, it is not unusual for one side to accuse the other either of having an incorrect approach to the problem or no policy at all. Much of this kind of rhetoric is dismissible in serious consideration of problems.

There is a third and more specific level of foreign policy application that focuses on the bilateral relationships among specific states and that is often ignored or downplayed in more grandiose, general treatments of the subject. This micro level is, in some important ways, where most foreign policy takes place in the bilateral relations between the governments of countries. It is often ignored or downplayed in general treatments of foreign policy, because so much of international relations at this level is less dramatic than broader foreign policy concerns, but in many important ways, it is where real foreign policy takes place. Much of this level of activity is relatively mundane—issuing passports or helping American citizens in foreign countries—but some of it is the very heart of American interaction with the world. Broad policy pronouncements offer some guidance and direction to bilateral relationships, but these are leavened by the peculiar circumstances of states, including their problems and the incompatibility of particular American policy positions and those of foreign lands. Broad policy preferences gain their meaning in the context of specific application to individual countries, and an understanding of foreign policy and the foreign policy process is self-limited when those specific points of interaction are not examined. Macro and intermediate foreign policy levels provide the broad brushstrokes on the canvas of foreign policy; microlevel bilateral interactions fill in the details.

Providing the kinds of details that complete the picture of foreign policy is the heart of the case for case studies, which is the content of this volume. It is a level of analysis that fairly infrequently finds its way onto syllabi or lecture series, because there is a great deal of material that can be covered in a one- or even two-semester sequence on the subject. Likewise, no course can devote its entire emphasis to the micro level of analysis without running the risk of examining so many trees that it forgets the trees are part of a forest.

This slender volume attempts to provide a vehicle to inject some microlevel material into the American foreign policy course by providing a series of case studies that can be inserted at appropriate points in a course and that provide the reader with useful information on American relations toward individually interesting places and situations in the world. It consists of seven chapters, each of which is devoted to a region of the world in which the United States conducts significant foreign policy. Each chapter, in turn, features case treatments of American interaction with two different countries in that region. The same internal structure is used in each chapter to facilitate the ability to compare policy interactions across as well as in particular regions.

In assembling the table of contents, I used three criteria to select what was included and what was not. The first criterion was regional inclusiveness. Thus, there are chapters devoted to all the inhabited continents of the world except Australia, with which the United States enjoys uniformly positive, noncontroversial relations. Thus, if an instructor wants to use these cases to illustrate points on a regional basis, cases addressing all the continents are available. Second, the cases for individual regions were chosen based on their importance, including controversy, in current and ongoing American policy. Some parts of the world are, quite simply, more important to the United States than others, either for historic or interest reasons, or because what is happening in them occupies more American time. Two chapters are, for instance, devoted to the Middle East for this reason. Parts of the Middle East are important to the United States for geopolitical reasons, chief among which tends to be that they possess petroleum in large quantities; others are important because they pose a particular threat such as being the source of terrorist threats. The third criterion is representativeness, trying to choose instances that are both of high salience but also that, individually or in tandem, are also typical of the kinds of problems and orientations the United States has toward different places.

Choosing appropriate cases was the most difficult task I faced in constructing this volume, and I realize that not all those who read the table of contents will be fully in agreement with all my choices. I realize that area specialists may argue that the criterion of representation of regions is an Achilles' heel of sorts, particularly Latin America and Africa. There is no South American case, because I chose to highlight two highly topical countries, Mexico and Cuba, rather than South American states to which not as much policy controversy attaches. The same criticism can be made of the chapter on Africa. There are fifty-two independent states on that continent, many of which are confronted with similar problems of multinationalism or ethnic and religious division. Choosing two was somewhat arbitrary, based on the level of complexity and controversy of one (the two Sudanese states) or size and foreign policy salience (Nigeria). Two of the studies, the Islamic State and the European Union, are not about states at all. Reviewers offered alternative suggestions, but all of them could not be accommodated without changing this slender supplementary volume into what I think would have been an unwieldy tome.

This volume seeks to serve as a supplement to comprehensive foreign policy textbooks by providing a compact and readable complement to them. More specifically, it has been designed to augment Donald M. Snow and Patrick J. Haney's *U.S. Foreign Policy: Back to the Water's Edge*, fifth edition, also published by Rowman & Littlefield. The Snow/Haney text provides three major points of emphasis common to other texts: the historical background of American foreign policy, the institutions through which it is made and implemented, and functional problems facing overall policy. As such, it is aimed primarily at the macro and intermediate levels of policy; *Regional Cases in U.S. Foreign Policy* provides more microlevel analysis illustrating contemporary policy as a complement to the general text. It should serve the same purpose for other texts as well.

As already noted, the book is divided into seven chapters. Each chapter begins with a brief regional overview, followed by two case applications. Each "mini" case is arranged in the same format, including overviews of the country, basic American policy toward it, and American options in dealing with it. There is a brief concluding section in each chapter, followed by discussion and study questions and a bibliography of sources either cited in the text or germane in obtaining additional information about its contents.

Chapters 1 and 2 examine aspects of the Middle East, because so much of contemporary U.S. foreign policy is directed at this complex and contentious part of the world. Chapter 1 examines the ongoing situation in the Levant, with emphases on the threat posed to the region and the United

States by the Islamic State (IS) and Iraq, which was the seedbed of the transformation of Al Qaeda in Iraq (AQI) and remains a major battlefield and recruiting ground in the ongoing war. Some discussion of Syria, where the war is also being conducted and which was the spark for energizing IS, is also included. Chapter 2 extends the discussion to two countries on the physical periphery of the Levant but which are major power players in the region, Israel and Iran. These two states are major antagonists and countries with which the United States has very different relations. Israel is America's major "ally" in the Middle East to which this country has the deepest security commitments, and Iran has moved from being a close and valued friend to a significant opponent. The role of nuclear weapons (Israel's possession, Iran's interest) is a major point of contention, as is Israeli policy toward the so-called occupied territories on the West Bank.

Chapter 3 moves the discussion eastward across the Asian continent. East Asia has been one of the most important areas to the United States because of its extensive economic ties to Japan, the Republic of Korea, and the People's Republic of China. It is a matter of foreign policy concern, because of negative changes in the region with regard to two countries that are the subject of the case studies. Of the greatest importance is Chinese-American relations. One source of concern is the economic relationship in areas such as terms of trade, the entanglement of the Chinese and American economies, the slowing of the Chinese economy, and ecological issues. The other concern focuses on military affairs, including the fact of and reasons for the Chinese military buildup of the past decade or so, particularly Chinese military activity in the South China Sea and its vast oil reserves. The other case is relations with the People's Democratic Republic of Korea (DPRK or North Korea). The major focus of that problem is the aggressive military policies of the DPRK, especially in developing nuclear weapons capability, potentially threatening many of its enemies, including the United States. The two states are linked in that the main potential source of taming North Korean behavior is China, which has been reluctant to do so for fear of the consequences of a fall of the Pyongyang regime.

Chapter 4 completes the odyssey through Asia, concentrating on the Asian subcontinent. The two major antagonists in this area of the world since 1947 have been India and Pakistan, the progeny of the granting of independence from British colonial rule. American-Indian relations have historically been cool because of Indian neutrality in the Cold War but have warmed since the early 1990s. India is the world's second most populous country and the world's largest democracy, forming a natural bond that was strained by India and Pakistan gaining nuclear weapons in 1998, but the possession of those weapons has stabilized relations between them. The other case has two emphases: Pakistan and Afghanistan. The AfPak countries, as they are often referred to in U.S. policy circles, are joined because of the importance of the outcome of the Afghanistan War to the United States. The AfPak countries share a long border, and both have significant Pashtun populations living on both sides of the frontier separating them, which residents in both countries ignore. The major U.S. interest is in seeing an end to the civil conflict in Afghanistan, and much of its ongoing dealings with Pakistan deal with how Pakistan can help facilitate that outcome.

Chapter 5 moves the geographic focus westward to Europe. The European continent has been in many ways a remarkably tranquil and positive part of the world since the end of the Cold War, but schisms have opened in some parts of the continent that are addressed in this chapter. Russian resurgence has been a major part of these difficulties and has focused on Russia's hardline actions toward former parts of the Soviet Union, notably toward Ukraine (including Russia's annexation of the Crimea). Russia is a "petrolist" state, and this adds to the difficulty of dealing with it. The other case emphasis is not on a country, but on the aggregation of most European states within the European Union (EU). For most of the period since the EU began to take form, its experience has been remarkably positive, but as the organization has moved toward full political integration, problems have emerged. These include the resurgence of nationalism in a number of states, reaction to national lack of control over refugees and other immigrants entering the EU area, and most recently, the British population's decision to leave the union (so-called Brexit).

Chapter 6 moves the discussion across the Atlantic Ocean to the Western Hemisphere. Most of Latin America has been a tranquil area for the United States—notably South America—but there are ongoing controversies with two states highlighted in the discussion. The first of these is the widely publicized and politicized disagreement between the United States and Mexico over unauthorized Mexican (and other Central American) immigration into the United States and has centered on the prospect of sealing the border through erection of a border fence across the 1,933 miles of common frontier, an issue that has additional aspects in terms of trade, illegal narcotics, and even the possibility of terrorists entering the United States by transiting the border. The other case deals with Cuba, centering on the resumption of relations between the two countries in 2015 after a fifty-five-year period in which they did not recognize each other. One of the most remarkable parts of this change has been the virtual lack of public resistance from anti-Castro Cuban elements in the United States.

Chapter 7 concludes the book with an examination of Africa. In foreign policy terms, Africa is the most underemphasized part of the world, despite the fact that its fifty-two countries are located on the second physically largest and most populated continent in the world. African problems, manifested in many continental states, are deep and difficult to resolve and generally do not involve the most obvious and important American interests, making their marginalization easier. This chapter looks at the problems of two of the larger and potentially more important African states. The first case deals with the Sudan, the southern part of which successfully seceded in 2011 to form the Republic of South Sudan. The basic divisions between the two Sudanese states are religious (Islam versus Christianity) and racial (Arabs versus "Africans") and resulted in virtually constant warfare between them since independence in 1956. In addition, the uprising in the Darfur region of Sudan has produced grisly casualty figures. Secession did not solve South Sudan's problems, and civil war involving the two largest tribes (the Dinka and Nuer) continues to roil their politics. Oil in South Sudan is also a factor. The other case is Nigeria. The continent's most populous country and one whose oil contributes most of its revenues, Nigeria is, like Russia, a "petrolist" state in which petroleum wealth enriches the country but lines the pockets of a thoroughly corrupt political system. The country has three ongoing or latent civil disturbances in different regions, largely ethno-religiously based. The most spectacular of these is the terrorist Islamist threat posed by Boko Haram, an affiliate of IS.

The potential menu of case applications of American foreign policy toward various parts of the world is virtually limitless, bounded only by the number of states in the world with which the United States must deal (around 220) and the various sources that can inflame disagreements. The fourteen cases examined in these pages offer no more than a glimpse at the variety and number of problems with which policy makers must deal. Appreciating that when "the rubber hits the road" in those relations is extraordinarily difficult, complex, and contentious; it is, however, a necessary part of understanding fully the subject of American foreign policy.

CHAPTER 1

The Middle East I

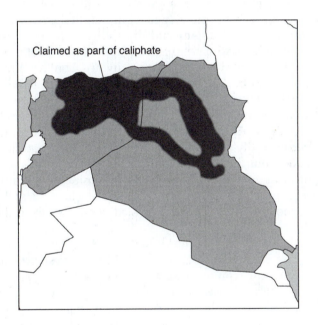

The Middle East has been the area of greatest concern for the United States in the twenty-first century. Prior to World War II, American interest in this region was minimal, basically tied to some concern about oil reserves and their exploitation. After the second global conflagration of the twentieth century, Middle Eastern oil increased in salience worldwide, including in the United States, and American interest increased proportionately. The creation of the Jewish state of Israel as a reaction to the Holocaust increased the importance of the region to foreign policy makers.

This status increased in the latter third of the last century, largely because of events driven by the Iranian revolution of 1979, discussed in chapter 2. The crowning event of the American foreign policy pivot toward a major concentration on the region and individual Middle East states was, of course, the September 11, 2001, attacks by Al Qaeda on the World Trade Center in New York and the Pentagon in Washington. Since then, the Middle East has been the fulcrum of American foreign, and especially national security, policy, a status it is unlikely to relinquish in the near term.

The Middle East is a complex and diverse, as well as dangerous and ironic, place. It is the birthplace of three of the world's great monotheistic religions, and yet it is also one of the most divided, conflictual, and uncivilized parts of the globe. The region's peoples are often bitterly divided by ethnicity, tribal affiliations, and, ironically enough, the religions they have created. The countries in which they reside are almost all artificial contrivances with little rationale for existence in their present form, and the result is often a deadly competition for power among the various groups who live in the countries but have their smaller groups as their primary loyalties. In most countries, the political dynamics are centrifugal with hardly any centripetal counterbalance. Some or all of these factors are found throughout the region, from the Mediterranean Sea to the steppes of central Asia.

It is difficult, and probably impossible, to identify and describe any set (or sets) of case interactions between the United States and countries of the area that are truly representative and that could lead to the conclusion that knowing how to deal with these countries will provide an adequate framework for assessing policy with others. Figuring out how to deal with Saudi Arabia, which is a current policy quandary given historic American dependence on Saudi oil and the involvement of Saudi citizens in support of organizations such as Al Qaeda and the Islamic State, does not provide much useful guidance for understanding how the United States should deal with Syria, Afghanistan, or Turkey. The Middle East is too idiosyncratic for much generalization. As I have put it in another volume (*The Middle East, Oil, and the U.S. National Security Policy*), the region is a "mess," and it is not clear what basic approaches and solutions can be generalized for the overall region or its constituent member states.

With that limitation in mind, the first two chapters seek to explore U.S. foreign relations with a sample of Middle East countries. This chapter focuses on the "hottest" spot in the region currently, the conflict in Iraq and Syria between the governments of those countries (especially Iraq) and the Islamic State (IS). It is chosen because the United States has an investment in Iraq that is over a decade old, dating back to the American invasion in 2003, and that investment is jeopardized by the aggressive attempt by IS to establish a territorial state in parts of Iraq and eastern Syria. American interest in Iraq's future and the disposition of IS are thus tied together. In addition, the disposition of IS has ramifications for a number of other Middle Eastern situations. The second chapter deals with Iran and Israel, two powerful states that serve, in effect, as bookends in the Iraq-IS conflict.

CONFLICT IN THE LEVANT

The concept of the Levant has become one of the shorthand ways to describe the conflict consuming Syria, Iraq, and IS. The Obama administration, for instance, liked to refer to the Islamic state by one of the descriptive titles given to it—ISIL (the Islamic State in the Levant), a term that IS itself does not employ. Part of the reason may be that the Levant concept is somewhat vague. Generally speaking, it refers to territory in the eastern Mediterranean region and areas of the Middle East with Mediterranean shores or that extend inward from those shores. There is, however, no universally agreed definition of what constitutes it geographically. The most inclusive definitions include most of the core Middle Eastern region: Palestine, Israel, Jordan, Lebanon, Syria, Iraq, parts of Turkey and Egypt, and even northern Saudi Arabia, as well as the eastern Mediterranean Sea and the islands in that sea (e.g., Cyprus). This inclusive version is not universally accepted, but IS has claimed all of the Muslim world as the ultimate goal of the caliphate it seeks to establish, and the broadly defined Levant is clearly a part of that ambition. Less expansive definitions limit the Levant to Syria, or that country and parts of the regional states surrounding it.

The Levant, or the core of its more inclusive depictions, is the current center of violent conflict in the region. The match that ignited the current conflagration was the Syrian civil war that began in 2011 as an offspring of the Arab Spring. That conflict has pitted a minority Shiite/Alawite government in Syria against a Sunni majority and has "featured" alleged atrocities including the use of chemical weapons and massive bombing by the government of its own population. The response to the Assad government's brutal crackdown included the formation of a large number of Sunni opposition groups to attempt to defeat and overthrow the government. One of these groups was the Islamic State, the reincarnation of Al Qaeda in Iraq.

Iraq and the Syrian/IS conflict are tied together in at least two important ways. First, Syria and Iraq are the countries from which at least the first part of the caliphate proclaimed by IS supposedly will be "built." In its more expansive proclamations, the Islamic State advertises a much wider territorial ambition for its holy empire based in highly Salafist, puritanical, and fundamentalist interpretations of the Koran, but eastern Syria and the Sunni areas of Iraq are the opening gambit. Making certain that expansion does not occur and that, indeed, the Islamic State in these two countries shrivels and disappears is an arguable basis for American and other Western policy toward the Levant area. Second, IS has its roots in the violent politics of both countries. IS was born in 2003 as a rump branch of Al Qaeda in the Sunni Anbar province of Iraq as part of the resistance to the American occupation, and although it disappeared from public sight during the so-called Anbar Awakening of 2007 (when the Americans convinced—some would argue bribed—Sunni tribesmen to oppose AQI), it reappeared in 2013 as a prominent element of the Sunni coalition seeking to overthrow the Syrian regime. It quickly emerged as the strongest element of that coalition and expanded its operations into Sunni Iraq as part of building the caliphate.

The result is a kind of triangular quandary facing the rest of the world, including the United States. The most obvious points are the disposition of the Syrian civil war and the IS threat. The United States opposes both the Assad regime and the caliphate and is rhetorically committed to destroying both. Unfortunately, doing so in whichever sequence is chosen—Syria first, then IS, or vice versa—creates automatic contradictions. Helping overthrow the Assad regime could create a Syrian void into which IS would move and extend the caliphate, and defeating IS would relieve Assad of the most formidable opposition to his rule. The third point is Iraq, which is primarily concerned about the outcome with IS. From an Iraqi vantage point (as well as that of many IS members), the conflict in Iraq is part of the Sunni-Shia confrontation for control of that country. IS represents an extremist branch of Sunnism, IS support is greatest in the Sunni areas of Iraq, the government in Baghdad is Shiite, and the defeat of the Islamic State indirectly is a form of support for the Shiism that is shared by the Iraqi majority and Iran. The result is a virtual maelstrom of conflicting foreign policy quandaries for the United States. The Americans have no inherent interests in the outcome of the confessional conflict within Islam, but regardless of what the U.S. government does, its actions will be interpreted as at least informally favoring one or the other. It is a difficult, arguably lose-lose situation. The horns of the resulting dilemma are illuminated by looking at the Iraqi and IS situations individually.

CASE: THE UNITED STATES AND IRAQ

The relationship between the United States and Iraq is both comparatively short and tumultuous. The country of Iraq did not exist until 1932 as the result of political forces in Europe (primarily Britain and France) that tried to create a post-Ottoman political map and ended by granting independence to a group of artificial states that have been in conflict ever since. Iraq was one of those states.

The United States and Iraq had virtually no political interaction before 1979, a pivotal year for the region. Iran had its revolution against the Shah, the Soviet Union invaded Afghanistan, Israel and Egypt implemented their peace agreement, and militants attacked the Grand Mosque in Mecca that year. In addition, a little known (outside of Iraq) Iraqi army colonel named Saddam Hussein seized power in Baghdad, beginning a reign that would last until 2003. In 1980, Hussein's armed forces invaded Iran, apparently, according to Polk, believing he could take advantage of the politico-military chaos that followed the Iranian Revolution (most of the Iranian military officer corps, for instance, were purged and either fled into exile or were arrested), allowing Iraq a quick and easy victory that would both defang the radical Shiite regime in Teheran and elevate Hussein to a heroic position in the Sunni Muslim world—even as a successor to Egypt's Gamal Abdel Nasser as the titular Arab leader. This calculation proved wrong, the Iranians rebounded from early setbacks, and the subsequent Iran-Iraq War raged inconclusively until 1988. During the war, the United States, acting on the "principle" that "the enemy of my enemy is my friend," became involved on the side of the Iraqis, helping to supply them with weapons with which to combat the Iranians. The downward spiral begins there.

The Iran-Iraq War largely bankrupted the Iraqi economy. To deal with the resulting economic crisis in Iraq, Hussein went to fellow Sunni states that had supported his efforts against Shiite Iran and had bankrolled the war, and asked them to forgive loans he had incurred and to grant him additional credits to shore up the economy. His major benefactors were Saudi Arabia and Kuwait, and both declined his requests. As Iraq's situation continued to deteriorate, Hussein unleashed his battle-tested military on tiny Kuwait in 1990 to seize the assets he felt were owed him. Kuwait was quickly conquered, and the Iraqis stood on the Saudi border, a quick dash from conquering the Saudi oil fields, a fate the Saudis could not physically prevent. Enter the United States.

Fearful of the consequences of an invasion, the Saudis accepted the offer by the United States to come to their assistance (in the process turning down an offer from a then-obscure veteran of the Soviet-Afghanistan war named Osama bin Laden). The United States quickly organized an international response it led, mounted Operation Desert Storm and, in the first Persian Gulf War, defeated the Iraqis in 1991 and evicted them from Kuwait. Iraq and the United States became adversaries in the process. Some neoconservative American analysts believed that the United States should have followed the retreating Iraqis and overturned the regime. President George H. W. Bush demurred, and those advocates would have to wait for the inauguration of his son to gain support to complete their task, which they accomplished with the successful May 2003 invasion and conquest of Iraq. That event and the subsequent eight-year occupation completed the process of transforming Iraq from a peripheral to a major American foreign policy concern. Current relations are a direct continuation of that transformation.

The 1990s reinforced this process of elevating Iraq in American policy. In the wake of his 1991 defeat, Hussein was faced by rebellions in the north by the Kurds and in the south by the Shiites. He responded brutally, including the renewed use of chemical weapons against the Kurds, many of whom fled to Turkey (where they were unwelcome but refused to leave, fearing the wrath of the Iraqi regime). The United States devised an interim solution that would satisfy both the Turks and the Kurds by declaring the Kurdish areas of Iraq a no-fly zone and sanctuary where the Iraqi armed forces would be excluded as part of Operation Provide Comfort, later renamed Northern Watch. The arrangement openly violated Iraqi sovereignty but protected the Iraqis *as long as U.S. and other aircraft enforced the ban.* It also meant that the United States was stuck indefinitely in Iraq: if they left, the Kurds (and Shiites) would be at Hussein's not-so-tender mercy. Northern Watch only ended when the United States invaded Iraq in 2003 and removed Hussein from power.

Iraq: A Physical and Political Sketch

Iraq as such is a fairly recent addition to the map of the world, although it sits on the site of one of the world's oldest and most notable places. The heart of modern-day Iraq is ancient Mesopotamia, and its most famous physical characteristic is that it is the area through which the Tigris and Euphrates Rivers flow, join, and form the Shatt al-Arab waterway that divides Iran and Iraq. Baghdad, Iraq's capital, has been historically significant since Biblical times.

In some ways, it is not a very remarkable place. According to statistics supplied by the 2016 *CIA World Factbook* (the source of statistical data throughout this book), Iraq is the world's 58th largest country, with an area of 168,888 square miles, about twice the size of Idaho. Its population in 2015 was about 37 million, ranking it 37th in the world, and its economy was $531.4 billion, also 37th in the world. Per capita GDP stood at $15,500

(104th among world countries). Were it in another part of the world, it would be just another developing country. The fact that it is in the Middle East, however, distinguishes it in three ways that help explain why it is a prominent regional actor.

The first factor is geographic, a matter of location. As the chapter-opening map shows, Iraq is the hub of a wagon wheel at the top of the Persian Gulf. The "spokes" of that wheel on its borders are Turkey, Iran, Saudi Arabia, and Syria, all regionally prominent and each with a conflicting interest in what happens in Iraq. It also has borders with Jordan and Kuwait. Much of this locational importance arises from the fact that Kurdistan, the aspirational state desired by the Kurds, would be carved from ethnic enclaves in Iraq, Iran, Syria, and Turkey, all of whose governments oppose this outcome with varying intensity.

Second, that location is augmented by the demographics of its population, which contribute to making Iraq a natural buffer area and object of competition by other regional states. The country is predominantly Arab (75–80 percent of the population), with 15–20 percent of the population Kurdish. Religiously, it is one of a handful of states with a Shiite majority (60–65 percent). Most of the remaining Iraqis are Sunni (32–37 percent). This is significant for a couple of reasons. On the one hand, the minority Sunnis ruled the country for most of its existence, ending after twenty-four years of Saddam Hussein's rule in 2003. Since their fall from power, Sunnis have been a restive minority that forms the Iraqi support base for the Islamic State. On the other hand, Iraq sits between the Persian Gulf region's most powerful Shiite (Iran) and Sunni (Saudi Arabia) states, making it a natural competition ground as well as buffer.

The third source of distinction is its natural resource endowment. Although fighting and instability have stifled the full blossoming of its potential, Iraq has some of the largest reserves of traditionally mined petroleum in the world. Estimates are that it ranks fourth in the world in reserves (behind Saudi Arabia, Canada, and Iran), and special characteristics of this resource add to its potential vitality to the global system, but also to some of Iraq's plentiful problems.

One potential advantage of Iraqi oil is its accessibility and cost of production. Largely because of endemic political instability, Iraq's oil has been among the least exploited of all major producers. As of 2006, only about two thousand wells had been drilled across the entire country, whereas there are over a million in Texas alone. That oil, moreover, is relatively easy to access, because it lies comparatively close to the surface, and refining it is also not difficult, because it is relatively "sweet" (low-sulfur content), making refinement comparatively inexpensive. As Polk puts it, "Iraqi oil is the world's cheapest to produce." From a producer's vantage point, Iraq is a tempting destination point.

There is also lots of oil to be accessed, and its potential is largely untapped. Current assessments put its availability at about 1.15 billion barrels, exploration has been relatively modest, and current politico-military conditions make further exploration daunting; as a result, no one is entirely certain how much more there may be under Iraqi soil. Given the relative lack of exploitation to this point, Iraq could be a future energy superstar.

The tumultuous politics of Iraq are a major qualification to this rosy depiction, and the distribution of Iraqi oil is simultaneously a part of the country's internal political instability. The problem mixes together ethno-religious habitation patterns with the presence or absence of petroleum. In broad terms, the southern part of Iraq is mostly Shiite (including the location of the two holiest sites of Shiism, Karbala and al-Najaf), and major oil reserves are found in the swampy marshlands of southern Iraq. The northern part of the country is dominated by the Kurds, many of whom harbor secessionist dreams in the form of Kurdistan, and the other major Iraqi oil reserves are located in the shadows of the Zagros Mountains of Kurdistan. The part of the country that lacks confirmed oil reserves is the central part of Iraq, the so-called Sunni triangle, of which contentious Anbar Province is the most important part.

This pattern, and its potential economic consequences deriving from how to distribute oil revenues from the oil-producing areas of the country, enlivens internal Iraqi politics. When the Sunni Baath Party ruled the country under Saddam Hussein, it was not a problem for the oil-poor Sunnis, but with power wrested from them, who gets what oil revenues is a critical matter. As might be guessed, the southern Shiites and the northern Kurds argue that most or all of these revenues should stay where the oil is produced, and in the post-Saddam and post-American period, new oil leases have been negotiated directly between the regions and oil companies, and these generally exclude or beggar the nonproducing Sunni areas. As a distinct minority in the country with no special claim to power, many Sunnis feel left out of this source of revenue, which constitutes the vast majority of Iraqi government tax revenues. This situation leaves the Sunnis feeling powerless in the debate over oil revenue distribution and helps explain Sunni anti-government activity, including support by some Sunnis for their Sunni IS compatriots.

Politically, Iraq is and has always been a classic instance of the *artificial state* phenomenon, a sovereign political entity with little (if any) historical base that places various and often antagonistic population elements under one political jurisdiction. The result is that the country is classically *multinational*, since the population elements view themselves more in terms of their ethno-religious roots than they do with the national entity. In a non-artificial state, the citizens would think of themselves first as Iraqis and then as Sunni or Shiite Arabs or Kurds (who are not ethnic

Arabs) rather than as Shiite Iraqis or simply Shiites. In Iraq, this has never been the case, largely because there was no such thing, physically or in the minds of the people, that suggested an Iraqi sense before the country was declared in 1932. Iraqi "nationalism" has never been a strong, overwhelming sentiment in a country where political processes and outcomes have generally had the purpose and effect of favoring one group at the expense of the others.

Before the American invasion, a Sunni dictatorship meant that the Sunni minority ruled at the expense of the Kurds and Shiites. When the Americans invaded and conquered the country, deposed the Sunni Baathists, and promised movement toward representative democracy, the majority Shiites were delighted. Shiite support for the concept did not necessarily represent enthusiasm for the prospect of a fully democratic society, but rather a power balance in which they could dominate and do the same bad things to the Sunnis that Saddam Hussein had done to them. The Kurds have always been on the outside of these arrangements, and thus it is little surprise that they are irredentist and secessionist, since they tend to lose regardless of which Arab religious group is in charge.

This set of problems was well known well in advance of American involvement with Iraq, and common wisdom among analysts was that Iraq was a country both to be avoided and was among the worst global locations for any attempts to change, and especially democratize, a country. When the neoconservatives proposed as one of their goals in 2003 to transform Iraq into a representative democracy, most analysts who knew anything about the country rolled their eyes in incredulity.

These political divisions are reinforced and even accentuated by Iraq's geopolitical location. There are Iraqi neighbors who profess a kindred relationship and interest in promoting the interests of each Iraqi group, and this often occurs at the expense of other groups. The most obvious connection is between the Shiite majority in Iraq and Iran, whose Shiite majority is more than 90 percent of the country's population. Iran's affinity arises partly because the Shiite holy places in Iraq are also of religious significance to the Iranians, and the co-religionists have long traditions of cooperation. Iran's Ayatollah Ruhollah Khomeini lived in exile in Iraq during part of the rule of the Shah, and most Iraqi Shiite leaders spent time in Iran to avoid persecution by the Hussein regime. The Iranians have invested financially in the Shiite leadership in Baghdad, and Iranian "volunteers" have participated in the fighting against IS. The two Shiite groups are not closer than they are because of ethnicity: the Iraqi Shiites are ethnic Arabs, whereas the Iranians are Aryan. Ethnicity, for instance, trumped sectarianism during the Iran-Iraq War, when Iraqi and Iranian Shiites fought one another.

The Sunni countries, and especially the oil-rich states of the Persian Gulf, have historically felt a similar affinity for the Iraqi Sunnis, and they felt a Sunni-controlled Iraq was an important bulwark against and barrier to Iranian penetration into their territories. This affinity has proven more rhetorical than substantive on occasion. As noted, co-religion did not cause the Saudis and others to forgive Iraqi debts after the Iran-Iraq War, and Iraq's Sunni brethren turned rapidly against the regime in Baghdad when it invaded Kuwait. The result is a kind of ambivalence with which the oil states grapple. In contemporary terms, it is manifested in official condemnation by Sunni governments of IS while private citizens with sympathies for the harsh Sunnism practiced by the Islamic State privately bankroll the terrorists.

Then there are the Kurds. As noted, the Kurds are an ethnic minority in several states in the region and have been attempting to fashion an independent Kurdish state from those territories (which are basically contiguous) since the end of World War I. Their irredentism has been consistently rebuffed by the states in which they reside (the reaction is probably most virulent among the Turks, which have the largest Kurdish minority—about 20 percent of the population), and this means that virtually every country in the region is anti-Kurdish to some extent. The Kurds were attached to Iraq after their petition for statehood was denied in 1919. The Iraqi Kurds are not Arabs, they speak a distinct Indo-European language, and since 2011, the Kurdish region has exercised effective autonomy within Iraq. Should Iraq dissolve into several parts (a real possibility discussed below), the Kurds would lead the secessionist parade.

The distinctiveness of the Kurdish situation and position is important to understand in light of recent developments. Because the Kurds live in parts of Iraq and Syria and do not practice the same ascetic form of Sunnism as IS, they have been subject to attacks and atrocities by the Islamic State. The Kurds are acknowledged as the fiercest of the non-IS fighters, and their militias, known as *pesh merga*, have been the most effective regional forces confronting IS in both Iraq and Syria. Some Westerners, including Americans, have translated this effectiveness into the idea that the Kurds should form the core of indigenous forces destroying IS. This advocacy ignores the fact that the *pesh merga* consider themselves a territorial defense force whose sole purpose is repelling IS in Kurdish lands. They have no particular interest in aiding the Syrians or other Iraqis, most of whom are their opponents, to solve *their* problems with the Islamic State.

Basic U.S. Relations with Iraq

On April 30, 2016, there was a major demonstration in Baghdad. Supporters of Shiite cleric Muktada al-Sadr, reacting to an anti-government and anti-American speech by the religious and militia leader who has been an opponent of the United States virtually since 2003, stormed the Green Zone in the Iraqi capital, seat of the country's parliament and most

major Western embassies. The protesters trashed the parliament building, temporarily causing the Shiite prime minister, Haider al-Abadi, to
flee the premises. The gist of al-Sadr's wrath was government corruption
and inattention to national needs. Among other things, he blamed the
United States for inadequately preparing the country for an independent
existence before it turned control over to the Iraqis. This demonstration
and recrimination occurred almost *four and a half years* after the United
States officially left the country and abandoned the occupation it imposed
in 2003. To paraphrase, Iraq has been a foreign policy gift that keeps on
giving for the United States.

The fact that demonstrations in Baghdad would have an American component reflects the distinctive nature of U.S.-Iraqi relations in the world.
The source of that distinction, of course, stems from the fact that Iraq was
invaded, conquered, and occupied by the United States for over eight years.
This was not only the sole time the United States invaded and conquered
a fellow member state of the United Nations (a direct violation of its obligations under the UN Charter); it was only the second time since the
United Nations came into existence that *any* member had committed such
an act against another. Ironically, of course, the other instance was Saddam
Hussein's invasion and conquest of Kuwait in 1990, a misdeed the United
States took the lead in decrying and rectifying. These bookend events offer
some insight into the unique relations between two countries that, until
the multiple Middle East events of 1979, essentially had nothing to do with
each other. The United States shattered the sovereignty of Iraq, suspended
and then moved to restore that sovereignty, and now tries to influence the
consequences of its actions.

The extraordinary American action of 2003 provides the watershed and
point of emphasis of relations between the two countries. As a result, U.S.-
Iraqi relations can be usefully divided into three distinct periods in terms
of American attention and concern. The year 2003 is the critical pivot in
this evolution. The first period is pre-invasion, when the United States first
developed an interest in Iraq that gradually got larger and more adversarial.
The second is the invasion and occupation, which began in 2003 and ended
formally at the end of 2011, but which did not fully resolve the fundamental issues of the Iraqi system and thus America's role in that country. The
third is the post-occupation period from 2011 to the present, where the
problems that remained in 2011 are still being worked through, not totally
successfully. Each is distinctive enough to merit individual attention.

Pre-Invasion Relations

During the period leading up to the crucial regional year 1979, American
relations with Iraq were decidedly minimal. For one thing, American policy

in the Persian Gulf region was focused on Saudi Arabia (and its oil) and on Iran, with which it had very close relations (see chapter 2). For another, Iraqi politics were decidedly unstable and hostile to the United States. Its Baath Party, along with other Middle Eastern states such as Egypt and Syria, flirted with the vaguely defined idea of "Arab socialism," and this led them to adopt generally less unfavorable relations than most of the rest of the region with the United States. Moreover, the various governments in Baghdad refused to allow concessions to American oil companies, a slight that was not important at the time due to the ready availability of Saudi and Iranian oil. U.S.-Iraqi relations for the first third of a century after World War II were decidedly distant and minimal.

The events of 1979 changed that equation and put relations on a roller-coaster ride that still exists. The fall of the Shah's regime and its replacement with a militantly anti-American Shiite theocracy made Iraq less uninteresting to the United States, and that interest gradually expanded. At the same time, Arab socialism was collapsing, and even though Saddam Hussein sought to replace Egypt's Nasser as titular leader of the movement, that effort did not survive long. The Iraqi invasion of Iran in 1980 was a way Hussein hoped to secure that mantle, but it foundered as the Iran-Iraq War settled into a stalemate that was partially manipulated by those supporting both sides.

The Iraq-Iran War began the transformation of U.S.-Iraqi relations. American-Iranian animosities led this country to oppose the Iranian side and even, in some quarters, to hope the Iraqis might succeed, overthrow the theocracy, and return Iran to some prerevolutionary normalcy. The Iraqis, however, had long been an adversary of the West, and thus their success was not a much better alternative than the success or failure of the Iranians. Various outside donors conspired implicitly to arm and rearm the combatants to levels where neither side could likely win or lose. In the face of the more numerous Iranians, the United States instituted military and civilian assistance programs to aid the Hussein regime, and by the end of the war, relations between the two countries were cordial, despite evidence of some Hussein regime atrocities such as chemical attacks against the Iranians and even against some Iraqi Kurds.

The courtship of Saddam Hussein ended abruptly with the Iraqi invasion and occupation of Kuwait. In these circumstances, American attention rapidly pivoted to protection of the Saudi oil fields, and the United States led the coalition (Desert Storm) that evicted the Iraqis from the small oil dome of a country. The downward spiral of relations followed.

As already noted, the decision by the first President Bush not to pursue the fleeing Iraqis into their own country and overthrow the government in 1991 left a lingering desire among many conservative Americans, notably the neocons, to "complete the job" by overthrowing Hussein and replacing him with a "democratic" government. The president had rejected this plan on the prophetic basis that it would likely lead to an open-ended civil war, and so the interventionists were rebuffed. They were purged from government during the eight-year Clinton administration, but their hatred for Hussein and desire for his removal did not abate. They returned to power with the George W. Bush administration in 2001. Events would soon revive the neocon dream.

Invasion and Occupation

Without the events of September 11, 2001, U.S.-Iraqi relations would likely have never devolved to what they became. The American reaction to the attacks created a vengeful sentiment among Americans in the form of support for the "war on terror" that could be used to justify militarized responses to the terrorist threat. The neocons, newly returned to positions of influence in the new administration, seized on this sentiment to reactivate their plans for Iraq. In retrospect, these schemes may seem flimsy and baseless (I have chronicled this period in *What after Iraq?*), but in the heat of the post-9/11 reaction, they resonated with (or cowed into silence) many Americans who might otherwise not have been inclined to support the invasion. The effort of 2016 U.S. presidential candidates to distance themselves from the 2002 resolutions authorizing military action on which the invasion was based are evidence of the questionable nature of claims made at the time that nobody wishes to acknowledge accepting.

The rationale for the invasion proceeded on two related rationales, which were backed by unsubstantiated accusations. The official justification was based on alleged Iraqi possession of weapons of mass destruction (WMD) that the Iraqis said they did not have (and which represented a violation of international treaty obligations to which Iraq was signatory) and ties to terrorism. The two accusations were linked by the awful prospect that Saddam Hussein might share WMDs—most frighteningly, possibly nuclear weapons—with terrorists such as Al Qaeda. These possibilities formed the underpinning for the resolutions authorizing the president to take whatever actions were needed to remove these threats.

The problem, especially in retrospect, was with the truth of these accusations. Despite concerted efforts during the occupation, no evidence of Iraqi WMD possession or manufacture was ever found, nor were ties to terrorists such as bin Laden discovered. The latter possibility was made more questionable by the fact that the militant Sunnism of bin Laden and the more moderate form practiced by the Iraqi regime made the two rivals, even enemies, not allies. None of the accusations have ever been substantiated. Whether they were knowing lies at the time has never been established, but without their acceptance, there would likely have been inadequate support for what followed.

There were also suspected motivations that were never acknowledged. One of these was the neocon dream to complete the job against Hussein that had been denied them in 1991 and the subsequent transformation of Iraq into a model Islamic democracy. The other was the pursuit of access to Iraqi petroleum. Officials at the time (and since) have denied that oil was ever a motivation, but the rich and largely untapped Iraqi reserves are both a tempting target and one given some cogency for the United States with access to Iranian reserves denied. Iraqi oil did enter the post-invasion calculus indirectly; occupation supporters argued that receipts from Iraqi oil exploitation would finance most of the needed postwar reconstruction and rehabilitation of the country. Like so much of the planning about Iraq, these projections also proved almost entirely false.

The occupation itself has been virtually universally excoriated. It began from a false proposition that the war and the occupation would be very short, meaning there would have been virtually no need for an occupation and thus little reason to prepare for one. The conquest of Iraq was indeed swift; it began on March 20, 2003, and by May, President Bush proudly proclaimed the war ended. Secretary of Defense Donald Rumsfeld declared that almost all American troops should have left the country by Labor Day, 129 days after the invasion. Obviously, they were both wrong.

The occupation lasted until the end of 2011, as specified by a Status of Forces Agreement (SOFA) signed by the United States and the government of Iraq in 2008 at Iraqi insistence. In retrospect, virtually everything about the war and its aftermath has been subjected to criticism and negative assessment. The decision to go to war has been widely criticized on the basis that the war was unnecessary since none of the premises of its justification have ever been demonstrated. Given the failure to demonstrate that the United States *needed* to go to war with Iraq, the entire rationale has been criticized as producing arguably the worst, most unnecessary war in U.S. history. Moreover, the premises of its conduct have been criticized largely on the basis that the United States had no realistic plans for the occupation and, quite simply, botched the job.

As a prime example of American ineptitude, one of the first major acts of the occupiers was to disband the Iraqi government, firing anybody with ties to Hussein's Baathist government, and to disband the Iraqi armed forces (most of whose officers were also Baathists). Getting rid of civilian functionaries left the country with virtually no Iraqis who had any idea how to run the government, and left day-to-day life in chaos, a contingency for which the arriving Americans had made virtually no provision. Firing the military left the former officer class in particular unemployed, and they drifted into opposition. Many of them now form the military leadership of IS. The major overriding criticism was that the Americans were unprepared for conducting an occupation, sent in unprepared and inexperienced officials to administer it, and had such unrealistic aspirations for what they could do that they blew the job and made Iraqi recovery worse than it probably needed to be. Some of this problem was institutional: the Department of Defense, with no particular expertise in nation-building, had power over the process and ignored prescient appraisals of the situation and remedies from other U.S. agencies such as the State Department and the CIA. Part of it was unrealistic goals and expectations, such as advocacy of outcomes such as Western democracy that were utterly alien to the problems and aspirations of most Iraqis.

The occupation spawned an asymmetrical military insurgency in 2004, mostly among the Sunnis who were driven from power and centered in Anbar Province. The road to American disengagement began in 2006, when the United States negotiated an agreement with Sunni tribesmen to join the Americans in putting down the rebellion in what was known as "Anbar Awakening." This action, secured by generous American monetary contributions to converted tribesmen, led to what General David Petraeus called the "surge" of 2007 that successfully quieted the situation enough for the United States to begin negotiations with Iraqi politicians to activate the process of American disengagement. In the process, the American goals of a vibrant Iraqi democracy were subordinated. Emma Sky, then an advisor to the Bush administration, described the new goal as "a nation at peace with itself, a participant in the global market of goods and ideas, and an ally against violent extremists (terrorists)." These were valid goals, but were they enough to justify the effort the United States put into their realization? They are also goals that arguably have not been attained.

Post-Occupation Relations

Although there have been no American combat troops in Iraq occupying or overtly influencing that country for over five years, the United States has not entirely left the Iraqi scene, and neither have the problems that the United States left behind. The Americans are still present, whether it be in the form of the largest American embassy in the world inside Baghdad's Green Zone or American military trainers working with the Iraqi National Army (ANA) or Kurdish *pesh merga* militiamen. Meanwhile, governance in that country remains a work in progress, or, as Sky argues, moving "from being a failed state to being a fragile state."

Two major categories of issues remain on the mutual American-Iraqi agenda. The first of these is internal in terms of the development of a stable Iraqi national political existence. When the Americans departed the country in 2011, the new prime minister was a Shiite, Nouri al-Maliki, who promised to form a multiethnic government in which the Shiites, Kurds, and Sunnis would be equal partners. That promise did not hold, and the regime alienated the other groups to the point of open talk of dismember-ment of the country. The problems with the Maliki regime were particularly blatant in the military. The prime minister appointed inept Shiite cronies to leadership roles within the ANA, which had two major negative results. One was that the ANA was progressively viewed by the Sunnis and Kurds as a pro-Shiite force opposing and potentially suppressing them. The other was that the ANA became increasingly ineffective as opposition to it began to mount. Kurdish forces were the best fighters the country could field, fur-ther debilitating Iraqi military capacities, since the Kurds were much more interested in defending Kurdistan than the rest of the country.

These problems came to a head with the emergence of IS in 2013. The initial actions of that organization were in conjunction with the civil war in Syria, but they quickly spread to the Sunni areas of Iraq, which are parts of the initial definition of the IS caliphate. In their initial encounters with IS fighters, the ANA performed abysmally. The American-trained and -equipped forces threw down their weapons and fled, leaving behind valu-able military equipment that IS appropriated into their own growing arse-nal. The only Iraqis who had any success were the Kurds, but they continue to show reluctance to leave Kurdish soil.

The United States has not taken an aggressive stance in the face of Iraqi problems. The Obama administration, after all, had campaigned in 2008 with American withdrawal as a major foreign policy goal, and viewed extrication as a major triumph. As Iraqi post-occupation problems have emerged, especially at the military level, this has created criticism and some advocacy of a more active American role, especially regarding the counter-ing of IS activity. How to deal with this problem may be the largest foreign policy problem with Iraq in the coming years.

U.S. Policy Options

When the United States ended its military campaign in Vietnam unsuc-cessfully in 1975, the country figuratively heaved a collective sigh of relief and put the Vietnam experience behind it. There were some recriminations and much soul-searching about what had gone wrong militarily that re-sulted in the world's most powerful military failing to defeat a third-rate Asian power despite the sacrifice of 58,000 American lives in the effort. Americans forgot about Vietnam as quickly as they could.

Something similar has marked the end of American involvement in Iraq. When the last American combat forces departed from Iraq in 2011, Americans similarly lost almost all interest in what happened next in that country. The effects were, of course, not so dramatic. In Vietnam, a communist regime came to power—the outcome the United States had sought to avoid. In Iraq, the Maliki government had American support, although that eroded as his regime became more aggressively pro-Shiite. Also in Iraq, the American departure was not as complete as it was in Vietnam. There is still an American mission remaining in Baghdad; the Americans left Saigon altogether.

The United States retains some interests in Iraq, even if its options to realize them are circumscribed. The future evolution of the state the United States helped shape is clearly at the top of the list, and it is an interest with two major aspects. One is the evolution of Iraq into a stable state, which effectively means the integration of all three of its major groups into a common structure with which each is satisfied and which it can support. Accomplishing that formidable task requires evolving a democratic order in which each is represented and which each trusts not to suppress it. A powerful symbol of this accommodation is a resolution of an ongoing controversy over the distribution of oil revenues from the north and south equitably. Currently, the Kurds and Shiites, in whose territories the oil is found, favor disproportionate distribution to them, leaving the Sunnis (whose regions have virtually no confirmed reserves) out in the cold. The Sunnis are also the least satisfied with current arrangements, so that a resolution would relieve some Sunni discontent. It has long been official U.S. policy to nurture the emergence of Iraqi nationalism that would discourage the splitting of Iraq into three separate states, an outcome that would further upset the international relations of the region.

The other, and currently more pressing, U.S. goal is to remove the threat to the government of Iraq posed by IS. This policy goal is clearly part of the overall American policy goal to eliminate IS altogether, but its Iraqi element also includes reducing the support of some Iraqi Sunnis for the radical Sunni group, thereby reducing centrifugal forces in Iraq. The two problems, Iraq and IS, are thus conjoined in the contemporary scene. The primary American emphasis is currently on IS, but how that problem is approached and resolved has real consequences for the future of Iraq as well.

CASE: THE ISLAMIC STATE

Before 2013, virtually no one outside the Levant itself had ever heard of the Islamic State. In that year, and especially since 2014, it has become a major power in the area with apparent ambitions that go well beyond the Iraqi and Syrian battlefields on which it now fights and which it claims as the beginning of the caliphate, a physical state that will be the launching pad for a "return" (the translation of caliphate) of the Islamic world to Koranic values and precepts. Whether its pretensions of forming a political union of Islamic peoples are realistic or delusional is not as germane as the fact that IS constitutes a menace to its immediate region and beyond, as evidenced by its terrorist attacks in Europe and threats of similar actions in the United States.

IS represents a special case and one that, on its face, does not seem to fit into a volume of case treatments of U.S. relations with other sovereign states. The uniqueness of dealing with IS arises from its status. Even if one strips away its more territorially ambitious pretenses and its apocalyptical intents and predictions (it foresees a climactic "end of times" scenario as its final act), the heart of dealing with IS begins with the question of exactly what the Islamic State *is*.

IS claims that the caliphate is a territorial state and, as will be discussed below, it has some of the characteristics and problems entailed by state sovereignty. Although international legal definitions are in some conflict, a fully independent country that is considered a full sovereign member of the international system typically has certain characteristics. These include a defined territory with a permanent population, a single government, and recognition as a state by other members of the international system. The Islamic State has some but not all of these qualities, and thus stands in the nether region of claims to sovereign statehood.

As an evolving political entity, the Islamic State is not exactly a state. It does have a core territory (the area surrounding its "capital" of Raqqa in Syria, for instance), and it does both control and govern the territory and population of the area that it occupies and claims. At the same time, the effective "boundaries" of IS are highly fluid and dependent on successes or failures in its domain. The physical entity and the population it governs are thus in a state of flux and, as will be argued, constitute an Achilles' heel of sorts for the future. The characteristic of a state on which IS most prominently fails is recognition as a state by other states and thus the ability to engage in diplomatic activities with other states. As of late 2016, IS was not recognized by any other state in the world as a sovereign state. Rather, to the extent it is accorded any status, it is as an insurgent or imperialist movement, since it seeks to enlarge its domain out of territories now parts of other sovereign states.

The question of IS has entered into American policy concerns in several ways. Most prominently, the caliphate sprang from the Syrian civil war as a leading part of the Sunni resistance to the continued rule of the Alawite Shiite regime. This placed IS on the American agenda in ambivalent ways, because the United States was (and still is) opposed to the Assad regime and thus has a natural affinity for its opponents. Early on, however, the United States realized the Syrian resistance was a very diverse amalgam of groups, some of which were radically oriented and affiliated with terrorist groups such as Al Qaeda, which the United States also opposed. IS heads the list of radical anti-Assad movements, meaning IS represents an opponent to the United States; this country finds itself opposing both the Assad regime *and* its leading opponent. The territory under siege by IS includes sizable parts of Sunni areas of Iraq. This also creates an American interest in IS, since the organization controls Iraqi territory and is in a state of effective war with the government of Iraq, the stability of which is an American interest. IS activity in Sunni Iraq is particularly troubling, because it weakens Iraqi control of its country. In addition, IS has some support in the Iraqi Sunni population as a reaction to what they perceive as Shiite suppression emanating from Baghdad and because sizable parts of the IS military are commanded by former Iraqi officers. Finally, the U.S. military campaign against IS in the form of aerial attacks has coincided with increasingly virulent IS terrorist threats against the United States as well as against American allies such as France and Belgium, who joined the American-led air campaign and were the subsequent victims of terrorist attacks.

IS: A Physical and Political Sketch

Unlike the conventional sovereign states that comprise the majority of studies in this volume, it is difficult, and likely futile, to try to describe the Islamic State in physical or demographic statistical terms. As an international phenomenon, IS represents an aberration. In some sense, it is a non-state actor like many of the internal insurgent groups that dominate the pattern of violence in the contemporary international system. Generally, the non-state entities are formed from indigenous parts of the population, aided and augmented by like-minded outsiders, who seek to overthrow a constituted government and to replace it. IS has some of these characteristics and goals, but not all of them. It is difficult to assign a national origin to those who are part of IS: some are Iraqi, especially in military leadership roles, some are suppressed Syrian Sunnis whose primary interests are in overthrowing the Syrian tyranny, but others are outsiders whose nationality is difficult to determine or catalog. Because the organization is very electronically savvy, it has made extensive and effective diverse progress in terms of recruitment. Precise figures are unavailable, but estimates, which are probably not very accurate, are that over 1,000 new recruits enter the IS system monthly, willing to serve as armed jihadis to fight in the IS war against nonbelievers. Some reporting suggests that as IS forces are killed (primarily through aerial bombardment), the flow of new recruits is adequate to replace fallen soldiers. Nobody publicly admits to the authenticity of these figures one way or the other. Certainly IS itself does not publicize such statistics, if it keeps them.

What is safe to say about the membership of IS may be that it is diverse in terms of national origin, and that assigning nationality to its members is futile. Borrowing from the literature on terrorism, the foreign recruits seem to share characteristics with people who join terrorist organizations. The recruits tend to be young men (and increasingly women) who are alienated from their surroundings (often ghetto conditions, especially in

Europe) who perceive little meaningful prospects in their lives, and who are attracted to the high adventure of the jihadi existence and are likely to be vulnerable to conversion to the extremely militant, fundamentalist interpretation of Islam that is at the heart of the IS message.

Estimates of the size of the support base are unreliable. Most approximations about the size of the force that IS possesses tend to be in the 20,000–40,000 "fighter" range, which is not very large considering the amount of territory that is part of the caliphate and which IS forces must control and defend from outside intrusion. IS does provide some governance in areas that it occupies, but how many supporters are committed to that governance is equally speculative.

As it burst upon the scene, outside observers (especially those unfamiliar with the physical area) were very impressed by extensive penetration including conquest and occupation of places such as the Iraqi city of Mosul and even a thrust in 2015 near the Iraqi capital of Baghdad. A look at the physical map appeared to show a relentless and very impressive momentum. At its zenith, the territory controlled by IS was estimated to be as large as 40,000 square miles (roughly the size of Kentucky), and in July 2015 those estimates stood at around 32,000 square miles, an area about the size of South Carolina. Reports in 2016 suggested that IS-held territory had shrunk by 10–40 percent, due largely to Kurdish and Iraqi government counteroffensives.

The amount of territory that IS conquered and annexed may have been physically impressive, but the extent of maps turning black (the color of the IS flag) was also misleading. On one hand, most of the territory was largely uninhabited wasteland with little intrinsic value or source of resistance (the areas in Syria that IS annexed earlier were places the Syrians did not bother to defend), and it encountered little resistance. This was particularly true in Iraq; Shiite armed forces showed little enthusiasm for defending Sunnis in Anbar, and the Kurdish *pesh merga* limited their major efforts to defense of Kurdish territories. Indeed, Kurd-IS fighting has been the major combat that has occurred in Iraq. This is not to discount the impressive success of an upstart armed force such as IS; it is to suggest that its early success was something less than meets the eye. The physical situation remains fluid, but the caliphate seems physically on the decline, not the incline.

The early success of IS seemed to be running out of steam in 2016. Not only was its physical territory in decline due to a combination of attrition through air strikes by Western forces led by the United States and reinvigorated military action to remove IS presence from as much Iraqi (Anbar) territory as possible. No one predicts the physical collapse of the Islamic State movement in the short run, but its inexorable success no longer seems inevitable either.

IS represents a unique political movement as well, and its distinctive political attributes distinguish it from other Islamist organizations. In combination, these characteristics have made subduing it a difficult task, but they also provide some hope for its eventual defeat and elimination. The roots of the organization are as a terrorist group. It is the direct lineal descendant of the Iraqi "chapter" of Al Qaeda (Al Qaeda in Iraq or AQI) that was formed in 2003 by a Jordanian expatriate and former Afghan *mujahidin* named Abu Musab al-Zarqawi as part of the Sunni resistance to the American occupation. Zarqawi was killed in an American air strike in 2006, and AQI went underground, waiting for an opportunity to resurface under a new leader, Abu Bakr al-Baghdadi, as part of the Syrian resistance in 2013. The newly christened Islamic State is clearly more than a terrorist organization, although terror is part of its "portfolio." A major aspect of its distinction from other organizations (including the Al Qaeda network from which it originally sprang) is its territorial ambition. Its desire to form the caliphate makes it a more difficult phenomenon to counter because it attracts greater membership and simultaneously makes it a more familiar kind of opponent, since it must engage in the traditional role of territorial defense, a burden not normally associated with movements that adopt a nontraditional approach to combat. Understanding the differences that distinguish IS from other opponents is a necessary part of understanding IS as a political problem.

In *The Middle East, Oil, and the U.S. National Security Policy*, I identified seven salient characteristics of IS that help categorize and comprehend it. These are (1) that it is a terrorist organization, (2) that it is a criminal enterprise, (3) that it has been very affluent, (4) that it has a strong religious basis grounded in extremist interpretations of Islam, (5) that its religious beliefs make it territorially ambitious, (6) that it has been much more successful than groups with less diverse characteristics, and (7) that it has demonstrated significant international appeal. All these characteristics are interrelated.

The first link in the chain is that IS was born as and remains a terrorist group in two senses. The first, already described, is in its origins. IS began as AQI, and that heritage remains. When it first resurfaced in Syria, it was considered just another terrorist threat, which made it dangerous but not extraordinary. Terrorist organizations present a limited threat to their adversaries. They can carry out outrageous acts that kill or frighten people, but they are generally too small and weak to do much more. The reason, simply enough, is that such groups are formed to influence some aspect of policy, and they can only try to do so by terror because the issue they choose has a very narrow appeal that does not attract many followers, and particularly enough followers willing to fight and potentially die for the cause. AQI had the goal of forcing an end to the American occupation; it failed, and it faded away. If IS had remained "simply" a terrorist group true to its origins, it would almost certainly not be worth including in this volume.

Terrorism remains part of the IS portfolio, and that is the second sense of IS as terrorist. Terrorist acts have as a major purpose frightening adversaries, and IS has shown a real affinity for this use of terror. The beheading of foreign journalists sends a clear and chilling message to others who seek to report on the caliphate, and the incineration of a live Jordanian air force pilot clearly was meant both to warn other foreign pilots (including Jordanians) what could happen to them if they attacked IS territory, as well as demonstrate the swift and summary method by which infidels were treated. The terrorist attacks in Paris and Brussels, in addition, occurred shortly after France and Belgium entered the air war and could be seen as both reprisals for those actions and a warning to others not to join the campaign.

Terrorism is part of the IS lineage and arsenal, but the movement is more. As terrorism expert Audrey Kurth Cronin notes, "IS is not truly a terrorist organization at all. If it is purely and simply anything, it is a pseudo state led by a conventional army." While this statement is also true, the Islamic State is more. For one thing, it is a criminal organization, once again in two senses of the term.

All organizations that engage in terrorism are criminal in that acts of terror—including harming or killing people and destroying things—are illegal activities punishable universally under criminal codes. Terrorists deny this criminality, arguing that the violent actions they commit are acts of war, and that their members who break laws are soldiers for whom the laws of war, not civil society, apply. Such a construction is intended to elevate the terrorists' status from common thugs to nobility. The old saw, to which terrorists ascribe, that "one man's terrorist is another man's freedom fighter," captures the distinction that terrorists prefer. Its victims reject this rationale.

Crime plays an integral part in the operation of IS; the commission of crimes is a major source of the income that finances the organization. Some revenue generation is always a part of terrorist activity, through acts of extortion (threatening to blow up valued objects if victims do not comply with demands) or kidnapping people for ransom. IS has raised crime for profit to a status that the hardest mobster would envy. When IS enters a town, one of its first acts is to "liberate" the local bank of whatever cash it has, which goes into IS coffers. IS sells protection to local merchants to ensure that their businesses are not attacked and destroyed—normally by IS itself. Formerly free roads suddenly become toll roads, with the tolls also going to finance the advance of the caliphate. As Peter Van Drehle summarizes the point, "Its armies are supplied from captured arsenals and are paid from money from looted banks."

The receipts from criminal behavior have been a major contributor to the comparative affluence of IS among groups with parallel goals and aspirations. Crime has been a leading source of IS wealth, but it requires a growing IS empire: once a bank in a town or city has had its money "liberated," there is nothing more left to steal, and extortion and other crimes against others can only go on so long until the well is dry. As Graeme Wood summarizes it, the current territory that forms the caliphate is "mostly uninhabited and poor." Thus, IS must expand the territory it controls constantly to maintain its wealth, or it must finance itself from other sources.

Two additional sources of funding stand out. One has been the exportation of Syrian oil from IS-occupied oil fields and refineries across the border into Turkey. The primary agent for suppressing this illicit trade should be the Turkish government, and the United States has taken two kinds of actions in this regard. One has been to encourage greater Turkish vigilance in not allowing this oil across the border from Syria, but these pleas have not been entirely honored by a Turkish government less committed to destroying IS than the Americans. The other action has been to assign some air missions both to destroying refineries in Syria (very unpopular with the Syrian government) and attempting to destroy oil tankers moving petroleum products to the Turkish border.

The other source of funding has been private contributions from wealthy Sunnis sympathetic to the ascetic ideology that IS preaches. The sharia-based, fundamentalist Sunni interpretation of Islam preached by Baghdadi and his followers is very similar to the Wahhabi sect's beliefs, and Wahhabism is the state religion of Saudi Arabia. Remittances from individuals in Saudi Arabia and other oil-rich Gulf states such as the United Arab Emirates have proven to be a valuable part of the three-legged stool underlying IS affluence.

These financing methods have been successful in the IS campaign to date. Using estimates that are probably inaccurate in detail, the budget of IS has been estimated at over a million dollars a day, which is a large amount to extract from the impoverished areas that are the heart of IS-held Iraqi and Syrian territory. Part of the strategy for dealing with IS has thus been to try to restrict the amount of income it receives from each of its criminal sources: stopping its expansion to deny it fruitful places from which to steal; interrupting its commerce in things such as petroleum; and forcing the governments of countries whose citizens have contributed to it to cease those payments. This latter initiative has caused some friction between the United States and the Persian Gulf states, especially Saudi Arabia. Impoverishing IS by drying up its sources of wealth is, however, a key to defeating the Islamic State.

The fourth characteristic of IS arises from the religious base that guides many of its actions and defines its aspirations. Under the charismatic leadership of Baghdadi, IS has articulated a religious philosophy based in the fundamentalist tradition found in both Sunni and Shia Islam that calls for religious purification and a return to the ways and virtues of the original rule of the Prophet. This strain has been a recurring theme in Islam, and, as Wood points out, "derives from a coherent and even learned interpretation of Islam." This tradition is far from the mainstream of modern Islamic belief and practice (which adds to its appeal in some quarters). The heart of the appeal is a return to seventh-century values and practices and a belief in the End of Days.

This strain of belief shares some pertinent common elements. These include elements of *Salafism* (which translates as "pious forefathers" and is often used to justify violence), a literal and extreme interpretation of *sharia* law (which derives much of its definition of crime and punishment from seventh-century sources in the Koran), asceticism that it shares with the Wahhabis, and even *takfir*, which "proclaims people to be apostate because of their sins," according to Wood. These sins include not accepting the IS interpretation of Islam and means that not only are non-Muslims apostates and thus subject to punishment (death), but so are other forms of Islam, including all Shiites and non-accepting Sunnis.

The extremely violent behavior that derives from these beliefs has created much of the shock value that attaches to the IS phenomenon in Western eyes. It projects a primitive fanaticism and willingness to engage in thoroughly uncivilized behaviors that most Westerners find so abhorrent, even bizarre, that the grounding of IS in minority views of Islam—its basis as a religious movement—gets lost. Islam is not, of course, unique in producing extremist interpretations of its meaning and imperatives, but it currently seems to be the purveyor of the most extreme manifestations. The fact that its message has a Koranic base that is recognized by Muslims makes it more difficult for them to join the condemnation with the same vigor as Christians and others more removed from their primitive pasts.

The fifth characteristic is the territorial ambitions that IS has and that are manifested in its pursuit of the caliphate. Territorial aims distinguish it from terrorist groups and even insurgent asymmetrical warfare movements. Terrorists and insurgents are not wedded to gaining and maintaining territory and, generally speaking, in governing sovereign territory. Doing so goes so far beyond the likely capacities of terrorist groups that they rarely espouse such interests and would, in all probability, have no idea how to govern if they did. Insurgent movements aim at overthrowing and replacing governments in states, but in pursuing their goals, gaining and holding physical territory is not a high priority, other than for instrumental purposes such as sanctuary. If they do gain power, it is often evident that they had given little thought to what to do next.

The pursuit of a sovereign, religious, and thus special state changes the calculation for IS, gives it some of the attributes of a more conventional political movement, and creates obligations that may prove to be its downfall. As Wood explains, "If it loses its grip on its territory in Syria and Iraq, it will cease to be a caliphate. Caliphates cannot exist as underground movements, because territorial authority is a requirement of statehood, one of the vulnerabilities of a state." IS must not only govern its territories; it must *defend them* or it will cease to be a state. By its own criteria, it would thus be a failure.

The obligation of sovereign statehood means that ultimately IS must become a conventional power, placing a priority on forming a military coalition of conventional forces that ultimately will invade the caliphate and push it out, even destroy it. For most terrorist and insurgent movements facing such a threat, their response would be simply to quit the field, disappear into sanctuaries, and wait to return and fight another day. *IS cannot do this without destroying itself.* It must stand and fight to defend its territory, because if it does not, the caliphate ceases to exist and it has lost. The ambitions of IS are thus its Achilles' heel, particularly since its potential opponents would be organized, trained, and equipped by the premier conventional military power in the world, the United States.

The sixth characteristic of IS has been its apparent success. The organization burst onto the world stage as it raced across Syria and Iraq, pushing aside all opposition and ruthlessly imposing its will on populations that stood in the way. The map of the region turned ominously black, and the bleeding looked as though it could spill into Baghdad and beyond. Their success was impressive at least partially because it was so surprising, but it was also at least partially illusory.

The major aspect of the illusion was that the sweep of IS forces occurred, as already mentioned, in generally vacant lands where there was little resistance because there were few people willing to resist. As Van Drehle puts it, "Al-Baghdadi's forces raced through northwestern Iraq . . . not because they were an unstoppable military force, but because no one wanted to stop them. In city after city, they met seething citizens eager for a champion. It was a cakewalk." In many cases, this "juggernaut" consisted of little more than ten thousand or so fighters who were viewed as liberators by the Sunni inhabitants as they arrived.

IS success could prove particularly transitory. Not only has much of their success been exaggerated, but their brutal methods—including some of the more primitive applications of *sharia*—will almost certainly alienate those whom they have liberated. Moreover, most of their military successes have been against poorly trained and motivated opponents, and the qualitative balance will likely change as anti-IS forces improve and as the need by IS to put increasingly raw recruits into the field to compensate for their own casualties degrades their forces. It is entirely possible that, as Wood puts it, "Properly contained, the Islamic State is likely to be its own undoing. No country is its ally, and its ideology guarantees that this will remain the case."

The final characteristic of IS has been its ability to recruit foreigners into its service. This international appeal has been aided by the sophisticated utilization of social media by IS recruiters, and it has had its primary impact on young, disaffected Muslims in Islamic countries and the West who are drawn to its ascetic life, to the promotion of Islam, and to participation in a cause that seems to give their lives meaning. The great fear in the West has been that recruits will go to the caliphate and, among other things, be trained as terrorists who will then return to their home countries to carry out terrorist mayhem. These fears are not ungrounded, but they are also enigmatic. The resort to terrorist methods is normally a sign of the weakness, not the strength, of a movement. There have been suggestions that IS terrorist activities in Europe have been reprisals for the killing of IS fighters by Western air attacks. These attacks are atrocious and kill innocent people, but they also demonstrate that IS can do nothing directly to keep the bombs from falling on them, and their resort to terror is an implicit admission of this shortcoming. The more terrorist attacks are planned and conducted, the more dismay and fright they will induce, of course, but it may also be that they are signs of the growing desperation and decline of the IS threat.

Basic U.S. Relations with the Islamic State

By definition, there have been no real state-state relations between the United States and IS. The Islamic State has existed for a handful of years, it does not meet all the criteria of a sovereign state, and it is not recognized as a sovereign entity by any state, including the United States. If there is any connection that predates 2013 or 2014, it is with the predecessor of IS, AQI, and that was not an interstate relationship, since AQI was an insurgent group at best, a terrorist group at worst.

Any relationship in a normal foreign policy sense derives from the interface between the United States and IS in the Syrian civil war. After the United States declared it to be American policy to help bring down the Assad regime, it had some level of contact with various opposition groups, and in some form, IS (if not necessarily by that name) was probably one of them. U.S. relations thus arise from two American interests, the disposition of the Assad regime and the territorial ambitions of IS in both Iraq and Syria. As noted, these goals are in apparent conceptual contradiction, leaving American foreign policy in a quandary.

The heart of the American dilemma, of course, lies in the determination of how to simultaneously pursue the overthrow of Assad and the dismemberment of IS without one goal's pursuit strengthening the other opponent to the point of making the objectives mutually exclusive. Can the United States lead the destruction of IS without weakening the opposition to Assad to the point that he survives? Would overthrowing Assad provide a carte blanche for IS to move into western Syria, where most of the population and certainly the wealth of Syria (which is a treasure trove IS would clearly covet) resides? When analysts advocate one concentration or the other, these residual questions often are ignored. They are, however, part of the equation of securing American interests in the region.

These policy quandaries were, of course, activated by Syrian atrocities against its own citizens (including chemical and air attacks) that outraged the international community and led the Obama administration to declare the removal of Assad a top foreign policy priority. That goal has never been renounced, and as he was preparing to leave office, Obama occasionally reiterated it. If rhetorical levels are any indication, however, the higher priority would seem to be the destruction of IS, because it represents a greater international peril, including a potential terrorist menace to the United States.

The U.S.-IS relationship boils down to how one answers three interrelated questions about the IS-Syrian quandary. The first question is, who is the greater enemy? In more formal terms, which of these adversaries represents a greater threat to American interests, including the physical safety of the United States? On the surface, the answer seems obvious, since Syria lacks the capability and has never shown an interest in posing a direct menace to the United States. Such a threat is posed by the prospect of IS-inspired terrorist actions against the United States, although the extent and deadliness of such threats may be questionable.

The second question is which of these adversaries should be defeated first. As a practical matter, the United States is extremely unlikely to commit the physical resources (including military forces) to mount an offensive simultaneously against them, and it is not clear that such an approach would be fruitful. The military problems are almost entirely mutually exclusive, attacking a government in control of most of its territory and possessing a reasonably powerful conventional forced (Syria) as opposed to an insurgent armed force in more tenuous control of parts of a country in which the United States is in a contest for popular support (Sunni Iraq). If a simultaneous campaign were possible, it would solve many problems, most prominently how one pursues one objective without making the other more difficult. Such an approach is, however, impractical: the real options are one or the other (or possibly neither), but not both.

This leaves the third question, which is the consequences of pursuing one goal for the other. If the United States can lead an effort to get rid of Assad but strengthen IS in the process (or vice versa), what is the effect of leaving one stronger: Syria under firm control by Assad, or a vibrant, expanding IS? The answer is not entirely an American choice, since the consequences will be felt more strongly by regional actors than by the United States in either case. To this point, countries of the region have not been forcefully outspoken on this goal. The Sunni states provide rhetorical support for getting rid of the Shiite regime in Damascus, and the Shiites wax enthusiastic against Sunni IS. In neither case has this translated into anything resembling real action against either. American policy options are thus constrained by what outcomes regional actors are committed to pursuing. The record to this point has not been encouraging.

U.S. Policy Options

On Mother's Day 2016, the *Washington Post* published a cautionary article regarding the progress of American efforts against IS, why they were in danger or faltering, and what many American analysts and officials felt needed to be done to rectify the situation. The analysis was entirely conventional: American efforts had made progress, but future progress was threatened by problems in the adjoining states to the caliphate, and only an expansion of *American* military effort could ensure progress. It was a familiar refrain and prescription; it also almost completely missed the mark on American policy options.

The heart of the argument was that progress was threatened by circumstances in the neighboring states of the region, those countries that are actually threatened by IS. The article suggested three separate problems: what it deemed to be political "chaos" in the Iraqi capital of Baghdad (hardly anything new), a "fraying" ceasefire in Syria, and political "turmoil" in Turkey. Each of these problems had a negative effect on an aspect of the anti-IS effort because they compromised the ability of each country to act against IS in terms the Americans advocated: Syrian efforts to aid in the liberation of the IS capital at Raqqa, Iraqi efforts to free Mosul, and Turkish assistance in efforts against Ramadi. These are all regional problems with regional consequences, and one would assume that they are rightly the responsibility of those regional powers affected directly by the IS threat. But internal factors compromise those efforts (assuming they would be forthcoming in any case), and the answer was increased effort by the participant whose interests are least affected among the relevant powers, the United States. Does any of this make sense?

The Turkish part of the quandary is illustrative. Turkey has a long border with Iraq and Syria, including areas controlled or menaced by IS. It is a large, heavily armed country that is a member of NATO and thus the only country in the region with which the United States has a formal defense treaty. It has also been mostly inactive against IS. It faces internal opposition from fundamentalists, some of whom are sympathetic to IS; it considers the Kurds (who make up 20 percent of its population) to be at least as much an enemy as IS; and it opposes the Shiite government of Syria, which is strengthened by an IS defeat. As a result, its support for the anti-IS effort has been, to put it kindly, lukewarm: it provides some host conditions for the Americans, it engages in a half-hearted sealing of its border with Syria, and it condemns IS rhetorically. It does not, however, provide any direct military involvement in the anti-IS effort.

This description leads to the question of American options. It has been an article of faith in some American quarters that the United States "must" be actively involved militarily. At a minimum, this means providing aid, training, and some military action, such as air raids and the insertion of Special Operations Forces (SOFs) as trainers and spotters for air attacks. The *Post* article, not atypically, suggested that the numbers of SOFs should be increased. A few analysts have even suggested the insertion of regular American ground forces, an option that has attracted little support.

What the United States should do goes back to the questions of what American interests are in the fight and what the consequences are *for the United States* of one outcome or another. By any measure, those consequences are less dire for the United States than they are for any of the regional actors but, for domestic reasons, they seem unable or uninterested in solving *their* Islamic State problem. In that context, one can identify three U.S. options for dealing with IS. None is so overwhelmingly attractive that it precludes consideration of any of the others.

The first option is to concentrate on one or the other of the conflicts (IS or Syria), and then turn to the other. This option provides for economy and concentration of effort, but also the probability that accomplishing one goal makes the other one harder and leaves the question of which one first. The current preference seems to be IS, then Syria. The second possibility is to attack both problems simultaneously. This option is the most decisive, but it requires a much larger commitment than the American public seems willing to accept. The third option is simply to abandon active pursuit of either goal, on the premise that these are regional problems the consequences of which affect the United States far less than they do the regional actors. The problem here is whether those regional actors will stand up to the problem.

CONCLUSION

The two problems discussed in this chapter are clearly related, physically and as U.S. foreign policy concerns. The key binding element is the American invasion and occupation of Iraq. The war was (and still is) highly controversial and is hardly defended by anyone any longer. It did, however, give birth to the problems the United States faces in its relations both with Iraq and IS. Had there been no American conquest, Iraq would probably still be ruled by a Sunni tyrant, either Saddam Hussein or a designated successor.

This would not have been the happiest solution, but at least Iraq would not be the unstable, destabilizing problem it now is. At the same time, there would have been no Sunni uprising against the occupation, thus little support for an affiliate of Al Qaeda, AQI, and no platform from which to produce an IS, whose support base even if created would have been minimal. When a heckler confronted then presidential candidate Jeb Bush with the taunt, "Your brother created ISIS," this disparagement of President George W. Bush was not entirely without merit.

The other parameter is how recent American involvement in this region is and thus how transient American interests may be. Prior to 1979, the United States had virtually no interest in the Levant other than protecting Israel and access to Saudi oil—both concerns on the periphery of the Iraqi/IS axis. That level of interest began to rise as the United States became a supplier of Iraq in its war with Iran and reversed as the United States led the coalition in driving Iraq from Kuwait. America returned to Iraq in 2003 based on reasons of questionable validity, left the country more politically unstable than it was under Hussein, and now finds itself enmeshed with the Islamic State, a pariah that probably would not have existed were it not for the initial precipitating events of 2003.

What residual interests does the United States have with Iraq or IS? A little over 21 percent of Iraq's exports (84 percent of which were in petroleum or petroleum products in 2015) are to the United States, but only one-twentieth of the things Iraq buys are American. The economic ties are not great. Historical ties are nonexistent, and it is not clear how the United States would be affected vitally by any Iraqi developments other than an annexation of the country by Iran (very unlikely). If there is a residual tie, it may be an American obligation to correct the ills it created in the country, a refrain of the "Pottery Barn" analogy crafted by journalist Thomas L. Friedman and popularized by general and former Secretary of State Colin Powell: "If you break it, it's yours."

The relationship between the United States and the caliphate is also more tenuous and ambiguous than is sometimes maintained. None of the core purposes of IS has much to do directly with the United States. Were a triumphant and expansionist IS to reach proportions that it could provide a menace to Saudi Arabia or Israel, then traditional American interests would be activated, but that possibility begs the question of whether Israel (which certainly would) or Saudi Arabia (which has shown no interest or resolve) would do something about the problem themselves. IS presents a terrorist threat to the United States, but one must ask why. The United States is not a potential part of the caliphate, and the only real basis for animosity between the United States and IS arises from the fact that American armed forces are attacking and killing members of IS, leaving their threats of attacks against Americans an arguable case of retribution or retaliation. If the

United States were to exercise the hands-off option and leave the problem to regional actors, would their motivation to threaten the United States not be reduced as well?

The Middle East, and especially the Levant area, is a maze of problems, mostly deep and long held. The subtitle of my 2016 Middle East book is "Intractable Problems, Impossible Solutions," and it is not a bad depiction of what one encounters when trying to make the situation there more attractive. Iraq and IS are poster children of these problems, but there are more, as described in chapter 2.

STUDY QUESTIONS

1. Characterize U.S.-Iraqi relations before and after 1979. What were the change events, and how have they influenced evolving relations?
2. Link the American intervention in the 1990–1991 Persian Gulf War to the decision process that eventuated in the invasion of Iraq in 2003. How has this decision continued to be relevant?
3. Trace U.S.-Iraqi relations through the three phases identified in the text. How did each phase contribute to current issues with Iraq?
4. What are the major U.S. interests and options in post-occupation Iraq? Relate these to the problem posed by IS.
5. How does the Islamic State pose a special problem for the Middle East and the United States? Elaborate.
6. What are the characteristics of IS that make it a special case? Elaborate on each.
7. Which of the IS characteristics are also sources of vulnerability for the IS future? Explain how.
8. What are U.S. policy options toward IS and Syria? How do regional politics complicate these? Which option makes most sense to you?

BIBLIOGRAPHY

Ajami, Fouad. *The Syrian Rebellion*. Palo Alto, CA: Hoover Institution Press, 2013.

Bacevich, Andrew J. "Even If We Defeat the Islamic State, We'll Still Lose the Bigger War." *Washington Post* (online), October 3, 2014.

Brisard, Jean Jacques. *Zarqawi: The New Face of Al-Qaeda*. New York: Other Press, 2005.

Central Intelligence Agency. *The CIA World Factbook, 2016*. New York: Skyhorse, 2015.

Chandrasekaran, Rajiv. *Imperial Life in the Emerald City: Inside Iraq's Green Zone*. New York: Knopf, 2007.

Cockburn, Patrick. *The Rise of the Islamic State: ISIS and the New Sunni Revolution.* London: Verso, 2015.

Cronin, Audrey Kurth. "ISIS Is Not a Terrorist Group: Why Counterterrorism Won't Stop the Latest Jihadi Group." *Foreign Affairs* 94, no. 2 (March/April 2015): 87–98.

Goldberg, Jeffrey. "After Iraq." *The Atlantic* 301, no. 1 (January/February 2008): 68–79.

Hashemi, Nader, and Danny Postel (eds.). *The Syrian Dilemma.* Cambridge, MA: MIT Press, 2013.

Isikoff, Michael, and David Corn. *Hubris: The Inside Story of Spin, Scandal, and the Selling of the Iraq War.* New York: Three Rivers, 2007.

Kristol, William, and Lawrence F. Kaplan. *The War over Iraq: Saddam's Tyranny and America's Mission.* New York: Encounter, 2003.

Lesch, David W. *Syria: The Rise and Fall of the House of Assad.* New Haven, CT: Yale University Press, 2013.

McCants, William. *The ISIS Apocalypse: The History, Strategy, and Doomsday Vision of the Islamic State.* New York: St. Martin's, 2015.

Polk, William R. *Understanding Iraq.* New York: HarperPerennial, 2006.

Pollack, Kenneth M. *The Threatening Storm: The Case for Invading Iraq* (A Council on Foreign Relations Book). New York: Random House, 2002.

Serwer, Daniel. "Iraq Struggles to Govern Itself." *Current History* 109, no. 731 (December 2010): 390–94.

Sky, Emma. "Iraq, From Surge to Sovereignty." *Foreign Affairs* 90, no. 2 (March/April 2011): 117–27.

Sly, Liz. "The War against the Islamic State Hits Hurdles Just as the U.S. Military Gears Up." *Washington Post* (online), May 8, 2016.

Snow, Donald M. *The Middle East, Oil, and the U.S. National Security Policy: Intractable Problems, Impossible Solutions.* Lanham, MD: Rowman & Littlefield, 2016.

———. *What after Iraq?* New York: Pearson Longman, 2009.

Stern, Jessica, and J. M. Berger. *ISIS: The State of Terror.* New York: Ecco, 2015.

Von Drehle, David. "The War on ISIS." *Time* 185, no. 8 (March 9, 2015): 24–31.

Weiss, Michael, and Hassan Hassan. *ISIS: Inside the Army of Terror.* Updated edition. New York: Regan Arts, 2016.

Wood, Graeme. "What ISIS Really Wants." *The Atlantic* 321, no. 2 (March 2015): 78–90.

CHAPTER 2
The Middle East II

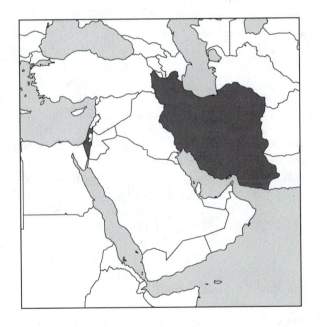

May 16, 2016, was the hundredth anniversary of the Sykes-Picot agreement that created some of the terribly imperfect boundaries distinguishing the countries of the Middle East, and especially of the Levant. It was not an occasion around which there was great celebration or positive remembrance. The boundaries formed the basis for creating Iraq, Syria, Lebanon, and Jordan in something very close to their present forms. Whether the region would have been less turbulent had the British and French diplomats done a "better" job is conjectural; the violence and instability of the area are not.

To this point, much of the instability, and particularly those parts that spill over into places and situations of direct and unavoidable American interests, has been bounded. Jordan and Lebanon have somehow avoided the worst of the maelstrom of the Islamic State phenomenon, and the other area of historic interest to the United States, the oil-rich Persian Gulf region, has managed to escape the central fray as well. Containing the instability emitting from Iraq and Syria remains the central regional concern for Washington, including those countries on the peripheries of the IS threat.

Two regional pillars stand at opposite ends of the Levant crisis. Neither was a part of Sykes-Picot in any direct way, which may help explain why both have been successful independent states throughout the contemporary period. The two states are very different by any physical or demographic measure, but they each serve as sturdy sentinels, in effect keeping the messiness of the Levant from spreading more widely. Both have been and remain important components in American foreign policy in the Middle East.

These two regional powers are Israel and Iran. Israel is a tiny country with a population of only slightly more than six million Jews within its internationally accepted boundaries (see below), but it is heavily armed and mobilized, and is the only regional state with nuclear weapons, an unacknowledged but critical element of Israeli national security. Israel has been a pillar of American Middle Eastern foreign and national security policy since the state of Israel was formally established in 1947. Its significance is further highlighted by the fact that the vast majority of adherents to Judaism reside either in Israel or the United States or, in some cases, both. In important ways, Israel and the United States are politically joined at the hip, but like all siblings, their relationship is not always tranquil. Politically, no American national politician or administration can avoid declaring that Israel's security is a top American foreign policy priority.

Iran, at the eastern end of the Levant, is an entirely different matter. It is the modern manifestation of Persia, the world's second-oldest continuous civilization. Among Muslim countries, it is third most populous (after Indonesia and Egypt), although it is the only one of the three that is predominantly Shiite. For the first thirty-five years after World War II, Iran was arguably America's closest Islamic partner (along with Sunni Saudi Arabia).

When the Shah of Iran, around whom that collaboration revolved, was overthrown, the relationship was turned on its head, and the two countries have been at serious odds ever since. If Israel and the United States are like international siblings, the American relationship with Iran is more like that of two former lovers. Opposition to the Iranian regime has been as basic a fixture of American politics since 1980 as has been support for Israel.

POWERFUL BOOKENDS

At first blush, Israel and Iran would appear to be an unlikely "pair" of states. They are certainly dissimilar by any objective measure: Iran is the physical behemoth of the region, the metaphorical Goliath, and Israel a small and beleaguered David in an "Arab Sea." A closer look at the two states, however, reveals more similarities than one might initially imagine, and each state occupies a large amount of the time and effort of American foreign policy makers.

The two countries are indeed the bookends of the Levant crisis, their presence containing the physical spread of the contest more broadly. Shiite Iran serves as a primary barrier to the physical march of Sunni IS further into Iraq and eastward, and the knowledge that expansion of the caliphate westward toward the Mediterranean would likely bring an Israeli military response helps cool IS pretension in that direction. The fact they are, by different metrics, the two most militarily potent states in the region adds to their dampening effect on others in the Middle East.

The two countries have had a schizophrenic relationship with one another. Cyrus the Great of Persia granted political rights to his Jewish population in 549 BCE that helped lead to the first Jewish state; indeed, the symbolism of his act was so great that President Harry S. Truman, in declaring American recognition of newly independent Israel on May 14, 1948, declared, "I am Cyrus." When the Shah ruled Iran from the early 1950s until 1979, Israel and Iran had positive relations, and Israel received much of its petroleum from Iran. When the Iranians replaced the Shah with a militantly Shiite regime, those relations deteriorated. Along with the rise of a regime in Jerusalem wedded strongly to keeping the West Bank, relations have been implacably oppositional ever since. Israeli threats to destroy the Iranian nuclear program militarily and Iranian support for the anti-Israel Hezbollah terrorist group symbolizes those relations.

The two countries share other regional distinctions, especially in the military realm. They are arguably the two most powerful states in the region—Iran by virtue of its population (the *CIA World Factbook* reports that there were over twenty-three million Iranians eligible for military service in 2010) and Israel by virtue of the acknowledged ferocity and proficiency of the Israel Defense Force (IDF) and its possession of a nuclear arsenal fully capable of destroying any regional power that might threaten or attack it. In a turbulent area, Iran has not been attacked since Iraq tried in 1980, and Israel has not suffered other than random terrorist attacks since 1973.

The nuclear edge of the relationship is significant and will be emphasized in this chapter. Israel is the only state in the region that currently possesses nuclear weapons (technically, the government neither confirms nor denies that they have the roughly 250 warheads generally ascribed to them), and most are on nuclear submarines impervious to preemption. The demographic nature of most Middle Eastern countries makes them highly vulnerable to nuclear attack, with populations concentrated in a few cities that could easily be incinerated. This fact makes even an implied Israeli threat against Muslim neighbors very effective; should other states such as Iran also gain nuclear weapons, Israel would be in a similarly perilous position, which is the strongest strategic reason for Israeli fixation with a possible Iranian ascendancy to nuclear weapons status. Iranian nuclear weapons would traumatize the Sunni states of the region and quite likely lead to a regional nuclear arms race as states such as Saudi Arabia sought to acquire them.

Israel and Iran share some common bases of relationship that affect how the United States approaches them, but there are also significant differences. American support for Israel is constant, a bedrock of American policy that no administration could deny. American politicians regularly vie for who can state the most unequivocal, militant basis of that commitment. U.S.-Israeli friction has been over relations with the current Israeli regime and its policies, and it has tended to focus on the question of continued Israeli possession of the West Bank of the Jordan River, a policy that infuriates the Muslim Middle East and strains Israeli relations with American allies in Europe and elsewhere. It is also a debate about the future of the Jewish State.

American relations with Iran are both more complicated and more antagonistic. American relations with Iran were very close for over thirty-five years when the Shah was in power, including close collaboration politically, economically, and militarily. That closeness, however, alienated traditional elements in Iran and contributed to a virulent anti-Americanism after the Iranian Revolution. The symbol of this reversal of relations was the Iranian hostage crisis of 1979–1981, a 444-day period when Iranian "students" occupied the American embassy in Teheran and held its staff prisoners as a way to force the United States to return the Shah, in medical asylum in New York, to Iran (the effort failed). The two countries have had no bilateral relations since, although they do interact through intermediaries. The signal example of Iranian-American relations is the agreement signed by Iran and the UN Security Council plus Germany by which Iran renounced any intention to acquire nuclear weapons.

CASE: THE UNITED STATES AND ISRAEL

American relations with Israel are unique for both countries. Israel is America's closest compatriot state in the Middle East, based in the unequivocal American determination to guarantee Israel's survival in a hostile geopolitical neighborhood. Other American interests, mostly grounded in the historic American dependence on Persian Gulf petroleum possessed by states hostile to Israel, occasionally clash with loyalty to Israel, but when they do, the ties to Israel normally prevail. The 1973 Arab oil boycott of the United States because it had supported Israel in the Yom Kippur War is emblematic.

Despite their closeness, the two states have very different worldviews. Unlike virtually all other states, Israel perceives itself in a desperate existential struggle, surrounded by hostile neighbors who wish to destroy both the Jewish state and its population, an effective extension of the Holocaust. This fear and actions to avoid it play a critical role in Israeli actions in the world and create animosities toward the Israelis. With the partial exception of the Soviet nuclear threat during the Cold War, the United States faces no parallel stress. Rather, the United States has global interests of which Israel is but one, and although it has adversaries, none seriously threaten the existence of the United States. The Israeli obsession with its existence and how to preserve it creates the greatest source of discussion in U.S.-Israeli relations.

The two friends are dissimilar in other ways. Israel is a tiny country that ranks physically as the world's 154th-largest in land mass and has a population that is 99th in world rankings. The United States, by contrast, has the third-largest landmass and third-largest population among countries of the world. The United States is, by most measures, the most powerful country in the world; Israel is a regional power.

The demographics of the relationship would seem to create a sense of proportion in the relationship, but such is not always the case. In another work (*The Middle East, Oil, and the U.S. National Security Policy*), I described the basic relationship in recent years as asymmetrical and inverted. Clearly, the asymmetry arises from any objective valuation of the relative importance of the two countries to one another. U.S. support is absolutely fundamental to Israeli security and prosperity: American provision of arms and training to the IDF and the provision of developmental assistance have been bedrock guarantees in Israel's posture toward the world, and Israel needs American support in a hostile world. As a result, Israel is very active in trying to influence American national security policy toward Israeli positions, most notably toward Iran. By contrast, the American loyalty toward Israel is more emotional (based in the reaction to the Holocaust), demographic (most of world Jewry lives in one of the two countries), and political (based on the influence of American supporters of Israel in domestic politics). By any objective standard, however, the basic asymmetry is that the United States is a great deal more important to Israel than the other way around.

The irony is that perceptions of this importance often seem inverted. The current Israeli government of Prime Minister Benjamin Netanyahu has formed an effective political alliance with conservative Republicans in the United States to produce enormous influence for Israel in American policy in Israel's favor. The "Israeli lobby" has long been an effective way by which Israel cemented American support for its positions (see Mearsheimer and Walt), but it has become more blatant over the dual issues of Israeli policy toward the "occupied territories" of the West Bank and the prevention of Iranian development and deployment of nuclear weapons. Both sides of the lively Israeli debate on its future are represented in Washington: the American-Israeli Public Affairs Committee (AIPAC) favoring the conservative position, and J Street representing liberal Israelis. The Trump administration appeared to tilt toward the conservatives when it nominated David Friedman to be U.S. Ambassador to Israel.

In this relationship, the interests of the two countries have seemed virtually inverted, with the Israeli prime minister in effect lobbying the U.S. government to support Israeli positions. Foreign governments always seek to influence one another, of course, but Israeli efforts have been particularly open and blatant. When Netanyahu addressed a joint session of the American Congress (at the most unusual invitation of the Congressional leadership and ignoring the president) in 2015, the appearance was of a senior, more consequential leader schooling a smaller and more dependent vassal, rather than the other way around.

The uniqueness of U.S.-Israeli relations is both difficult to understand and idiosyncratic. No comparably sized state exercises the degree of influence that Israel does over American foreign policy, and American support for Israel provides a safeguard for the Israelis that is difficult to analogize anywhere else in the world. This uniqueness has historic, physical, and political bases, and they give a unique cast both to those relations and in the interaction of American interests and options in the world.

Israel: A Physical and Political Sketch

The idea of a state of Israel is ancient, dating back to the time the Old Testament was produced, but the existence of a formal Jewish state has mostly been an aspiration throughout history. Much of the Old Testament is a history of the travails of the Jewish people to carve out a suitable homeland in a hostile environment in a part of the world where there are multiple claimants to virtually all territory, either divinely or historically justified.

The Jewish claim is based in their interpretation of God's will; actual possession of the territory currently occupied by Israel has been a long and tortuous journey. The political right particularly embraces this claim. As one spokesperson, Ayelet Shaked, puts it, "I do believe in the historic right of the Jewish people to the land of Israel." Israel, in this vision, encompasses the occupied territories on the West Bank, a position held strongly by Netanyahu and his supporters.

The movement that successfully promoted the modern state of Israel, Zionism, has its roots in the nineteenth century among Jews who mostly lived in Europe but desired to build a state on God's "promised land." Jewish immigration to what became Israel began in earnest after World War I when the territory of Israel, which had been part of the Ottoman Empire, came under mandatory control by Great Britain. The great push to relocate what was left of European Jewry came after World War II and the Holocaust, as displaced Jewish people sought refuge from the unsettled conditions in war-ravaged Europe. Officially, their migration was discouraged by the major powers, but embarrassment over the slaughter by the Nazis had created a massive guilt complex that made these exhortations largely hollow. The "exodus" became a flood, and when the new settlers demanded that a formal Jewish state be carved out of parts of Transjordan, the United States and the Soviet Union co-sponsored the resolution in the UN Security Council that brought Israel into the roster of sovereign states in 1948.

The creation of the state of Israel was controversial. When the Jewish state was declared, the neighboring Muslim states declared war on the new state and vowed to push the Israelis into the sea. Their military effort was uncoordinated and inept, and the Israelis repulsed it and, in the process, added more territory. Many Palestinians fled into exile in the surrounding countries, creating a refugee problem that remains. Much of the ongoing animosity between the Jewish and Palestinian populations dates to the late 1940s, particularly in terms of rights of occupation and citizenship in territory jointly claimed by Jews and Palestinians.

The first twenty-five years of Israeli existence were marked by concerted efforts of its Arab neighbors to confront, defeat, and destroy the Israelis, efforts that uniformly failed and generally resulted in increased Israeli advantage. In 1956, Israel joined Britain and France in the Suez War, as those European powers moved to seize the Suez Canal back from Egypt's Nasser, who had nationalized it the year before. The British and French were forced to withdraw, but Israel gained territory on the Sinai Peninsula. In 1967, Egypt, Syria, and Jordan attacked Israel and were soundly defeated. In the process, Israel acquired territory from each: Sinai and the Gaza Strip from Egypt, the West Bank of the Jordan River from Jordan, and the Golan Heights from Syria. The occupation of Sinai was ended by the Egyptian-Israeli peace accord of 1982, and the Israelis relinquished control of Gaza in 2006; the other territories remain matters of ongoing contention. In 1973, Israel's adversaries struck again and enjoyed enough initial success that Israel allegedly armed its nuclear arsenal to prevent its defeat and the Soviets threatened to intervene to aid Egyptian forces trapped with their back to the Suez Canal. The result was a short but tense confrontation between the Americans and the Soviets that ended when the Soviets agreed not to drop troops into the war zone and the Americans agreed to guarantee the repatriation of the Egyptian army trapped against the canal.

The 1973 war was an important watershed for Israel in at least three enduring ways. First, its opponents had given their best shot at defeating or destroying Israel, and they had failed. None of them has tried since, and the only real military purposes for which the IDF has been used are Israeli incursions into neighboring countries (e.g., their largely unsuccessful 2006 foray into Lebanon to destroy Hezbollah) or into the occupied territories of the West Bank or Gaza to quell uprisings or to suppress suspected terrorists. Second, the 1973 experience disillusioned Arab states, and especially Egypt (the physically largest state opposing Israel), with the Soviet Union, which had not, in their estimation, acted in a timely manner to resupply and support their forces. The process of excluding the Soviets militarily from the region effectively occurred after 1973 everywhere except for the naval enclave the Russians still maintain in Syria. Third, any ambiguity that may have surrounded Israel's unacknowledged nuclear arsenal and their willingness to use it to guarantee their survival (or to take down their enemies with them) was laid to rest by reports of the arsenal's activation. From that point forward, Israel's enemies knew that confronting Israel militarily potentially posed an existential threat to *them*, a sobering judgment.

The geopolitical situation of Israel was fundamentally altered by the events of 1967 and 1973. The Six-Day War put Israel at physical advantage by providing possession of territories harmful to Israel in the hands or others (such as the Golan Heights, from which its enemies had historically launched artillery attacks again Israeli settlements), and it created leverage because Israel now had something the others wanted back. In a geopolitical sense, 1973 was the icing on the cake; Israeli actions created an atmosphere in which its enemies no longer perceive any advantage in threatening or waging war against the Jewish state. Since 1973, Israel has been the target of terrorist attacks and insurrection from the occupied territories, but it has not been at war in the way it was four times in its first quarter-century. Israel arguably is still not entirely secure from its enemies, but it is far less insecure than it used to be. The security threats it now faces—notably the fate of the occupied territories and the prospect of an "Arab bomb"—are matters either of its own creation or concerns over which it has some leverage to influence.

This evolution is at least partly a tribute to the Israelis and their unique state. At one level, Israel is a very ordinary place. The physical area recognized by the international community (essentially the boundaries before the 1967 war) is 5,822 square miles, which is slightly larger than New Jersey. The Occupied Territories, by contrast, are slightly less than one-third the size of Israel and are about the size of Delaware. A fair proportion of this area is virtually barren desert, meaning that the inhabitable space available to the state is less than its gross size; only 15.45 percent of Israel is considered arable, and it has modest natural resources that include timber, potash, copper ore, and natural gas. Physically, Israel is not an impressive place. Israel's boundaries are with states that are current, former, or potential future opponents, notably Egypt, Syria, Lebanon, and Jordan (in roughly descending order of opposition).

Israel's strength is its people. The country has a population of approximately 7.8 million, of whom 91 percent live in urban areas (over 5 million live in Tel Aviv/Yafo, Haifa, or Jerusalem—not including contested East Jerusalem). Of this population, approximately 6 million are Jews, 1.2 million are Palestinian Arabs, and the rest are Christians and others.

Population statistics and their implications are slippery, largely due to whether people living in the occupied territories are included. *CIA World Factbook* figures reported in 2016 suggest that there are approximately 557,000 Jewish settlers in the occupied and contested areas: 341,400 on the West Bank, 18,900 in the Golan Heights, and 196,700 in East Jerusalem. These numbers change rapidly, based primarily on the opening of new settlements by the Israelis, and are in areas that could eventually become part of Israel, Jordan, Palestine, or Syria. It has been reported that the Palestinian population of the occupied territories is almost four million, and there are numerous Palestinian refugees in exile in the surrounding Arab states, many of whom seek to return. It is misleading to ascribe too much precision to any of these figures, but they do have some potentially ominous implications for Israel.

These demographics are consequential. The Zionist mandate called for bringing as much of world Jewry to Israel as possible, a mandate reinforced by the religious belief that Jewish possession of Israel was a promise made to the Jews by God—the basis of the "promised land" claim that is a prominent feature of Israeli justifications of many of its acts. There are, however, two demographic realities that confront this aspiration. One is that there is simply not enough physical space in pre-1967 Israel (the boundaries accepted as legitimate by the vast majority of the international community) to accommodate much of the remaining Jewish population outside Israel. The other is that the inhabitable territory within internationally defined Israel has, for all practical purposes, been used. Advances in science such as conversion of salt water to potable water could increase the available land slightly, but pre-1967 Israel is about as populated as it can reasonably get.

These physical facts collide with Israeli aspirations, especially as they are articulated by the Netanyahu government. When the terrorist attacks occurred in Paris over the Christmas season of 2015, he was one of the heads of state who visited France to offer his condolences, but he also came with an extraordinary offer to French Jews, who he said would be welcome immigrants to Israel. The Jewish population of France is not great (about one percent of the French population of sixty-six million), but unless his offer was entirely hortatory, it raised the question of where Israel would physically put the influx of any sizable number of the invitees. The answer was that Israel lacked the ability to accommodate a large number of French émigrés within the 1967 boundaries, leaving two possibilities: either the invitation was an empty gesture, or Netanyahu was in fact inviting French Jews to live on the occupied West Bank. The latter possibility had potentially ominous implications for the disposition of the occupied territories, one of the major sources of disagreement between Israel and the United States.

Within its confined space, Israel is a remarkable country, particularly given the physical "neighborhood" in which it resides. Israel does exist in a condition of existential threat that is unique. One can argue, and both Israelis and students of Israel do, about how lively the present level of threat is: how likely is it that some state or states will actually launch an existential attack against the Jewish state? Such a discussion, from an Israeli vantage point, is prejudiced by their circumstance. The purpose of the Holocaust was a genocidal elimination of European Jews (the term *genocide* was invented in 1944 to describe the Holocaust), and pogroms and forceful incarceration in ghettos and the like have created a not surprising paranoia among Jews toward those around them. This paranoia has been reinforced since independence: the purpose of the botched attack on the new state in 1948 was to drive the Israelis into the Mediterranean Sea, and Islamic governments (Iran, for instance) and terrorist groups (Hezbollah as an example) have threatened the Jewish state ever since. It is arguable that nuclear weapons have reduced the objective prospect of an attempt to destroy Israel, which has made no bones about its firm intent to take down any state that tries to destroy it—a task for which nuclear weapons are well suited. This mind-set may be difficult for most people to understand or accept, but that it resonates with large numbers of Israelis should be less surprising and should condition any critical appraisal of Israel.

One thing that makes Israel distinct from other countries in the region is that it is the only functioning full democracy in the Middle East. The franchise is available both to the Jewish majority of Israel and to its Palestinian minority, both of which are represented by multiple parties in the

Knesset, the single (unicameral) legislative body of the state. The head of government is the prime minister, who is the elected leader of the coalition of political parties that forms the majority in the chamber. Over fifteen parties are currently represented in the Knesset (the largest being Netanyahu's Likud-Beiteinu coalition with 23.6 percent of the vote in the 2013 election), making it both a multiparty and contentious body. Like Great Britain, Israel has no formal written constitution but governs on the basis of democratic processes embedded in English and other common-law traditions. Unlike its neighbors, freedom of speech makes for a very lively and spirited quality of debate within both the government and the public. The fact that Israel is democratic and that its factions resemble political opinions within the United States adds to the affinity between politicians of the two countries.

American relations with Israel are closer than they are with any other country in the Middle East. The American practical guarantee to protect Israel from the worst actions its enemies may conjure has been a bedrock of Israeli security, and while there are differences, sometimes heated rhetorically, about the steadfastness of that relationship, hardly anyone in either country seriously questions the symbiosis between the two countries.

Basic U.S.-Israeli Relations

U.S.-Israeli relations begin from a basic expression of the incongruity of the inversion of relations between the two countries. Israel's view and relations with the world represent a central focus: the survival of the Israeli state in a hostile world that poses an existential threat to it and that might succeed in that destruction without the single focus of Israel on its avoidance. This goal is so overriding that it cannot be entrusted to any other state(s); only the state of Israel can ensure it. The foreign country on which it most relies for assistance in this goal is the United States, and this relationship is so important that Israel does and will do whatever is necessary to ensure that the United States will perform its role. If, however, the two countries clash, many Israelis believe the existential threat overrides even friendship and that Israel must be prepared to act unilaterally, regardless of international opinion.

The American perspective is broader. The well-being and continued existence of Israel is a primary value of the United States, but it is by no means the only important interest of America in the region and certainly the world. Historically, the American hierarchy of interests in the Middle East, for instance, has consisted of three primary concerns that are not always compatible with one another: secure access to petroleum, Israeli security, and regional peace and security/Soviet exclusion.

The three foci are largely intuitive. Since the end of World War II, the primary global importance of the Middle East has been its possession of the world's largest petroleum reserves, and most countries, including the United States, have been dependent on that energy resource and thus on secure, reliable, and economic access to it. Achieving that security has not always been automatic, as American relations with Iran discussed in the next section reveal. That dependence is contracting for the United States due to reduced demand and new sources such as shale oil and gas, but Middle Eastern petroleum remains the major source of regional geopolitical importance. Israeli security is a major *American* interest, but it is not shared by other regional actors. Before its demise, limiting or eliminating Soviet influence in the region was seen as a major vehicle to help attain both other goals. It has been replaced by the pursuit of regional stability, including democratization, as a way to reach the other goals.

From an American viewpoint, reconciling the need for petroleum energy and ensuring Israeli security have always represented the horns of a dilemma of American Middle East policy. Both are fundamental, vital U.S. interests: petroleum for energy security and economic prosperity, and Israel's existence for emotional and humanitarian reasons dating back to Hitler's genocide. The problem, of course, arises from antipathy between Israel and its Islamic neighbors; both consider the other to be enemies of varying but significant degree. Some of the Arab states have posed active, open existential threats to Israel over time, and although those calls are less frequent and arguably more symbolic in a world of Israeli regional nuclear monopoly, they remain a vital concern of the Israelis. At the same time, the Arab states remain antagonistic toward Israel and some Israeli policies, ensuring that antipathy between the Jewish and Islamic states does not disappear.

The perspectives are not entirely reconcilable. U.S. policy has tried to balance the three points of its interest triangle. It assures Israel of its fidelity in a variety of ways, including generous economic assistance to its military, and it seeks to assure the oil-possessing states of its continuing support for them in ways such as coming to the military aid of Saudi Arabia when it was threatened by Iraq during the Persian Gulf War of 1990–1991. Since the Soviet Union folded in 1991, promoting peace and stability in the Muslim Middle East has become a primary initiative to reconcile the two incompatibilities. Its premises include the idea that stabilization, and especially democratization, of the Arab world will reduce their differences with Israel and allow the two sides to reconcile. When the United States invaded Iraq in 2003, one of the hopes of the neoconservatives in the Bush administration who pushed hardest for the war was that it would have this result.

The American and Israeli perspectives on the Middle East are at odds due to these conflicting views of the region. American policy can only succeed if it can balance and reconcile its conflicting interests of a secure Israel and a peaceful, stabilizing Islamic region. For the United States, the result is the need for a balancing act, where the United States seeks to dampen manifestations of conflict between Israel and its neighbors, promotes greater cooperation (or at least the absence of conflict) between them, and creates a more peaceful environment in which it can pursue *all* its interests. It is a difficult, possibly impossible set of priorities simultaneously to pursue, and it is made more difficult by both domestic American and international objections.

The primary domestic barricades come from overt support for Israel from American citizens, both overt supporters of Israel from the Jewish population in the United States (which is not monolithic in its support for various expressions of any particular issue) and from non-Jewish conservative elements in the country who admire the Israeli state. These advocates demand strong and frequent paeans for Israel, even when these are antagonistic toward Arab positions the U.S. government is also attempting to accommodate. Likewise, conservative Israelis either reject the possibility of reconciliation with their neighbors (and thus dismiss such efforts) or believe that the underlying existential threat is so great that Israel simply cannot afford to take chances by extending an olive branch that could be dispatched by an Arab sword.

These varying perspectives frame the critical elements of U.S.-Israeli relations. Most dealings between the two countries are close and cooperative: Israel and the United States are, indeed, the best of friends, but, as the old saying goes, "what you see is where you sit." Israel's concerns in the world—and especially the region—are conditioned by history, size, location, and the primacy of the threat it faces. Whether one believes its concern is excessive or not, the seriousness of its perspective means Israelis believe they cannot be wrong and make a decision that could endanger their existence.

The American perspective is very different. Americans do not feel themselves to be at the same degree of existential risk as the Israelis, and American interests are much broader than those of Israel. The security of Israel is *one* American interest in the world and in the Middle East, and even though it is a very important interest to the United States, it must compete and be reconciled with other interests. The consequences of being wrong may be substantial for Americans, but they rarely involve the survival of the United States.

These differences create different, sometimes conflicting, American and Israeli views on issues of common interest to them. The emotional and very articulate expressions of Israeli positions compete with a somewhat less fervent American position on the same matters, simply because the issues and their outcomes may be more important to one of the two sides. Moreover, when these debates become public, the very democratic nature of both countries amplifies the expression of those differences, in some cases arguably to the extent of distorting them in the public dialogue. The result may be to constrict or even distort how the issues and their resolution occur. The two issues that will be examined are the most extreme expressions of this dynamic—the issue of the Palestinian State/West Bank, and the issue of Iranian acquisition of nuclear weapons. The Palestinian question will be addressed in the next section; the Iranian nuclear program will be introduced there as well but will be developed in the Iranian case that follows.

U.S. Policy Options

No two issues highlight the differences in policy and perspective on the world more clearly than the disputes over the fate of Palestine and Iranian nuclear weapons ambitions. The outcomes of both disputes are seen in existential terms: failure to achieve the Israeli position could mean confronting Armageddon in the hottest rhetoric, and this belief creates a sense of intransigence that makes a negotiated compromise difficult if not impossible. The United States believes both issues are important, but they do not affect basic American security. Rather, they reflect ways in which America's multiple interests in the region can be attained. Israeli policy on both has been inflexible. It will discuss solutions to the Palestinian problem, but generally only in terms it knows the Americans and Palestinians will not accept—out of a conviction that only its position ensures Israeli survival. It has regularly threatened military action against Iran to destroy its nuclear infrastructure in the same way it did in the twentieth century against Syria and Iraq, a proposal the U.S. government has deemed both ineffective and likely to lead to regional war. Neither side has been effective in moving the other toward its position on either conflict. Examining the two problems shows how even the best of friends sometimes cannot reconcile their differences and frustrate one another.

The Palestinian Question

In essence, the Palestinian problem surrounds who should exercise sovereignty over the West Bank of the Jordan River (formerly a part of Jordan) and the narrow Gaza Strip along the Mediterranean Sea (formerly administered by Egypt). The problem has remained an unsettled sore for a half century; both territories were occupied by Israel after the 1967 war. Efforts to resolve the question of sovereignty over the two areas were attempted in the 1990s (the Oslo Accords), and eventually sovereign control of Gaza was turned over to the Palestinian Authority in 2013. The West Bank is the real prize, and it remains unresolved and the source of U.S.-Israeli disagreement.

The Palestinian question is in essence a real estate problem over who has rightful claim to the West Bank of the Jordan River, an area that was part of the Kingdom of Jordan before the 1967 war. The Jordanians no longer pursue the area, leaving the Israelis and the Palestinians the contending parties for sovereign control. Each has a different and what it feels more compelling claim. Most countries of the world side with the Palestinians, who consider it to be the site of the sovereign state of Palestine. The Israelis disagree.

The Israeli claim, voiced most forcefully by Netanyahu, is based on three concerns. The first is geopolitical. The Israelis realized during their early wars that if their enemies controlled the West Bank, they faced a geostrategic threat. At its narrowest point, the distance from the West Bank to the Mediterranean Sea is only about ten miles, meaning that an Arab thrust from the West Bank to the sea could cut Israel in half and leave it in a compromised, even untenable military situation. Control of the West Bank creates "strategic depth" for Israel by moving the distance back to the Jordan River itself and making defense more tenable. Another Israeli geopolitical fear is that a Palestinian state could become a sovereign sponsor of terrorism against Israel that would be much more difficult to control than it is within current conditions. The second is religious. Netanyahu and other devout Zionists believe that God willed the entire Levant to Israel, of which the West Bank is part, thereby giving the claim divine imprimatur. Third and possibly most important in current terms, continued control of the West Bank provides additional living space for Jewish "settlers," mostly immigrants from other countries. As noted, there are now about a half-million Jewish residents of the West Bank and East Jerusalem, and they would have to be evicted, relocated, or assimilated should the West Bank become Palestine.

The Palestinian position is more straightforward. Large numbers of Palestinian Arabs fled Israel in 1948 and have remained a stateless population ever since, residing in greater or lesser deprivation in various surrounding countries, including the West Bank. Their desire is to have a state of their own. This position is endorsed by most members of the international community. The West Bank is the only available and appropriate site for such a state.

Palestinian Options and Disagreements

There have been two basic visions by which to resolve the Palestinian problem. The most common is some form of the *two-state solution*, by which a Palestinian state is created on the West Bank to exist side by side with Israel. This position has historically been the American preference, although it is opposed by some because it contradicts the Netanyahu position. Conservative Israelis (especially the settler community) also oppose this outcome, although it is supported by liberal Israelis. The official Israeli position does not dismiss this outcome out of hand but is sufficiently vague in terms of steps to implementation to frustrate proponents of Palestine.

The issue begins with a dilemma. Israel was created as and remains a state that is both Jewish and democratic, but continued occupation and especially incorporation of the West Bank into Israel might make these goals incompatible. As Israeli demographer DellaPergola explains, "The state faces a conundrum because it has three fundamental goals . . . to preserve the state's Jewish identity, democratic character, and territorial state." The problem is demographic. Israel within the essential 1967 boundaries is heavily (five to one) Jewish and can maintain that identity indefinitely. The population growth rate is much higher among Palestinians than Jews in the territories, however, and if the West Bank is part of Israel, Muslims will eventually outnumber Jews in the larger state. Then the conundrum kicks in: if that happens, Israel can be either Jewish or democratic, but not both. A democratic state would have a majority Arab population, and not be Jewish. A state in which Jewish citizens had greater rights than non-Jews (effectively what President Jimmy Carter referred to as an apartheid state) could remain Jewish but not fully democratic. From this analysis, the only way for Israel to retain its preferred identity (Jewish *and* fully democratic) is to adopt a two-state solution, where there is a basically permanent Jewish majority in Israel and a Muslim majority in Palestine. This analysis is accepted and forms the base of liberal Israelis' position. As expressed by Tzipi Livni, "For us, it's about keeping Israel a democratic state. The only way to do that is by dividing the ancient land of Israel into two states." Benn says Netanyahu holds the opposite view: "In their view, Israel is a Jewish state and a democratic state—in that order."

The Israeli government essentially ignores the liberal argument as expressing future concerns and continues to populate the West Bank with settlements that increasingly look like efforts they would not abandon, and these settlements are absolutely necessary for a continued Zionist policy of bringing all or most Jews to Israel. They also soften the demographic effect by compensating somewhat for Israel's fertility rate, but they can only delay, not prevent, the ultimate demographic "time bomb."

Most American government officials have maintained that only a two-state solution serves Israel's long-term interest and that of the United States, which is in regional stabilization. Here the policy perspectives diverge and disagreement blooms. The U.S. perspective may place Israel at the head of its regional imperatives, but it has other perspectives as well, such as peace and stability to enhance energy flow. For Israel, the situation is starker: beginning, as it does, from the existential security threat it faces, it is unwilling to take any actions that might endanger its position. If a Palestinian state proves not to be a responsible member of the Middle East cast of countries, the United States will still survive. Israel might not. Other major barriers to creating two states include a Palestinian renunciation of the so-called right of return (the desire to reclaim property abandoned in 1948 within Israel) and adjustments of the 1967 borders to accommodate at least those Israeli settlements adjacent to those boundaries. The future of Jerusalem (i.e., can it be the capital of both states, as each claim?) further exacerbates the issue. Solving these problems will be difficult. From an American vantage point, they are also necessary for long-term regional health.

Iranian Nuclear Weapons

The same stark contrast basically surrounds the question of alleged Iranian intentions and actions to gain nuclear weapons. There is agreement both in Washington and Jerusalem that Iranian nuclear possession would pose serious regional problems that could directly imperil nuclear-armed Israel and possibly set off a race to create a "Sunni bomb" to match Iran's "Shiite bomb." The Iranians have denied any intention to create nuclear weapons, which meets with sharp skepticism in Israel and among America's most vocal supporters of the Jewish state. The question is what to do about this problem.

Nobody in the international community approves of the idea of Iranian nuclear proliferation, but their reasons and the methods they would employ to prevent it differ. At the most general level, there is agreement that *any* nonnuclear weapons states gaining the capability is a negative, because, by definition, each possessor increases the number of "fingers on the nuclear button"—the number of states that could start a nuclear war. Most of the potential aspirants are developing world states with some instability—a category that encompasses Iran—and this increases aversion. In the case of Iran, possession could start a regional nuclear arms race to procure the Arab Sunni bomb, which could mean negotiating access to Pakistani weapons or one of the oil-rich states starting its own program. Given regional instabilities, these possibilities are not comforting.

American policy toward Israel may change significantly under President Trump. On December 18, 2016, the president-elect announced that he would nominate David Friedman, a bankruptcy lawyer with no prior diplomatic experience, as ambassador to Israel. Friedman's public positions include opposition to the two-state solution, further development of West Bank settlements and possible annexation of the territory to the Israeli state, and moving the U.S. embassy to Jerusalem (thereby accepting all of Jerusalem as the Israeli capital). These positions reverse historic policy and, if implemented, would have serious consequences regionally and in future Israeli-American relations. Friedman's stance on the two-state policy is at odds with positions Trump took during the 2016 campaign, and his position on the disposition of the West Bank contradicts the general position of Netanyahu, who rhetorically accepts the two-state solution. These changes could affect American policy toward Iran as well.

CASE: THE UNITED STATES AND IRAN

U.S.-Iranian relations have been schizophrenic since World War II. At the end of the war, the Soviet Union cast a hopeful eye on Middle Eastern oil, and given their long common border, Iran seemed a reasonable place to launch a quest southward from their southern republic of Azerbaijan through the Iranian province of the same name. Recognizing the potential peril involved, the United States moved naval vessels into the eastern Mediterranean Sea and threatened military action if the Soviets did not abandon their initiative. The Soviets reluctantly complied, and the roller-coaster ride between Iran and the United States was engaged.

It has proceeded through several stages. The first began after the Azerbaijan crisis in 1946 and ended in 1953. Reza Pahlavi, the son of Reza Khan, who had united what became modern Iran in the 1920s, had arisen as the Shah (king), assumed the Peacock throne, and was immediately courted by Americans who saw Iran's oil reserves and other assets as a great opportunity to make money. They presented the Shah, who was thirty at the time and had grown up outside the country, with an elaborate developmental plan the heart of which was Western control of Iranian oil reserves, at the time the second-largest in the world. The plan had opponents, notably nationalist Mohammad Mossadegh, and in 1950 the Shah was overthrown and replaced by the only truly democratically chosen government in Iranian history under Mossadegh's leadership. Among the heretical (and described at the time as "communist") actions of the Mossadegh regime was to discard the economic development plan devised in Washington and to nationalize Iranian oil, thus giving control over Iranian oil revenues to the Iranians themselves. This move was so traumatic that officials in the United States, notably the Dulles brothers (see Kinzer 2013), conspired with the CIA to overthrow Mossadegh and bring the Shah back from exile. After a convoluted process, American-recruited elements successfully overthrew the Iranian regime on August 19, 1953, an action justified on the grounds of communist influence in Iran's government, and the Shah returned from exile. Iranians continue to remind Americans critical of Iranian politics that the United States overthrew the only freely elected government in their history.

The removal of Mossadegh ushered in a quarter-century of close collaboration and friendship in U.S.-Iranian relations. During this period, the Shah bought into American designs for Westernized development first articulated in the 1940s and rejected by Mossadegh. Military collaboration burgeoned as part of an effective trade-off whereby the Iranians were equipped and trained on the most advanced American military systems, in return for which they enforced freedom of access to the Persian Gulf, thereby ensuring the free and unfettered flow of oil to the West. From the vantage point of the Shah, the purpose of the collaboration was to reestablish the old glory of the Persian Empire in the form of a new Peacock Kingdom of Iran. From the American perspective, the arrangement provided a surrogate enthusiastically committed to guaranteeing an American strategic imperative without the direct application of American forces. It was a bargain that endured until 1979, despite evidence that things were not as idyllic as they first appeared.

Although it was apparent to very few at the time, the relationship was built on a faulty premise, the execution of which would eventually doom the collaboration. The premise was twofold: that the basic problem American intervention sought to overcome was the spread of Soviet communism to Iran, and that the solution was an effort that would Westernize and modernize Iran into a developed Western country wherein communism would have no appeal. The fallacies of the approach were that the evidence of communist activity—the rejection of Western development programs designed to increase American interests and to make money, and the nationalization of Iranian oil—were more nationalist than anything else. Communists were undoubtedly present in Iran, but they were not the problem. The second part of the premise, that Westernization would effectively "communist-proof" Iran, was also flawed: deeply conservative Iranian Shiites wanted religious purity, not the materialism of secular Western development. Iran was probably the most unpromising place on the face of the earth to try to Westernize in 1953 (Iraq, where the United States would try again in 2003, was probably second on the list).

The Shah, with grandiose pretensions of Iranian renaissance and his own potential as a modern Cyrus, bought into the American plans and moved to implement them. The major transformational tool was something called the White Revolution, the purpose of which was the rapid economic modernization of the country. The chief collaborators in this enterprise were a new entrepreneurial, technocratic class of Iranians and American advisors and consultants. Iranian students flocked to American universities, where they seemed ubiquitous during the 1960s and 1970s. American advisors flocked to Teheran and other Iranian urban centers created or expanded by the program. Under the Shah, those who embraced Westernization thrived and became a privileged, advantaged class. Unfortunately, not all Iranians enjoyed that fate.

While the Shah's revolution was entrancing Americans, the situation inside the country was not so positive. The Shah was aloof and aristocratic, and he was not especially popular with the Iranian masses. Many viewed him as a tyrant and the actions of his secret police, known as SAVAK, included the suppression, including torture, of those who opposed him, charges the Shah dismissed. Secularization was a major outgrowth of the Westernization program, and it deeply offended the profoundly sectarian

Shiite peasants who lived in the countryside and the slums of Iranian cities. Reforms also robbed the Shiite clergy of traditional land holdings and control of certain legal functions generally part of Western civil law. The peasants and clergy were natural allies, and increasingly they coalesced in opposition to the regime. The clergy led this opposition, which came to be focused in the forbidding visage of Ayatollah Ruhollah Khomeini.

By the mid-1970s, this opposition began to boil over, although it was not recognized in the United States. Two factors became crucial as the Shah's control crumbled. First, Jimmy Carter was elected president in 1976. One of his major emphases in foreign policy was human rights: supporters would be rewarded, and violators would be punished. In Iran, the Shah's government was forced to curtail its most abusive policies, resulting in less intelligence on dissident activity and less rosy depictions to Americans, who had been relying on SAVAK for most of their intelligence on the country. Dissidents had less to fear from SAVAK. At the same time, the Shah was diagnosed with cancer and had to undergo treatments that substantially debilitated him and his ability to make decisions as the opposition grew in the form of increasingly massive urban demonstrations that the government did not suppress, presumably because the Shah was too debilitated to order it.

The opposition reached a crescendo during January 1979 when the Shah left Iran on an advertised vacation that was universally interpreted as an abdication of the throne. Within days, Ayatollah Khomeini returned to Teheran in triumph, and the Iranian Revolution was joined. For a period of months, more moderate, pro-democratic factions (who had also not prospered under the Shah) competed with conservative religionists who supported Khomeini for control. Ultimately, the conservative clerics prevailed, and the result was the declaration of the Islamic Republic of Iran.

The final nail in the coffin of U.S.-Iranian comity was driven on November 4, 1979, when Iranian "students" stormed the American embassy in Teheran and captured and held captive embassy personnel until January 1981. The official cause of the takeover was that the Shah had been admitted to Bellevue Hospital in New York, and the Iranian revolutionary government demanded he be returned to Teheran for a predictable fate. The U.S. government refused the request, and the hostage crisis was front-page news for fourteen months. The period of American-Iranian friendship had given way to the "era of bad feelings" that is the third period of those relations and that continues to this day.

Iran: A Physical and Political Sketch

Iran would not be a major concern if it were just another state in the Middle East, but it is more than that. One way of ranking the importance of states (discussed in Snow, *Cases in International Relations*) is by employing a threefold categorization. At the top are the major powers, countries with power and interests that transcend regional boundaries and global power players. At the bottom are the more minor states, countries with limited abilities, interests, and aspirations within the world's regions.

Between these two extremes are the *pivotal states*, regional powers that by virtue of history, size, self-sense, and a variety of other measures are the most important states within specific geographic regions. These states generally lack global reach or aspirations, but within their regions, they cannot be ignored and generally cannot be manipulated, even by the major powers. Within their parts of the world, their role in regional international relations is thus pivotal to how the region functions and the extent to which outsiders can operate in that region. In the Middle East, Iran is the pivotal state.

Iran occupies a unique place in the world. It is the world's second-oldest continuous civilization (after China), and it has been a major world power whenever the Middle East has been a prominent part of international politics. Its place in the international sun has waxed and waned: it was the source of the mighty Persian Empire 4,500 years ago, but it was also subjugated as part of the Ottoman Empire until the end of World War I. The glory of Persia is central to its national myth, however, and since the removal of the Ottoman yoke, Persia as Iran has clearly yearned to reassert its place among the world's powers. That was the clear intent of the Shah's rule, and it is an aspiration of its current religious leadership.

Iran's claim to pivotal state status begins with its size. Its physical size is 631,659 square miles, slightly larger than Alaska and about three times the size of Arizona, making it the eighteenth largest country in the world in area. As such, it is also the second largest Muslim state (after Indonesia) in territory. It has a population of 81.8 million, making it the third most populous Muslim state (after Indonesia and Egypt) and by far the most populous Levantine state (Iraq is second with about 32 million, Saudi Arabia third with about 27.5 million).

Within Islam, Iran is the world's largest country with a distinct Shiite majority, with roughly nine of ten Iranians professing Shiism. Unlike most other Middle Eastern countries, its people are not Arab but are instead Persian Aryans, creating a further distinction between the Persians and their Arab Sunni regional counterparts and fueling part of the regional tensions. The only other countries with Shiite majorities are Iraq and Bahrain.

Economically, Iran has the world's third-largest reserves of petroleum and, despite Western sanctions, has been the world's sixth-largest producer and third-largest exporter (at about 2.5 million barrels a day) of oil. Western boycotts of Iranian oil have forced the country to exploit other markets, notably, according to Bakhtiari, in China and Russia. According to CIA figures, the gross domestic product (GDP) of Iran is about 7.8 trillion dollars (twentieth in the world) and likely to grow with many economic restrictions loosened as part of the 2015 nuclear weapons agreement. As evidence of the impact of sanctions, GDP per capita stands at $17,800, ninety-fifth in the world.

Iran is a regional pivot in another way. Like next-door neighbor Iraq, Iran sits in the middle of Asia and thus has both interests in and effects on continental affairs by virtue of its location. It sits at the top of and commands the eastern shoreline of the Persian Gulf, the waterway through which a large percentage of the world's oil flows from refineries along the Shatt al-Arab waterway that divides Iran and Iraq. It also borders the strategic Strait of Hormuz, through which petroleum must flow from the oil-rich Sunni kingdoms to reach world markets. When the Shah ruled and guaranteed that flow, he was a valued ally; since 1979, Iran has been viewed as a potential interrupter of that flow and is the prime reason for an American naval presence in the Gulf. Iran currently serves as a major inhibitor to the expansion of IS from the west (as discussed in chapter 1) and as a balancer of power with the Sunni oil states to the south. To the north, Iran borders on former Soviet states, providing Russia an entrée into the region in a working relationship involving Iranian oil and Russian non-weapons nuclear technology assistance. To the east, Iran has developed a relationship with oil-hungry China that could provide the model for a similar arrangement with India in the future. All Asian roads may not lead directly through Iran, but it is certainly not far from those roads either.

The volatility of Iranian politics adds to both its importance and the sense of concern in which it is held. Prior to the Iranian Revolution, most of the Western world viewed Iran very favorably, as the most modernized and generally stable and friendly country in an unstable and hostile part of the world. Much of this impression reflected the very positive image that had been nurtured for the Shah, a handsome and forbidding visage with a beautiful wife and family who regularly traveled through the most glamorous parts of Europe and exuded an aura of Western culture and sophistication. In the United States in the 1960s and 1970s, American universities had large numbers of Iranian students studying science, engineering, economics, and business to become integral parts of the White Revolution, and many American collegians had Iranian friends and compatriots. The Iranian military was ubiquitous at American military facilities, collaborating with their American counterparts and being trained to operate the sophisticated American equipment with which they were lavished. Other than Israelis, Iranians competed with the Saudis as America's best friends in the Middle East. As noted earlier, the Israelis and Iranians also collaborated with one another, adding to animosity by many Sunni Arabs toward the Persian Shiite Iranians.

The revolution burst this image. The Shah's overthrow would probably not have been so shocking had his public relations efforts not created a kind of Potemkin village about Iran and his relationship with it. Americans (and other Westerners) believed the people loved the Shah, and while those he enabled (the White Revolution's technocratic class) did, many others did not. As the revolution spread across the country, hardly anyone came to the defense of the old regime, and those Iranians most closely associated with the Shah found themselves under siege. Many—and especially the military leadership who trained and collaborated with the Americans—found themselves in physical peril that many did not survive. Revenge was loudly proclaimed in terms of religious fanaticism, adding to the image of a country unhinged. As Iranian demonstrators circled the captured U.S. embassy chanting death to the "Great Satan," the image of Iran was turned completely on its head.

The shock of that period continues largely intact to this day. The United States and Iran have not had formal relations with one another since 1979, and that situation is unlikely to change anytime soon. In important symbolic ways, both countries view the other as the "Great Satan." The United States gains this title for its sponsorship of the Shah and role in the White Revolution, major parts of which are viewed as apostasy by the religious majority. From the American standpoint, the hostage crisis still casts an indelible image of atrocity and barbarism, reinforced by forbidding visages of the various ayatollahs glaring ominously from billboards and condemning the Americans. The Iranians and the Americans still communicate with one another, but it is through intermediaries, generally in guarded and unpublicized forums. It is all the American public will allow.

Dealing with the regime of the Islamic Republic of Iran, as it was declared on April 1, 1979 (the date that is formally celebrated as Independence Day), is difficult both because of the visceral animosity of the two countries toward one another and because Americans do not truly understand the nature of the Iranian system. The *CIA World Factbook* refers to Iran as a "theocratic republic," suggesting it contains elements both of sectarian underpinning (which is a common trait in Muslim countries) and of some representative character. The result is government where two different strains coexist and compete for control of the political system.

The religious element is symbolized by and revolves around the office of the head of state (normally a symbolic position with few real powers in Western countries) or Supreme Leader. This position has been held since 1989 by Ali Hosseini Khamenei, who is also an ayatollah within the Shiite religious hierarchy. His secular powers are largely informal but impressive. He must certify candidates for major office (on grounds of Koranic purity), and more secular figures contest his authority at their own peril. His true role is to monitor and maintain the religious purity of a regime based on conservative Muslim beliefs, and he is informally assisted in these efforts by semi-autonomous bodies such as the Revolutionary Guards and Courts and the Councils of Guardians and Experts.

The republican aspect of government is represented by the legislative branch, the Majles. It is an elective body chosen by the people from a slate of candidates approved by the Supreme Leader. The Majles is a unicameral body that forms a government from its multiparty system. Although it is not always the case, the legislature and its leading figure, the prime minister, are somewhat more secular and moderate than the religious leadership, and it is with representatives of these bodies that Western efforts in dealing with Iran are focused. The major public figure in the Iran nuclear deal, for instance, was Prime Minister Hassan Rouhani, who was elected in 2013 and is thought of as a "moderate," a designation that must be taken in an Iranian context. The other figure who was prominent in negotiating the nuclear weapons ban was Rouhani's foreign minister, Javad Zarif.

Dealing with the Iranian political system is difficult, tricky work. The Supreme Leader and his associates do not interact directly with apostate Westerners and are generally suspicious of any dealings with a West that had defiled their Islamic society under the Shah. The leadership of the Majles more directly represents more secularized, even democratic remnants of the prerevolutionary era and is thus less hostile toward interacting with the West. Its authority to negotiate, however, is circumscribed by the informal veto that the Supreme Leader possesses over what it does, both constraining a leader such as Rouhani and conditioning what Americans and other Westerners can expect from that leadership. This combination of accumulated animosity and mystery makes dealing with Iran difficult.

Basic U.S.-Iranian Relations

Iranian-American relations have varied from extremely close and intimate to virtually nonexistent. The two countries can, and have, chosen not to deal with one another on the regularized, sustained basis on which most countries interact. The dual reality that the United States is a global power whose interests extend to the Middle East and Iran is the pivotal regional state means the countries and their interests come into contact and must be dealt with. Mutual animosity over the past third of a century makes doing so more difficult than it might be otherwise.

U.S.-Iranian affairs touch all three parts of the triangle of U.S.–Middle Eastern relations. Israeli-Iranian conflict over terrorism and nuclear weapons directly affects the American objective of guaranteeing Israel's security. Iran is an oil-rich state that once supplied and protected American access to that oil. It no longer does either, and has been an impediment to American secure oil access. The potential confrontation between the Sunni states led by Saudi Arabia and Shiite states led by Iran adds that aspect of the triangle to those concerns as well. Americans and Iranians have more mutual concerns than they generally care to admit.

In the contemporary situation, Iranian-Israeli problems have been the lightning rod. Iran has flirted with a nuclear program at least since the turn of the millennium. Most of the time, it has argued that its efforts are not directed toward weapons production, but rather to peaceful nuclear energy generation. Its opponents in Washington and Jerusalem reject this explanation, arguing instead that Iran's program has been, at a minimum, compatible with nuclear weapons aspirations, that the regime is unstable and hostile, and that aggressive, possibly including military efforts, should be undertaken to destroy the program. Unlike previous programs in Iraq and Syria, however, the Iranian effort has been built in heavily protected underground locations, making air strikes against it (the Israelis' preferred solution) problematical.

The nuclear weapons problem is a mirror of U.S. and Israeli foreign policy toward Iran and the region. Reflecting their existential obsession, the Israelis find the Iranian program more menacing than do the Americans, for whom the existential prospects are remote and distant. American concerns arise more from a general opposition to nuclear proliferation (the spread of nuclear weaponry to current non-possessors), the desire to support Israel to the extent possible, and worries about the regional effects (e.g., an Islamic nuclear arms race) of the Iranian program. All these are important matters, but they do not rise to the intensity of Israeli fears. As a result, the U.S. government has been unwilling to embrace the more extreme Israeli solutions, although some American supporters of Israel have.

Iranian motives have never been entirely crystalline. Certainly there are elements within the country's political hierarchy who support the idea of nuclear weapons possession and have expressed the position that it is within Iran's international rights to pursue the nuclear weapons option if it chooses (as a member of the Nonproliferation Treaty of 1968 banning such development, it could withdraw by giving proper notice, something it has never done) and that such possession would enhance Iran's return to great power status. The religious hierarchy has consistently denied any nuclear weapons intent and has allegedly issued a *fatwa* (punishable religious edict) against anyone attempting to do so. At the same time, progress has continued in the construction of nuclear facilities that could be adapted to weapons uses.

The details of the program, its progress, and the reliability and honesty of the Iranians in their anti-weapons statements remain highly controversial, mostly along partisan lines in the United States and Israel. The situation began to change with the election of Rouhani, who entered office in 2013 intent on serious nuclear negotiations. In September 2013, Rouhani and

President Obama talked directly with one another by telephone, by far the highest level of communication between the governments of the two countries since 1979. In November 2013, talks between Iran and the so-called 5+1 Western powers (the United States, Britain, France, Russia, and China, plus Germany) produced an interim agreement by which Iran would renounce any weapons intentions, restructure its program, and open its facilities to international inspectors. After a series of setbacks, in which both sides accused the other of cupidity, a comprehensive nuclear agreement was announced on July 14, 2015.

The agreement has not, of course, removed all controversy from the issue. The agreement itself is highly technical, including its provisions and standards by which those provisions are monitored. Most of the partisan dialogue on both sides of the debate comes from a likely incomplete knowledge and understanding of its provisions, and the terms are apparently not as categorically unfavorable to the Iranians as some Americans and Israelis would have preferred (had they been, the Iranians almost certainly would not have accepted them). Anti-treaty partisans in both countries have typified the treaty as badly, even "fatally," flawed, but it remains in force in a nurturing environment that is poisoned by the long-standing animosity between the Iranians and the Americans and Israelis.

The agreement is now in force. Because of partisan opposition, the Obama administration did not treat it as a treaty, because that would have required Senate acquiescence, a problematical outcome given general hyper-partisanship in contemporary American politics. Instead, it has been treated as an executive agreement between the heads of government of the two states, and this is a more fragile and reversible condition than full treaty status would afford it. At the same time, the agreement is not strictly a U.S.-Iranian document. It is an agreement between the five permanent members of the U.S. Security Council and Germany (the 5+1) and Iran. All the other Western powers support the agreement, and thus an American effort to rescind or drastically alter its provisions would have to gain the support of the other powers, a more difficult task than opponents who wish to brush it aside often imply. Iran's international renunciation of nuclear ambition embedded in the agreement may not be carved in stone, but it is certainly cast in wet cement that is rapidly drying.

The American issue with Iran extends beyond nuclear weapons to Iranian sponsorship of Shiite terrorist organizations, notably Hezbollah. That organization operates primarily within Lebanon, and although it does more than engage in terror against Israel, that has been a prime focus of its activities. Leaders of the group have episodically proclaimed the destruction of Israel as a long-term goal, and although how seriously it takes these proclamations is debatable, it helps fuel the continuing animosities between Israel and Iran, concerns of which the United States continues to take notice.

The second major concern of the United States is with petroleum flow from the Persian Gulf area. This concern has evolved. The period when the Shah served as guarantor of that flow gave way to a period of animosity where Iran, occupying one side of the Persian Gulf littoral, harassed and threatened to interrupt that flow. The result, particularly after the Persian Gulf War of 1990–1991, has been a permanent American naval presence in the form of one (and occasionally two) American carrier flotillas in a body of water ill-suited for such a presence (the Gulf is too small and narrow for optimal protection of the naval formation) to protect the oil flow. Reflecting the overall change in relations, the Americans have gone from being naval partners to adversaries because of Middle Eastern oil.

The dynamic of that disagreement is changing as well. Due to a combination of conservation, alternate energy sourcing, and the movement toward reliance on domestic shale oil and gas, the U.S. dependency on Middle East oil has been reduced greatly in recent years, and it will be only a matter of a few years until the United States can, if it chooses, virtually end its reliance on Middle Eastern sources altogether. The possible impacts are discussed at some length in *The Middle East, Oil, and the U.S. National Security Policy*, but they include a receding, possibly disappearing, permanent American military presence in the Persian Gulf area. Doing so might complicate the situation for American allies who cannot make the same transition (a factor affecting American choices), but it also would greatly reduce a major irritant between the United States and Iran.

The final thrust of American Middle Eastern interest is American preference for growing regional peace and stability. As already noted, this process includes Israel, since Israeli intransigence on the Palestinian state issue is a major inhibitor to reducing Israel's rivalry with its Islamic neighbors. In more contemporary terms, the major source of instability has been IS and the Levantine crisis, in which the United States and Iran have some coinciding and some conflicting interests. This situation in turn affects the possible destabilization of the region in a Sunni-Shia conflict led by Saudi Arabia and Iran, a confrontation in which it is difficult to imagine *any* outcome that would benefit the United States.

The IS situation was raised in chapter 1. As a matter of U.S.-Iranian relations, however, it is clear the two countries have mutual interests that their overall animosity makes difficult to realize. Both countries desire the defeat of IS, if for different reasons (the terrorist threat for the United States, the Sunni-Shia schism for Iran). As a classic example of the old saw that "the enemy of my enemy is my friend," they both have an interest in seeing IS expelled from its base in Sunni-dominated Iraq. The United States does not want to conduct this expulsion personally because it would reopen wounds from the 2003 war. In its stead, the offense against IS in the area has been led by the Iraqi army and Shiite militias from Iran. The United States embraces the Iraqi Army but barely acknowledges the militias because of the tenor of relations with Iran and the fact that many Anbar Sunnis hate the Iranians because they are Shiite. Any collaboration by the United States with the militias must be covert for fear of further destabilizing Iraq and thus strengthening IS. At the same time, the Americans oppose the Shiite regime in Syria, which the Iranians support.

The twisted U.S. and Iranian interests in the Levantine struggle further illustrate the convoluted nature of entanglements for the United States in the region. Further complicating the IS struggle is, as noted, covert Saudi private financial support for IS, and this lends a regional Sunni-Shia conflict potential to destabilize the situation even further. In recent years, there has been increased discussion of a potential major confrontation between the two sects of Islam, most dramatically stated as a possible parallel to Europe's religious wars of the seventeenth century.

Whether such an exigency will in fact happen is conjectural, but two things about it are clear. The first is that it would be profoundly destabilizing for the region, and especially the oil industry that is the heart of the global interest in what happens there. Saudi Arabia and Iran, who would be the major contestants in the struggle for supremacy, also happen to be, along with Iraq, the largest petroleum reservoirs in the region, and interrupting that flow through sectarian violence would have major negative effects globally. The second clear thing is that the United States has no interest in who might prevail in such a conflict. This is certainly true on religious grounds, and although American relations since 1979 have been more closely associated with the Sunni Gulf States than Shiite Iran, the latter does remain the pivotal country in the region and, if the conflict did not spread beyond the Middle East, would likely prevail in some way. None of the contingencies one can conjure benefit the United States other than avoiding the turmoil and instability a clash would produce. An American capacity to influence the regimes in both the Sunni and Shiite capitals would seem the best way to influence events in this direction.

U.S. Policy Options

What should the nature of U.S.-Iranian relations be? For nearly forty years, they have been emotional enemies that have avoided one another with a fervor unsurpassed in American foreign policy since the United States ignored the existence of China between 1949 and 1972. That policy was driven by the capture of political power on the mainland by the Chinese communists and found itself instantiated as American forces faced Chinese "volunteers" on Korean battlefields. Even suggesting the possibility of dealing with China's "illegitimate" leadership was politically perilous for anyone who might propose it. The same has been true of U.S.-Iranian relations since 1979.

Post–World War II history has created and reinforced animosity on both sides. The countries' perceptions are near mirror images: each thinks of the other as the "great Satan" that has wronged it. To some extent, both are right: it is true that the United States did overthrow Iran's only truly democratically chosen government and supported what many Iranians considered an apostate dictatorship run by the Shah. For their part, the Iranian Revolution did overrun the U.S. embassy in Teheran and subject American diplomats to a humiliating captivity. At the end, both demonized the other; the Americans led the imposition of harsh sanctions against the Iranian regime, some of which were finally relaxed after the 2015 nuclear deal was signed.

Had none of these events occurred, the two countries would probably have dealt with one another the way major and regional powers more normally interact. The Iranians would have recognized American interests in oil and Israel, and the United States would have recognized Iran's self-perception as the area's premier regional power. From an American vantage point, that is what relations were like during the Shah's rule; the problem was that it occurred without an adequate appreciation of the domestic costs of the Shah's modernization to parts of the Iranian population. Any future improvement must begin by somehow overcoming the negative legacies of the past.

There are policy items on which the two countries have similar, if not identical, interests. The most notable of these is the IS-Iraq crisis. During the long reign of the Shah, Iran arguably contributed to the American achievement of all three of its goals in the region. Its strategic relationship with Israel provided some protection and a source of oil to the Jewish state, it protected the flow of regional oil to Western markets, and it acted as a stabilizing force within the international politics of the region. It may be impossible to reprise that role—and the Iranians may not be interested—but it is possible to think of a less vituperative, mutually reinforcing relationship between the two countries.

Iraq policy probably offers the best opportunity, but it is a complicated possibility rife with difficulties and contradictions. The two countries have a common interest in the defeat and destruction of IS, but for different reasons that affect the outcomes each favors. American interest in erasing IS arises mostly from its interest in protecting the United States from possible terrorist activity directed at it by IS. Secondarily, the defeat of IS could contribute to the stabilization of Iraq and thus the region, one of America's three regional goals.

Iran also desires the defeat of IS, but for different reasons. The existence and success of IS in Iraq threatens a fellow Shiite regime for which Iran has provided considerable assistance, as well as relieving pressure on the Assad regime in Syria (a goal the United States does not share). American and Iranian goals partially contradict one another, and this problem is nowhere clearer than in Sunni Anbar Province, the primary battleground of the IS-Iraqi conflict.

Both the United States and Iran want IS forcefully removed from Iraq, and the United States has shown great reluctance to commit the ground forces to territories claimed by the caliphate. The Iraqi army has recently shown some capacity for competing with IS forces, but their removal requires more. Sunni states seem unwilling or unable to fill the role, and the Kurds are only interested in protecting their tribal lands. That leaves Iran as virtually the only state available to provide the force necessary. The question is whether the United States and Iran can overcome or set aside their animosities enough to make at least informal common cause toward this mutually desired end.

The further question is how both sides can approach some reduction in hostility, assuming they can both agree that doing so might be mutually beneficial (an assumption not to be accepted easily in either capital). Since the Iranian Revolution, American policy has featured negative, coercive actions toward the Teheran regime—military containment, assistance for Iraq in the Iran-Iraq War, severe economic sanctions by impounding Iranian assets in the United States, and diplomatic non-recognition and isolation, to name the most obvious "sticks" as the defining instruments in the relationship. The Iranians have responded by loud, confrontational condemnation of the United States and opposition wherever they could mount it (e.g., support for the Syrian regime, funding for Hezbollah). The first softening of relations came with the ascension of Rouhani, and the Iranian nuclear agreement provides at least some tentative steps toward relaxing hostilities—the Iranians have agreed to permanent on-site inspections of their facilities by International Atomic Energy Agency (IAEA) inspectors, and the United States has released some of the Iranian funds frozen in American financial institutions to the United States. Because of ongoing suspicions and opposition in both capitals, these "carrots" have been tentative and limited. The question is whether they can serve as the basis for further improvement of relations.

CONCLUSION

American relations with both Israel and Iran have been cast in terms of the three pillars of American foreign policy in the Middle East since the end of World War II: the security and survival of Israel; secure access to Middle East petroleum for the United States and its allies; and the promotion of peace and stability in the region since the demise of the Soviet Union. One can argue about the ordering of these priorities, and one must recognize that they are not necessarily compatible with one another: support for Israel and access to Muslim-controlled oil is the primary example. From an American perspective, a major goal is to make them more reconcilable: greater stability, for instance, might reduce Israeli-Muslim tensions, as might resolution of the Palestinian problem.

Relations between the United States and the two strategic "bookends" demonstrate how difficult fashioning foreign policy toward regions and countries can be. The United States may be more or less wedded to its trinity of objectives, but individual states such as Israel and Iran are not. For the Israelis, the Iranian nuclear threat is its major regional challenge because, as Shaked admits, "there is no threat that a big army will invade Israel." This focus can put the United States and Israel at odds, and Israeli open advocacy of attacking and trying to destroy the Iranian nuclear program shows the extent to which interests and objectives can collide. The Iranians, for their part, remain intransigent toward American overtures to stabilize the region, and their deep suspicion of American intentions makes mutual consideration of alternatives difficult. Iran clearly wants to be treated as the region's pivotal state, and the United States, sensitive to the fears of Iranian opponents such as Saudi Arabia, fears that such recognition would further destabilize an already unstable situation. Antagonistic relations between the bookends do not further American efforts at nurturing peace and stability in the region.

The relations between the two countries also reflect what can only be described as the paranoia of the region. Paranoia is not always irrational or unfounded: sometimes there are in fact forces out to get you. In the Middle East, however, this dynamic is virtually institutionalized. It has, for instance, been a standard aspect of the argument for opposing (including destroying) the Iranian nuclear program that, unlike other states who have gained nuclear capability, Iran would actually use that capability to destroy Israel. No state has ever actually done this, of course, and it is entirely clear (including, presumably, to the Iranians) that such an act would result in its own destruction with the same kind of weapons. That is, after all, why Israeli nuclear forces are on invulnerable submarines that would survive a nuclear attack and be able to retaliate. The paranoid basis of the argument implies that Iran/Persia, the world's second-oldest civilization, would willfully engage in its own utter destruction because it hates the Israelis. The only way one can make this argument is to assume that the religious leadership of Iran is so removed from reality that it would find the sacrifice of its country acceptable. Such a calculation is, of course, conceivable, but is it reasonable?

The subtitle of my book on the Middle East already referenced is "Intractable Problems, Impossible Solutions." It is arguably somewhat hyperbolic and overstated, but it suggests the deep divisions that exist in the region and their high resistance to solution, especially by outsiders. The subtitle suggests that the quest to "solve" Middle Eastern problems and to achieve all three of America's regional goals in the face of bilateral dictates of dealing with countries as diverse as Israel and Iran may represent a variation of Don Quixote's "impossible dream." Instead, the admonition of Willy Brandt, the West German chancellor during the 1960s, may be the more appropriate standard. "Real problems," he said, "cannot be solved. They can only be worked."

STUDY QUESTIONS

1. What are the elements that make Israel and Iran "powerful bookends" in the contemporary Middle East conflict? How do these commonalities justify their pairing as cases in this chapter? Elaborate.
2. How do differing worldviews create different perspectives for the United States and Israel in their approach toward foreign policy and the world? How are those relations asymmetrical but inverted?
3. What has the Israeli military experience since its founding been? How did the 1973 war and Israel's nuclear arsenal contribute to changing that experience? How does that change affect Israel's relationship with Iran?
4. The United States and Israel have their deepest disagreement over the occupied territories and the establishment of the Palestinian state. What is the position of each side on this issue? How to their differences reflect differences in national interests? Can they be resolved?
5. Why has the U.S.-Iranian relationship been described as schizophrenic, a competition between Great Satans? How did it get that way?
6. Why was the Iranian Revolution such a turning point in U.S.-Iran relations? Explain how the revolution came about, how the United States was implicated in it, and why that experience has so influenced the contemporary situation.
7. What does it mean to describe Iran as a pivotal state? Why is this position pivotal to Iran's self-image and to its position in the region? Why does it put the Iranians at odds with other regional powers such as Saudi Arabia?
8. Why has Iran's nuclear weapons program been so controversial? Include regional effects and Israel's fears about potential Iranian use of those weapons in your answer. How has the issue been resolved for the time being? Could cooperation on implementing the treaty help create U.S.-Iranian cooperation in other areas, such as dealing with IS?

BIBLIOGRAPHY

Aslan, Reza. *No God but God: The Origins, Evolution, and Future of Islam.* Updated ed. New York: Random House Trade Paperbacks, 2011.

Bakhtiari, Bahman. "Iran's Conservative Revival." *Current History* 106, no. 696 (January 2007): 11–16.

Benn, Aluf. "The End of the Old Israel: How Netanyahu Has Transformed the Nation." *Foreign Affairs* 95, no. 4 (July/August 2016): 16–27.

Bregman, Ahron. *Cursed Victory: A History of Israel and the Occupied Territories, 1967 to the Present.* New York: Pegasus, 2015.

Carter, Jimmy. *Palestine: Peace Not Apartheid.* New York: Simon & Schuster, 2006.

Della Pergola, Sergio. "Israel's Existential Predicament: Population, Territory, and Identity." *Current History* 109, no. 731 (December 2010): 383–89.

Gilbert, Martin. *Israel: A Revised History.* Revised and updated edition. New York: HarperCollins, 2008.

Goldberg, Jeffrey. "How Iran Could Save the Middle East." *The Atlantic* 304 (July/August 2009): 66–68.

Harel, Amos. "Israel's Evolving Military." *Foreign Affairs* 95, no. 4 (July/August 2016): 43–50.

Kaplan, Robert D. "Living with a Nuclear Iran." *The Atlantic* 306, no. 2 (September 2010): 70–72.

Kinzer, Stephen. *The Brothers: John Foster Dulles, Allen Dulles, and Their Secret World War.* New York: Times Books, 2013.

———. *Iran, Turkey, and America's Future.* New York: Times Books, 2010.

Livni, Tzipi. "Anger and Hope: A Conversation with Tzipi Livni." *Foreign Affairs* 95, no. 4 (July/August 2016): 10–15.

Mearsheimer, John J., and Stephen M. Walt. *The Israeli Lobby and U.S. Foreign Policy.* New York: Farrar, Straus & Giroux, 2007.

Muravchik, Joshua. *Making David into Goliath: How the World Turned against Israel.* New York: Encounter, 2015.

Owen, John M. "From Calvin to the Caliphate: What Europe's Religious Wars Tell Us about the Modern Middle East." *Foreign Affairs* 94, no. 3 (May/June 2015): 77–89.

Polk, William R. *Understanding Iran: Everything You Need to Know from Persia to the Islamic Revolution, from Cyrus to Ahmadinejad.* New York: Palgrave Macmillan Trade, 2011.

Ross, Dennis. *Doomed to Succeed: The U.S.-Israeli Relationship from Truman to Obama.* New York: Farrar, Straus & Giroux, 2015.

Shaked, Ayelet. "Ministering Justice: A Conversation." *Foreign Affairs* 95, no 4 (July/August 2016): 2–8.

Shavit, Ari. *My Promised Land: The Triumph and Tragedy of Israel.* New York: Spiegel and Grau, 2015.

Sick, Gary G. *All Fall Down: America's Tragic Encounter with Iran.* New York: Random House, 1985.

Snow, Donald M. *Cases in International Relations.* 6th ed. New York: Pearson, 2015.

———. *The Middle East, Oil, and the U.S. National Security Policy: Intractable Problems, Impossible Solutions.* Lanham, MD: Rowman & Littlefield, 2016.

Van Creveld, Martin L. *The Land of Blood and Honey: The Rise of Modern Israel.* New York: Thomas Dunne, 2010.

CHAPTER 3

East Asia

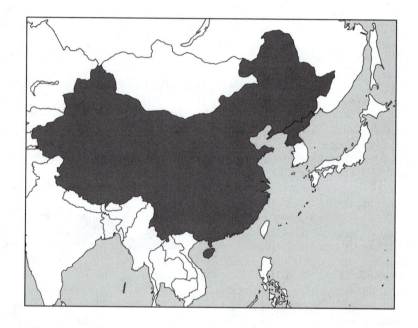

Asia has been an area of fascination and allure for Americans and others for a long time. The discovery of North America was, after all, basically an accident. Columbus's 1492 voyage was undertaken to find a quicker route to Asia and its "riches" than was previously available, and it bumped into the Western Hemisphere on the way. In the early days of the American Republic, seafarers from New England fashioned graceful clipper ships to provide faster transit across the Pacific to the Orient. The Panama Canal was built at the beginning of the twentieth century to allow the United States to project power both toward Europe and toward Asia.

World War II thrust Asia indelibly onto the American foreign policy agenda. The war with Japan was partially presaged by American imperialist actions in the 1890s: the annexation of Hawaii by overthrowing its indigenous monarchy and the acquisition of the Philippines as part of the spoils of the Spanish-American War. Both created concrete American presences that would eventually impede Japanese imperial aspirations along the Pacific Rim. Participation in the Boxer Rebellion and the subsequent American intrusions on Chinese sovereignty in China created a conflict there as well.

The fascination with East Asia is understandable. China, the physical heart of the region and the world's oldest civilization, carefully guarded that civilization from outside pollution until Europeans intruded on it in the nineteenth century, and boasts the world's largest population (a distinction it could yield to India in the future). Distinct cultures and civilizations emerged throughout the region across time, notably the isolationist kingdom of Japan and a reclusive Korean peninsula. Americans historically knew little of these places until the 1800s, but they have had to learn.

World War II and its outcome forced East Asia into the center of American foreign policy, a place it has never relinquished. The most obvious cause was the defeat, occupation, rebuilding, and refashioning of Japan as a democratic state. Japan has evolved as America's closest ally in the region, even if has been an economic rival of sorts some of the time. The Philippines was granted its independence from American colonial rule in 1947 and has been a close American ally ever since.

Two parts of the region have been more problematic, and it is for that reason that they are paired as the cases in this chapter. By far the more important has been China. When World War II ended, China resumed its massive civil war, pitting the Kuomintang (or Nationalist) government of Chiang Kai-shek against the communists of Mao Tse-tung. The fighting between them had been suspended effectively in a national effort to expel the invading Japanese and reignited after the Japanese surrender. In 1949, the communists drove Chiang's nationalists off the mainland and they ended up on Taiwan, where they still reside. The United States refused to recognize the new People's Republic of China until 1972.

The other problem occurred on the Korean peninsula. Korea was always a single country, but after the war, it was divided into "temporary" occupation zones, with Americans as the occupying power in the southern part of the country and the Soviets in control in the north. On June 25, 1950, the northern communists invaded the south in an attempt to reunify the peninsula under their rule. The United States led a UN coalition that evicted them, and the country has been divided between the southern Republic of Korea (ROK) and the northern Democratic People's Republic of Korea (DPRK) ever since. The deeply secretive, reclusive DPRK has been a progressive thorn in the side of American foreign policy, particularly since it has acquired nuclear weapons.

The two countries are also tied to other cases already introduced. China is both a major economic partner and geopolitical rival of the United States—a true "frenemy" (part friend, part enemy) in the words of Stephen Colbert—and that multifaceted relationship has extended to places such as Iran, where the Chinese compete with Russia (among others) for influence. The precedent of DPRK nuclear weapons and their brandishing is often cited as a prime reason for opposing an Iranian quest for nuclear weapons, on the basis that Iran might prove as "crazy" as the North Koreans. Further, if any country can exercise influence over the DPRK, it is the Chinese.

A MOST CRUCIAL AND CONTENTIOUS AREA

The two countries reviewed in this chapter were selected because they are either the most consequential state in the region (China) or because they were the most contentious and confrontational (the DPRK). China is obviously of great importance because it is the most populous state in the world, has the globe's second-largest economy, has great military power that raises it to near-superpower status, and is intimately related to the United States because China has become the retail manufacturing base for American consumers. At the same time, China retains an authoritarian political system in which citizens have relatively few political rights, has one of the most polluted ecosystems in the world, and is at odds with the United States and many of its neighbors on numerous issues mostly related to Chinese pretensions as a world power. The current fracas over Chinese military activity in the South China Sea is an emblem of these concerns. Americans and Chinese view one another warily, tied as they are economically but politically worlds apart.

North Korea is in a category all its own. It shares with China the "distinction" of being one of the world's four remaining communist states (the other two are Vietnam and Cuba), and it is one of the most withdrawn and backward states in the world. The DPRK is scarcely able to feed itself, and exists amid recurring clandestine reports of malnutrition and starvation, but it boasts one of the developing world's most active (and expensive) nuclear weapons programs. It is constantly at odds with virtually all its neighbors, but especially the residents of the ROK and the United States, which serves as the guarantor of South Korea in its confrontation with the north. The country is very isolated, with its main borders with the ROK and China, as well as an eleven-mile frontier with Russia. The DPRK is still technically at war with the United States from the Korean conflict of 1950–1953, and it publicly declares the defeat of the United States with nuclear weapons as a prime foreign policy goal.

Both countries are important to broader American objectives in the region. The closest American political and economic ties in East Asia are with the ROK and Japan, both of which were occupied by the United States and nurtured into democratic societies by the Americans. China and Japan, as the historically most important regional states, have a long history of opposition to one another that was moderated historically by their practiced isolationism. Japan invaded China during the 1930s and remained militarily active there throughout World War II, including numerous reports of massive war crimes by the Japanese against the Chinese (e.g., the Rape of Nanking). The two are mainly economic rivals. At the same time, the North Koreans, located across the Sea of Japan, are a constant irritant to the Japanese, and as their nuclear capabilities increase, potentially a military problem as well.

China and the DPRK are tied together as an American foreign policy matter because China is the only country that has any noticeable impact on North Korean behavior. The Sino-DPRK border is North Korea's entrée into East Asia, and many destitute North Koreans cross the Yalu River into China to work (at very low wages) in Chinese industries. The relationship between the two is complex and inherently unstable: being identified as the DPRK's only friend in the world is embarrassing to China, but they also fear that should the Kim Jong-un government fall, the country would be unified under ROK control, putting potentially hostile neighbors on their frontier. This prospect played a role in Chinese intervention in Korea in 1951; no one wants to test the hypothesis that it might not once again.

It is against this backdrop that the chapter is written. The two states that are featured are, as noted, very different. China is one of the world's largest and most consequential states, with a long history of dominance in Asia that it seems intent on re-creating. North Korea, on the other hand, would be one of the most marginal states in Asia—if not the world—were it not for its possession of nuclear weapons and persistent threats to use those weapons against its neighbors or, more ominously for the United States, against American territory. Both are significant for different reasons.

CASE: THE UNITED STATES AND CHINA

In the last chapter, Iran was identified as a pivotal state, an intermediary position between the mass of nonpowerful countries and the most powerful. Throughout its history, China has at a minimum been such a state, but for most of the past millennium, China's self-imposed isolation from the international system meant that it never truly demonstrated aspirations of being a more prominent power in any traditional sense: China represented, in its own estimation, a superior civilization, and interaction with the world could only taint its culture. Keeping the barbarians out was China's idea of foreign policy.

The problem for China was that the once superior culture stagnated, and the rest of the world caught up to and passed China in important, power-related ways. This change became evident in the nineteenth century—what is known in China as the "Century of Humiliation"—when Europeans and others forcefully "opened" China and were able to occupy parts of the country, including the effective partition of parts of its vast mass into effective vassals of the culturally inferior Westerners. The Boxer Rebellion epitomized this humiliation early in the twentieth century, and it continued through World War II. When the Chinese communists successfully defeated the Nationalists (Kuomintang) in 1949 and sent them into exile on Taiwan, one major agenda item for China's leadership was to restore China's stature in the world.

Returning China to its "proper" role in the world has been the major foreign policy burden of the leadership ever since. Mao's communists had promised a transformation of the country into a Marxist-Leninist worker's paradise, and the first quarter-century of their rule was dedicated to this Quixotic quest. Things did not change until 1979, when the diminutive Deng Xiaoping (he stood less than five feet tall) assumed leadership of the Chinese Communist Party (CCP) and announced his Four Modernizations in the areas of agriculture, science and technology, industry, and the military. Their purpose was to strip away the most debilitating effects of literal adherence to Marxist dogma and to bring China into the modern world. The most dramatic action was to create the Special Economic Zones (SEZs) in eastern China, where what the Chinese argued was their special form of private enterprise would be permitted. The SEZs have been the primary sites for the transformation of China into a world-class economic power.

For the past thirty-five years, China has been an international phenomenon, one of the fastest-growing countries in the world. China is now far more than a pivotal power; it is a "rising power," a country that, by virtue of increased economic, military, or other power, plays or has the potential to play a more prominent role in the international system than it heretofore has played (this definition comes from Snow, *Cases in International Relations*, sixth edition). In the case of China, that rise appears to be in the direction of approaching major, even superpower status, a position unilaterally held by the United States since the collapse of the Soviet Union in 1991.

The question for international relations and American foreign policy is the kind of major power status to which China aspires. China has become an economic superpower whose economy by most measures is surpassed only by that of the United States. Competition in this realm creates some problems for the United States, but is partially conditioned by problems that may arise within China in the coming years. The major area of concern is military: will China engage in a military buildup that also challenges American prowess? China has made some tentative steps in this area within its physical region, an arguable reassertion of the suzerain relationship it has historically had with its neighbors. Whether its aspirations are greater is a larger part of the concern for American policy. Will China seek to become America's partner (as it has been in economic affairs), its military adversary, or, more ambiguously, its "frenemy"?

This evolution occurs within the context of a distinct American mythology about China and its relation to China. Americans have long had a fascination with China and unlocking the key to the "riches of the Orient" at a time (mostly the nineteenth century) when those riches were actually in abeyance. Trying as best it could to hide behind its centuries-old veil of isolation, China was forced to endure Western incursions, such as the arrival and proselytizing roles of American missionaries, actions that probably did not impress the Chinese very much but that caused some Americans to embrace the idea of a "special" link between the American and Chinese peoples. When the government of Chiang Kai-shek was defeated, some Americans felt betrayed that their government had "allowed" this to happen, despite the lack of any concrete interest or ability to have influenced the outcome. The shock was so great that the United States refused to accept the reality of the communist government in Beijing from 1949 until 1972 and preferred to believe that the "real" government resided across the Taiwan Strait in Taipei. It took the actions of the most overtly anti-communist president of the United States, Richard Nixon, and his secretary of state, Henry Kissinger, to expose the myth and begin relations with China.

China: A Physical and Political Sketch

By any measure, China is a huge and consequential country. Chinese civilization has existed for over 7,000 years, longer than any other culture in the world, and for most of that period, it was a world leader in terms of advancement. Its superiority was so extolled within the country that it largely cut itself off from the outside world and, in the process, began to stagnate.

As noted, the Western world caught up and surpassed China in areas such as science and military power in the nineteenth century, and China entered a downward cycle from which it only began to escape in the latter part of the twentieth century. The Chinese leadership is dedicated to reversing the negative experience and to restoring China's "rightful" place in the world. Chinese actions in the international system are best understood as a concerted effort to reassert China's mantle as a world power—a rising power ascending to great power status. The question is what form that ascendancy seeks to create. For Americans, the question is the extent of such an ascent at the expense of the United States.

China begins its quest for global status with impressive credentials, although some of these are double-edged. It is the world's largest state in terms of population at roughly 1.36 billion (India is second with 1.24 billion people; the United States is third at 330 million). Geographically, China is the world's fourth-largest country with an area slightly smaller than that of the United States, which is third behind Russia and Canada. It occupies the strategic center of East Asia, an area it has dominated for millennia, and there are sizable Han Chinese enclaves in most regional states. The traditional relationship between China and its neighbors was based on suzerainty, a relationship where the other countries exercised sovereign internal control but bore periodic tribute to China. Its symbol was the ka-tow, in which tribute bearers prostrated themselves at the feet of the Chinese emperor sitting behind a screen where he could not be physically seen by the tribute bearer.

China is a basically homogeneous country. Its Han majority constitutes about 92 percent of the population, with the other 8 percent divided among Kazakhs, Koreans, Mongols, Tibetans, and Uighurs. Most of these groups do not consider themselves Chinese in terms of race, background, even religion, and most harbor desires either for independence or at least substantial autonomy. They tend to be concentrated in the western parts of the country where their grievances are not well advertised, with the exception of the Tibetans because of the activism of the Dalai Lama. Among the other groups, the Uighurs, who are Muslim, have been the most troublesome. Although none of these groups poses an immediate threat, Tuttle points out that "regions of China that are dominated by non-Han people constitute roughly half of Chinese territory. If non-Han Chinese citizens formed their own country, it would be the 11th largest in the world," between Mexico and the Philippines in gross area. This may be a remote prospect, but it does condition claims about the overall homogeneity and possible stability of China.

The heart of Chinese global ascendancy has been the growth of the Chinese economy since the announcement of the Four Modernizations. The engine of the Chinese economic "model" has been the adoption of capitalist economic practices in the SEZs, which have fueled an economic growth rate of around 8 percent; that rate has only recently begun to slow somewhat, but it remains among the world's leaders. The heart of Chinese economic growth has been in the manufacturing sector, where Chinese firms collaborate with Western firms to produce basic consumer goods at substantially lower costs than can be done in the West. The result has been an enormous increase in Chinese profits and a very positive trade balance with the world and especially with the United States, which absorbs much of the consumer output of the country. The result has been large budget surpluses within China that have facilitated a Chinese initiative to help finance development in many of its neighboring states.

Each of these impressive accomplishments comes with caveats. China's long history and sense of superiority has created resentment among the barbarians toward the Chinese, and the sizable Chinese enclaves in most states are not popular with the natives—a source of regional difficulties. China has land boundaries with fourteen countries, and it has been in conflict with most of them at one time or another. Because Chinese foreign enclaves are resented almost everywhere, the Chinese find it necessary to admonish those in other countries not to mistreat their citizens. This became a particular problem at the end of the Vietnam War, when Vietnamese "boat people" fled communist conquest and headed for neighboring countries. What was not widely publicized at the time was that most of the boat people were ethnic Chinese, and that the People's Republic of China (PRC) was not terribly interested in having them return to the mother country.

China's status as the world's most populous country is also a mixed blessing. The Chinese population has become basically stagnant because of reduced fertility rates that are the partial result of the Chinese "one child" policy enacted in the 1980s (it was a crime for a couple to have multiple children) that have reduced the pool of eligible young people of child-bearing age in the population. During the period of forced birth control, there was also a marked preference for male children, meaning many females were either abandoned or aborted. As a result, there is an imbalance of males of reproductive age, further reducing fertility.

The population is also aging. At one level, this is a decided achievement for the regime. Since the communist takeover, life expectancy has more than doubled from roughly thirty-five years in 1960 to around seventy-five today. The effect, however, has been to age the work force on which the Chinese economic miracle is based. According to French, the combination of fertility-created reductions and attrition of aging citizens has meant that "the working age population shrank by 4.87 million" in 2015, and this effect will be progressive. He also notes that while China currently has five workers for every retiree, "by 2040, this highly desirable ratio will have collapsed to about 1.6 to 1," and China will become "one of the older societies in the world."

This situation is by no means unique to China, but it does pose problems. There are two models for dealing with a collapsing ratio of working to retired citizens: the Americans and the Japanese. This problem has effectively derailed the "Japanese economic miracle" of the last century, because the Japanese have been unable to find replacement workers: fertility rates remain low, and the Japanese, for racial reasons, are reluctant to import foreign workers from other places. The United States, on the other hand, has traditionally solved this problem through the immigration of young workers from other countries, leading French to conclude that "immigration sustains American prosperity."

For the Chinese, the problem is much more similar to that facing Japan than the United States. Chinese reluctance to import outsiders approaches that of Japan, although a small number of North Koreans do regularly cross the Yalu River to work in Chinese industries along that border. The other possible source of additional workers could come from minorities within China itself, but most of these people are alien to the Han Chinese and are unacceptable as immigrants into Han-dominated regions (where virtually all of the industrialization has occurred).

A final conditioning factor is both economic and political in nature: the drag of the State-Owned Enterprises (SOEs). Although the vast majority of Chinese prosperity comes from the activities of private enterprises concentrated in the SEZs, the majority of Chinese businesses, upward of 70 percent of the employment base of the country, is concentrated in businesses owned by the state. These enterprises underachieve in economic terms, but they serve political purposes. They are, for instance, the source of funding for much of China's military efforts (the military owns a sizable number of them) as well as by members of the political elite. The SOEs are an economic drag on China, but they are an integral part of the CCP's means of control. As long as the SOEs control two-thirds of the country's work force and resources but only produce less than one-third of its output, they will inhibit China's ascendancy in the world.

Possession and access to natural resources are also a major Chinese problem. This is especially true in the area of energy. One of the reasons for the rise of China as an industrial power was an offshoot of the global warming problem. When the Kyoto climate control process created emission standards and reduction schedules for many European countries and the United States, one solution was to export the most energy-intense, polluting industries to China. This solution had two advantages: very low Chinese wages meant low-technology goods could be produced at lower prices by underpaid Chinese workers, thereby making these goods cheaper for consumers. At the same time, this relocation of industries meant energy uses declined in those states exporting the industries, making their ability to meet carbon-reduction standards more feasible. Corporate profits and civic responsibility seem to coincide, a win-win solution.

The Chinese welcomed this movement with open arms, because it stimulated the SEZs, where the relocations occurred. The problem, however, was that the transfers solved European and North American problems by making an already existing Chinese problem much worse, a net negative for the global environment. Among its limitations, China is basically energy deficient in terms of accessible, usable forms of energy. The only energy source it has in abundance and reasonable proximity to the place energy is used is coal, the most polluting of all the carbon-based energy forms. The Chinese government, for which economic growth was a much higher priority than environmental impact, geared its energy—and thus economic growth—strategy to coal production and burning. In 2013, for instance, Economy and Levi report that China consumed about 70 percent of the coal burned in the world. The result, painfully evident to anyone who traveled to the 2008 Beijing Olympics or to eastern China generally, is atmospheric pollution and environmental degradation unmatched virtually anywhere in the world.

This is a very serious problem for China, because energy consumption is the single most reliable indicator of economic success. The continuation, and especially the expansion, of Chinese economic supremacy is premised on coming to grips with this problem. There are three possible solutions, none of them particularly appealing from a Chinese standpoint. One is a reduction of manufacturing activity to make the Chinese environment healthier for the population and less damaging to the world. The second is to continue what they are doing, thereby maximizing Chinese prosperity and power at the expense of Chinese and world environmental health. The third is to find alternate sources of energy, preferably less polluting in nature. Prejudicing the choices is the publicly declared intention by the government greatly to increase citizen access to private automobiles, a further major pollutant.

To this point, Chinese policy has been a combination of the second and third alternatives. Finding some form of less polluting energy is on the face of it the most attractive, since it potentially allows China to continue to manufacture, even to increase its activities, while lowering its noxious impacts. There are two avenues China can pursue in this quest: identifying and buying energy from abroad, or developing internal sources. Both have their limits.

Chinese attempts to obtain foreign energy have tended to be directed toward Middle Eastern oil, and particularly toward making arrangements with Iran when the West was boycotting Iranian crude. The problem with this solution is that it requires constructing a pipeline from Iran to China that must traverse potentially hostile territory such as some former Soviet republics in Central Asia such as Turkestan, as well as Afghanistan and Pakistan, all problematic routes from a Chinese security standpoint. The alternative is to arrange for oil to be shipped through the Persian Gulf, but that solution also faces barriers, including the future of American naval presence in the Gulf and the potential vulnerability of shipping lanes, such as the Strait of Malacca and through the South China Sea. None of these avenues for increasing badly needed imports is without difficulties, which is one reason for exploring other alternatives.

The other thrust has been internal development in a broad sense. The most controversial aspect of this strategy has centered on Chinese activities in the South China Sea. There are significant oil reserves under the surface of this body of water that are claimed by several states, notably China, Vietnam, and the Philippines. China considers the South China Sea to be part of its territorial waters, and has taken specific actions to reinforce this claim. One has been to declare the sea off-limits to transit by other countries, and especially naval vessels. The United States is included in this ban, which is a source of conflict between the two countries. The other action has been to build artificial islands in the sea, which China claims as part of Chinese soil, thus reinforcing the territorial waters claim. The Philippines has sued China over its actions at the International Court of Justice (ICJ). The United States supports the suit, but its advocacy is compromised by the fact that the United States is not a signatory member of the United Nations Convention on the Law of the Seas (UNCLOS), the provisions of which form the basis of the suit.

Another, and in the long run possibly the more promising, strategy is through the exploitation of China's shale oil and gas reserves. China possesses the world's largest known reserves (Canadian and American shale deposits are the second largest). The advantage of exploiting these deposits is that it creates the ability to move from coal to natural gas as a way to power electricity plants; natural gas emits only about half the carbon of coal and injects far fewer particulates into the atmosphere. Four problems stand in the way of exploiting this alternative source.

The first problem is technological. The process by which shale oil and gas are extracted is known as hydraulic fracturing, more commonly called "fracking" (see Snow, *The Middle East, Oil, and the U.S. National Security Policy*, chapter 4, for a discussion). The basic techniques for fracking were developed in the United States a half-century ago to recover the last product from largely depleted traditional oil wells in the Southwest, and their application to wringing oil and natural gas from shale formations has given the United States and Canada a virtual monopoly on production of this resource. China, like most other countries, lacks this history and thus knowledge and experience in hydraulic fracturing.

Even if it had the knowledge, it lacks the other essentials for exploiting shale. Its major shale formations are in remote areas of southwestern China, which are infrastructure deficient. Thus, the second and third limits on a movement toward shale are geographic: the remote location of the resources and the lack of a transportation system that could move finished products to market. Both would be expensive propositions and will take a long time to accomplish. Moreover, the entire enterprise assumes Chinese indigenous development of shale technologies or the ability of the country to negotiate access to American technology.

There is a final barrier, which is water. China is a water-deficient country, with water tables that have been dangerously lowered across the country, creating problems of citizen health, air pollution and respiratory problems, economic consequences in terms of agricultural industries and the availability of foodstuffs, and resulting social unrest. The government has not done much to address this problem to this point, and it would be exacerbated by a movement to shale production: fracking requires the use of large amounts of water in a "cocktail" that leaves the water seriously polluted and nonpotable. There are techniques for water purification, but they are expensive and wipe out much of the economic advantage of shale exploitation. To make matters worse, the areas where shale deposits are located are among those parts of China where water table lowering has been the worst.

The political part of the landscape also remains problematical. For all its impressive economic growth, China remains an authoritarian state with the Chinese Communist Party as the sole source of political power. The regime, sensitive to outside scrutiny, tries to downplay its more overtly authoritarian foundations, but no other political entity is allowed to compete in the country, citizen dissent is regularly suppressed, and forums of citizen expression such as the Internet are monitored and censored. There is little evidence that the CCP has any intentions of changing the basic political power arrangement in the country.

As Chinese economic prominence emerged, the CCP made an implicit bargain with the people. In essence, this bargain said that if the people accepted the political fact of the CCP monopoly of power, the regime would make them prosperous by providing them the tools of capitalist economics that would fuel prosperity. This bargain was attractive in the eastern SEZs, where the Chinese exercise a large amount of freedom in areas such as travel and are unimpeded in the exercise of that freedom as long as it does not extend to political matters, such as criticism of the regime. Chinese students, for instance, are enrolled in large numbers in universities worldwide, where they are encouraged to pursue curricula that will provide skills useful to economic development. Those who choose to extend their educations to political levels are generally discouraged in their efforts and often do not return to China, where they might become dissidents and thus challengers of the regime's monopoly of power. The Chinese leadership has struggled with the apparent contradiction between economic freedom and political repression and has not reached what it considers a satisfactory conclusion. China remains rhetorically committed to Marxism-Leninism, but it is far more Leninist (politically repressive) than it is Marxist (economically socialist). The Soviet Union tried to be both Marxist and Leninist, and it ultimately failed. Whether China can do better with a mixed system remains to be seen. So far it has been successful.

This discussion has reflected the initial comment that China's rise has been a double-edged sword containing dynamics that cut both to China's advantage and disadvantage. Part of the impressive quality of Chinese growth is that it began from a modest level and in physical and human circumstances where change created impressive statistical and physical growth. The Chinese ability to exploit its circumstances has been very impressive as well, and it has created the impression of China as a virtually inexorable growing force in the world. As the discussion has shown, however, China's phenomenal growth may be slowing as it encounters problems not present in underdeveloped China, such as a shrinking work force, the environment, energy, and even available water. These are problems the Chinese can and certainly must address, but their solutions will also bring China "back to the pack" in terms of the dynamics of its ascent. China has clearly risen and will continue to do so; where the ceiling of that growth is located is a question that must be raised in the context of U.S. policy toward China.

Basic U.S.-Chinese Relations

Americans disagree on the basic nature of relations with China. The political right tends to retain images cast in the adversarial period ushered in by Chinese intervention in Korea and the memory of Chinese and Americans clashing on the battlefield there. This view is framed in the image of America having "sold out" the Nationalist government in the civil war and the subsequent near quarter-century of pretending that the PRC was not the legal government of China and thus neither a regime that the United States would acknowledge nor one with which it would interact. China may have been the junior partner in the communist side of the Cold War, but it was nevertheless the enemy.

Denying the existence of the government that ruled nearly a quarter of mankind made little geopolitical sense, and it took the conservative, anti-communist, geopolitically oriented combination of Nixon and Kissinger to destroy that fiction (when Nixon visited China) and open informal relations, formalized by President Carter on January 1, 1979, the same year that the Four Modernizations began. Those modest beginnings have evolved into the extremely tight economic relations between the two countries since then, making it possible at that level to think of the two countries as "friends," or at least as interdependent entities.

The dual legacies of rivalry and cooperation have left Americans and Chinese ambivalent about one another. They are both great powers. The United States has been the sole global superpower for over a quarter-century, but at least in the economic realm, the Chinese have challenged that position, and China's geopolitical aspirations are the current source of disagreement and apprehension. The United States has maintained the East Asian balance of power for most of the post–World War II period, but China has raised itself above pivotal state status to that of a rising power challenging that supremacy. Americans are concerned with China's apparent desire and efforts to widen its range of influence. Economic and geopolitical concerns frame the major thrusts of U.S.-Chinese relations.

China has clearly been on a path of trying to increase at least its regional influence in Asia. Historically, this has meant a limited but clearly understood subservience of those within China's sphere of influence through the suzerain relationship. The key elements of Chinese power relationships have been aimed at perpetuating China's superior status, but they have not been expansionist beyond those areas China thought of as inherently theirs. The major purpose of creating and reinforcing those relationships has been isolationist and defensive. The Great Wall of China is the major symbol of historical Chinese foreign policy: a physical barrier to keep the barbarians out and to protect the sanctity of the Chinese empire and civilization from pollution by outsiders.

The question is whether that goal has changed, if so, how, and what any shifts may mean to the United States and its interaction with China. At one level, Chinese actions can be seen as largely defensive, seeking to repair the barriers that maintained Chinese isolation and that were breached, events like Japan's invasion in the 1930s and American excursions into places historically part of the Chinese domain such as Korea and Southeast Asia. Taiwan, which has resisted reincorporation into China except on terms that would not subjugate the island to PRC rule, remains a matter of contention as well.

U.S.-Chinese security relations flow from the basic question of Chinese assertiveness. Military enhancements were one of Deng's four modernizations, and the Chinese have acted to increase the size and capabilities of their armed forces. Using 2015 figures from *The Military Balance*, China is the only country in the world with larger active duty forces than those of the United States (2,233,000 to 1,433,000), and its defense budget is second to that of the United States (roughly $129 billion to America's $581 billion—about 22 percent). Historically, the bulk of Chinese capabilities has been ground forces with the major task of territorial defense, but as the budget has grown, that force has been diversified to accommodate greater power projection capabilities beyond Chinese soil. This has been true both of naval expansion (e.g., the commissioning of aircraft carriers) and air assets. The army has actually shrunk somewhat, and these changes make some observers believe the Chinese are intent on challenging the traditional American role of oversight of the western Pacific.

There is policy disagreement about what Chinese military expansion means for U.S.-Chinese relations. American economic ties with East Asia are clearly extensive: Japan, South Korea, and China are among America's largest trading partners, and much of that commerce has been by ship under the watchful eye of the U.S. Sixth Fleet. China has shown no interest in interrupting these relationships, but has shown interest in other naval assets, notably the South China Sea. To this point, Chinese military spending growth has been impressive, but is still on a scale that hardly qualifies it as a challenger to the United States. As Cumings puts it, "No one would be rash or stupid enough to challenge the core of US presence in the Pacific." Whether the Chinese will eventually try to mount such a challenge remains a concern in relations between the two countries, however.

The United States and China do have specific security concerns. Three are prominent and deserve mention: the status of Taiwan, the South China Sea, and North Korea. The longest standing involves Taiwan. The island of Taiwan (Formosa) is across the Straits of Taiwan from China, a distance of about 110 miles. It became a security issue when Chiang Kai-shek's regime fled there after losing the Chinese Civil War in 1949. The Nationalists quickly took control of the island (to the chagrin of many native Taiwanese) and established the Republic of China (ROC) there. Both the PRC and the ROC (if not the Taiwanese themselves) consider Taiwan part of China, but they clearly disagree about who should rule both on the island and the mainland.

The possibility that China would mount an amphibious invasion across the straits as a way to annex the island has been a problem ever since. The United States, with its historic ties to the ROC, has interposed itself in the straits to prevent Chinese aggression against the island, and Taiwan has evolved as one of the most prosperous parts of East Asia. Periodic threats and crises have occurred, but any movement toward forceful union has largely disappeared in the new millennium. Ties between Taiwanese firms and the SEZs have become quite close, and Taiwanese investors are the most active foreigners in China. Current tensions, such as they are, focus on the terms of peaceful reunion between the two territories, although some form of military action still remains a remote possibility.

The second, and currently most contentious, disagreement is over the status of the South China Sea, a body of water that washes the southeastern shores of China, the Philippines, most of Southeast Asia, and some of the northern islands of the Indonesian archipelago. China has declared the sea part of its territorial waters and "closed" it to transit by the vessels of other countries. To reinforce its claim, it has built a series of artificial islands in the territorial sea that serve as naval stations. No other states accept the Chinese assertion of control over the sea other than in internationally defined territorial waters. The United States has been a major denier of this status and has challenged it with military exercises on and over the sea.

The South China Sea is geopolitically consequential for two main reasons. First, it is a major part of trade routes from East Asia to the Asian subcontinent and Middle Eastern petroleum resources. Controlling the South China Sea (along with the Straits of Malacca) provides substantial leverage for China or any country that exercises it. This assertion of control roils relations with the United States, both in terms of the American policy of freedom of the high seas and because it could interrupt a great deal of commerce in which it and trade partners engage.

The other source of South China Sea importance arises from the vast reserves of oil under its waters. China and the other states washed by the sea all claim the reserves as theirs, and the assertion of sovereignty by the Chinese is the basis of their claim. It is of great importance to China, which currently imports 5.4 million barrels a day (third most in the world) and has limited reserves of its own (other than shale)—ranked fourteenth among countries of the world. No other country recognizes the Chinese assertion of possession of the rights to South China Sea oil, and the resolution of the issue has ramifications for the pace of development of shale oil and gas and the urgency of penetrating the Middle East oil markets. The issue is of importance to the United States because of its ties to other claimants, notably the Philippines.

The third area of national security concern is the DPRK. As discussed in the next section, the DPRK is one of the most remote, impenetrable countries in the world. Its hostility toward the United States, most clearly manifested in its nuclear program, is a major U.S. concern, and it is clearly in the American interest to exercise some restraint on the military expansionism of the Kim Jong-un regime. The problem is how to accomplish this.

China offers the best (or least bad) alternative for putting pressure on the North Koreans. The frontier with China is North Korea's longest (virtually only) land border, and a portion of the funds available to the government comes from taxing North Koreans working in the PRC. Moreover, China came to the DPRK's aid in the Korean War. If the DPRK listens to anyone, it is the Chinese.

The problem with this logic is that it puts China in a bind. China finds itself embarrassed and exasperated by North Korean policies, and supports change in the DPRK. At the same time, it is reluctant to put great pressure on the government, for fear that it might collapse. If that were to occur, the likely result would be unification with South Korea, and the Chinese adamantly oppose this outcome because it would mean having a potentially hostile neighbor on its border, the avoidance of which was one reason for Chinese intervention in the Korean War. China faces the unattractive alternatives of an eccentric DPRK regime over which it can exercise a modicum of influence (although not as much as the United States would like) or a possibly hostile neighbor.

The other form of contention is economic, and it also has two aspects. The first regards the bilateral trade relationship between the two. In simplest terms, the United States buys much more from China than China does from the United States, resulting in a sizable balance of payments deficit for the United States. Much of the surplus that China accumulates is reinvested in the United States, including American government bonds and the like, meaning the U.S. government is indebted to China. Much of the funding for the Iraq and Afghanistan wars came from funds borrowed from China, and some American observers believe this potentially compromises the United States in its relation with the PRC. As a result, there is pressure to reduce imports from China and to renegotiate terms of trade with the Chinese more to America's favor and to increase American exports to China.

This nervousness is partially compensated by the fact that America owes so much to China that China has a vested interest in the strength of the American economy. The last country in the world whose economy China wants to see weakened is that of the United States, since it devalues the American dollars it currently holds. Lieberthal calls this a "dollar trap," and Miller describes its dynamic: "In truth, the United States and China are holding one another hostage. The United States needs China to buy its obligations, and for the foreseeable future, China will have few other places than the U.S. dollar to store the foreign currency it has accumulated."

China in particular is thus a necessary champion of American economic success, because if the American economy weakens, it would have two obvious deleterious effects on China. One of these would be to undercut the market for its goods. Much of the Chinese economic miracle, after all, has been built on the production of fairly unsophisticated consumer products; the technological base has to be imported. The United States is both the major consumer of these goods and the major source of the technology on which those products are based. A serious weakening of the American economy could seriously threaten the basis of Chinese prosperity, which is hardly good business for the Chinese entrepreneurial effort. At the same time, a weakening of the American economy could also result in the devaluing of the dollar. Since much of the world's—including China's—wealth is held in U.S. dollars, the result could also be very damaging to China.

The result is that China and the United States are, in many important ways, economically interdependent, the mutual children of 1990s-style economic interdependence. This relationship has largely reverberated as Chinese advantage in many popular discussions, including calls from major political figures such as President Trump to "level the playing field" in areas of economic policy such as tariffs, price fixing and subsidies, and the manipulation of currency values. China holds some of the advantages in this debate, but so does the United States. Economic competition between the world's two largest and most dynamic economies is to be expected, but there are realistic boundaries on how cutthroat it can become without resulting in self-inflicted wounds being administered to whoever wields the economic instrument of power.

The other economic problem involves Chinese initiatives to use its economic might to increase its international influence. Chen points out two instruments by which it is doing so. It has established, along with the other BRICS countries (Brazil, Russia, India, China, and South Africa) a New Development Bank (NDB) to help finance developing world projects, as well as an Asian Infrastructure Investment Bank (AIIB) to finance projects. Visitors to Asian cities report that Chinese-financed projects are evident almost everywhere. Some worry that political influence will follow these initiatives.

These examples illustrate the ongoing nature of relations between two of the world's mightiest countries. Between powers that have historically opposed one another, the relationship is not entirely cordial, and there are clear differences between them. For now, those differences are basically confined to East Asia, since that is where China is primarily engaged in its apparent quest to elevate itself through rising power status. The problems that divide the two countries are not inconsequential, but they are far less stark than they were a generation ago, when analysts talked about prospects of war. How these relations will evolve and how the kinds of differences described here will be resolved depends, to a great degree, on the kind and tenor of options both sides exercise in the future.

U.S. Policy Options

Finding the proper content and tone that American foreign policy should take toward the PRC is not a simple matter. There are major philosophical and substantive differences between the two powers, and all of these cannot be definitively resolved. China, for instance, either will or will not abandon or enforce its proclaimed control over the South China Sea, and there is not a great deal of rhetorical room for change that does not appear a capitulation on the issue by one side or the other. The United States is less than enthused about Chinese military modernization, but until or unless that program produces capabilities that directly confront and endanger American assets and the protection of American assets in the region or beyond, it is not clear what this country can do to cause the Chinese to change course.

The relationship is no longer between a clearly superior and inferior power. China has always had impressive physical assets such as its large and increasingly productive population, and in the past quarter-century, China has clearly risen from being a regional pivotal state to being a rising power. The geopolitical question is whether China's ambitions include becoming a comprehensive superpower that can challenge American power in the world. Doing so would represent a vast departure from the inward-looking, regional emphasis that has historically marked Chinese activity in the world, but China's impressive economic credentials mean it may have the wherewithal to mount a challenge. Some American observers look at the Chinese military buildup—still modest by American standards—and wonder darkly about whether China is intent on usurping the American superpower mantle. No one can be certain.

It is in the economic area that China's efforts have been most successful and where the greatest concerns arise. Gross measures of economic activity are indeed startling: China's GDP is the second largest of any country in the world (third if the European Union is included as a "country"), and although its GDP/capita is less impressive (120th) because of its population size, it is a manufacturing juggernaut whose accumulation of international currency makes it a force that must be considered. One American response to this rise, much of which has been the result of Chinese-American economic relations, has been to question U.S. trade policy, and particularly trade with the Chinese. It is probably foolhardy to assume that recent growth will continue in a linear manner due to demographic and other difficulties in the Chinese economy, but future U.S.-Chinese foreign relations will be conditioned by China's economic might.

The extent to which Chinese military and economic growth is a major concern for the United States depends, to a great degree, on the way China develops in the future. Like all change, that direction is not entirely predictable. China has unquestionably ascended to the rank of a major rising power—arguably *the* leading country in that category. There are two questions that form the parameters of future American options toward China. What, if anything, can the United States do to help condition and steer continued Chinese development in what America considers a positive, constructive direction—one compatible with American interests? That question leads to the second, which is the vector and velocity of China's rise: where is China headed? The answers to both questions remain clouded. As Minxin Pei put it a decade ago, "China may be rising, but no one knows if it can fly."

CASE: THE UNITED STATES AND THE DPRK (NORTH KOREA)

North Korea is an international enigma. A divided Korean peninsula did not exist before 1945, and the creation of two Koreas was the result of post–World War II occupation politics, not any felt or expressed desire on the part of the Korean people to live in separate political jurisdictions. Rather, the Koreans are a single nationality, and if anything, they fall into the category of divided states, a Cold War artifact. The other two prominent examples of this phenomenon were Germany and Vietnam, and both of these countries have been reunited. The Koreas are the only remaining exception.

Through most of Korean history, there was no such thing as a divided Korean peninsula in a political sense. From approximately 300 CE, when Korea won its freedom from China, to 1910, when it was occupied by Japan, Korea was a unified state. The division of the Koreas was a post–World War II accord between the victorious allies on how to occupy the territory as it was liberated from the defeated Japanese. The country was divided into Soviet and American occupation zones in 1945; in the Soviet case as a reward for agreeing to participate in what was projected as a very bloody invasion of the Japanese home islands. At the time, the division was supposed to be temporary and to end with unifying elections in 1948. This arrangement rapidly proved untenable (the United States withdrew in 1948 from the south, but the Soviets remained in the north), and the two occupation zones became the ROK (Republic of Korea) and the DPRK (Democratic People's Republic of Korea).

The DPRK tried to unify the country by force in 1950. On June 25, North Korean forces armed with Soviet weaponry stormed across the demilitarized zone and rapidly spread throughout the south, which lacked the size of forces and armaments to defend themselves. On June 27, the Truman administration announced their intent to come to the aid of the southerners, and the Korean War ensued. Fighting ended formally on July 27, 1953, when an armistice was signed at Panmunjom. No formal ending of the war ever occurred, and technically the United States, the ROK, and the DPRK have remained in a state of hostilities ever since.

The two halves of the peninsula have evolved very differently. The ROK is slightly smaller physically than the DPRK (38,502 square miles as opposed to 46,540 square miles for the north, about the difference in sizes of Pennsylvania and Virginia), but the ROK has a population almost twice that of the north (forty-nine to twenty-five million). The ROK is a fully functioning democracy, whereas the DPRK is one of the world's four official remaining communist dictatorships. The economic comparison is especially stark. The ROK is one of the "Four Tigers" of Asia: it has a GDP of $1.67 trillion (thirteenth in the world), and a per capita GDP of $33,200 (twenty-seventh). By contrast, the DPRK has a GDP of $40 billion (106th in the world) and per capita GDP of $1,800 (197th). In terms of the comparative quality of life, the differences in GDP per capita are particularly instructive in understanding the physical plight of Koreans on opposite sides of the frontier dividing them.

At the end of the Cold War, only Germany and Korea remained divided countries (the result of the Vietnam War was to unify that country in 1975). At that time, there was discussion about reuniting both Germany and the Koreas. Both had communist halves that were far less developed than their Western counterparts, and there was concern about how the communists could be absorbed without lowering standards of living too greatly in the non-communist state. There was also speculation about political integration. The two former German states were rejoined in 1990 and have managed to integrate their economies. Politically, the East German communists lost power when forced to compete openly and freely. That experience was not lost on the DPRK leadership, which could only assume that their fate would be similar to that of the German communists in a unified Korea. Unification talks have never gotten off the ground on the peninsula and likely will not in the foreseeable future.

North Korea is one of the most forlorn, isolated places on the globe. Much of this isolation is traditional and purposive. The DPRK has long been known as the "Hermit Kingdom," a designation long held and valued, at least in part because of North Korean "celebration of racial purity and homogeneity," in Myers's depiction. The result is what Myers calls "a paranoid nationalism that has informed the regime's actions since the late 1940s." At the same time, the contrast in quality of life between the DPRK and the ROK could scarcely be more striking, and the regime clearly does not want North Koreans knowing how much better their relatives in the south live for fear of the political unrest that could result. The regime in Pyongyang must rely on the utter isolation of its people from outside influence to avoid invidious, regime-threatening demands from its citizenry.

Part of the contrast is political. The North Korean regime has one of the most inbred and politically repressive governments in the world. All the leaders of the country are the direct descendants of Kim Il-sung, the original communist leader anointed by the Soviets, and nepotism runs rampant in the military and civilian bureaucracies. The North Koreans are notorious for their harsh treatment of their own citizens, and hundreds of thousands of North Korean citizens languish in political labor camps. As recently highly publicized cases have demonstrated, harsh treatment extends to visitors who commit infractions and find themselves behind DPRK bars.

For all these reasons, the DPRK is one of the most marginal countries in the world and would scarcely seem to warrant inclusion in this volume except, of course, for its possession of nuclear weapons and its bellicose threats about their potential use against American and Asian countries. If North Korea did not have an active nuclear program that includes both the development of increasingly sophisticated atomic weaponry and ballistic means of delivery over ranges that include some American soil, no one other than its neighbors would have any reason to pay much attention to what goes on north of the 38th Parallel (the boundary between the DPRK and the ROK). It would be, in Lankov's assessment, a country "on a par with Mozambique or Angola." Under the current leadership of Kim Jong-un, who assumed power as Chief of State on December 17, 2011, North Korea's nuclear arsenal and the stridency and erratic nature of its threats have made it impossible to ignore a country that would rightfully attract virtually no international attention otherwise. With nuclear weapons, the world has no choice but to take notice of the Hermit Kingdom. That, of course, may be the principal reason for the program. In North Korea's case, "the nukes make the man."

The DPRK: A Physical and Political Sketch

North Korea is a relatively unimportant state amid much more consequential countries, including its sibling state of South Korea. Its maritime exposures are to East Asia's traditional great powers, China across Korea Bay and the Gulf of China and Japan across the Sea of Japan. Even when united, Korea is not a large or populous enough place to fend off the forceful blandishments of either rival and has had to rely on inward-turning regimes in both. The peninsula is connected to the Asian continent by a roughly 900-mile land boundary, almost all of which is with China (except its short border with Russia). This physical contiguity, along with the geopolitics of ending World War II, helps explain why the north part of the peninsula became communist in the 1940s.

The DPRK is also a desperately poor place that has, upon frequent occasion, shown itself to be physically incapable of feeding and sustaining its own people. The *CIA World Factbook* describes its economy as "one of the world's most centrally directed and least open," and the result has been an economy that does not perform competitively, even adequately. Less than 20 percent of its land is considered arable, but 35 percent of its workforce is classified as agricultural. Its industrial/manufacturing sector is minuscule but employs 65 percent of the DPRK's laborers. Five-eighths of its exports (mostly minerals and basic industrial products such as textiles) are to China; South Korea buys one-fifth of its exports. Similarly, China and the ROK are the leading exporters to the DPRK. The DPRK does not produce statistics on matters such as percentage of the population living in poverty or standard of living. The military is known to have first priority to the North Korean budget. The country is particularly energy deficient and has to import most of its petroleum and coal, largely from the PRC.

Politically, the DPRK is a tightly controlled authoritarian regime. The country is ruled by the Korean Workers' Party (KWP), and the authority of the Chief of State technically derives from his position as Secretary-General. In fact, the country is run by a coalition of the KWP and the North Korean military, which has a high priority on access to power and resources. One of the major sources of tension within Pyongyang has been the attempt by the current leader to exert more control over the military, and this has resulted in the purges and executions of some leading military leaders (including some relatives of the leader himself).

Essentially all power resides in the chief of state, and the means of governmental succession has been nepotism. Since it was formed, North Korea has been ruled by three members of the same family. Kim Il-sung, the first leader and patriarch, ruled from 1948 until his death in 1991. He was succeeded by his son, Kim Jong-il, who reigned until his death in 2011 and was succeeded by one of his sons, the current leader, Kim Jong-un. Kim Il-sung was officially designated as the "Great Leader," his son as the "Dear Leader," and his grandson the "Great Successor," presumably as a way for the people to show their affection and loyalty for the family.

Kim Jong-un has proven to be a much more difficult leader to deal with than his father. He is very young for the leader of a communist state; he was born in 1983 and is the first DPRK leader born after the birth of the country. At age thirty-three in 2016, he was the youngest chief executive of a country in the world and in 2015 was ranked by one poll as the forty-sixth most powerful person on the globe. He was personally chosen over several siblings for ascension by his father before Kim Jong-il's death.

The younger Kim has proven to be both a ruthless and aggressive leader. He moved quickly to consolidate his power both in the KWP and within the armed forces. His rise within the military was accompanied by the arrest and execution of several top generals, including one of his uncles. Under his rule, dissent is even less tolerated than under former rulers; this intolerance has been extended to foreigners who visit the country and break North Korean law. An American student who, in 2016, was convicted and sentenced to fifteen years of hard labor for attempting to steal a propaganda poster from a Pyongyang hotel is a case in point.

There is no publicly known opposition to the young Kim's rule. Given what Myers calls "a paranoid nationalism" that includes "the celebration of racial purity and homogeneity," Kim Jong-un's radical, aggressive anti-Americanism probably strikes a national chord in a country where there is virtually no access to contrary information about what is happening in the world. America is the enemy, the roots of all the DPRK's ills, intent on destroying the worker's paradise. Americans cannot imagine why they would feel this way, but they do.

At both the rhetorical and policy levels, the negativity of relations between the DPRK and both the United States and the ROK has escalated. The most troubling manifestation has been in the area of nuclear weapons, where the DPRK has accelerated both its attempt to develop thermonuclear warheads and ballistic delivery systems capable of long-range delivery—

including to American targets. The North Koreans already have the ability to attack Japan and the ROK with these weapons, and both countries rely on the deterrent threat from the United States to prevent such an attack. DPRK programs have not reached viable fruition, but it is probably a matter of time until they do, at which point the United States will face even more difficult choices than it already does about what to do. North Korean saber-rattling has also increased toward the ROK, and while a renewed war on the peninsula makes virtually no geopolitical sense, Kim Jong-un has nurtured the reputation of erratic behavior to the point that no one is entirely certain what he might do.

Basic U.S.-DPRK Relations

A National Committee on North Korea report summarized U.S.-DPRK relations succinctly in a November 2015 publication: "There are few bilateral relationships in the world which have been more consistently difficult than the relationship between the U.S. and North Korea." Two countries that could scarcely be more unlike have been at one another's throats for over sixty-five years, and there seems little reason to believe that the situation will change in the foreseeable future. Both are thorns in the side of the other.

If it were not for the Korean War and its unending aftermath, U.S.-DPRK relations would likely be unremarkable and very limited. North Korea is a small, impoverished country far from American shores, and one with which one would otherwise not expect more than the most cursory, bland relations. If anything, the generally wretched conditions in the northern half of the Korean peninsula would probably be the source of some sympathy, even humanitarian assistance to relieve the suffering. That has hardly been the case. The signal reason for the absence of tranquility comes from the fact that the two have technically been at war since 1950.

The tenor of U.S.-DPRK relations begins with the Korean War and that, particularly for the North Koreans, is a conflict that has never ended and whose consequences continue to dominate the dynamics between the two countries and form the heart of the issues that divide them. From an American vantage point, there are three issues on the agenda with the DPRK. The first two are strategic and direct legacies of the Korean War: the control of the North Korean nuclear weapons program and the stabilization of relations between the two Koreas. In tandem, both are aimed at reducing the likelihood of war between the ROK and DPRK, which could spread and destabilize the Far East and possibly beyond. The goals are obviously related to one another: "denuclearizing" the peninsula would reduce the potential consequences of renewed war, and reaching some kind of accord would reduce the probability of war. The third issue, at a lower order of priority, is addressing the DPRK's dismal human rights record.

From an American vantage point, dealing with the DPRK nuclear program is the more pressing, since the North Koreans have publicly threatened to use nuclear weapons against the United States. In one sense, the United States bears some responsibility for this problem. Beginning in 1958, the United States began moving so-called tactical nuclear weapons into South Korea to help deter a second DPRK invasion, and this may have provided the initial incentive for the northerners to start their own program. As Norris puts it, "the fact that North Korea was threatened by nuclear weapons during the Korean War, and that for decades thereafter U.S. weapons were deployed in the south, may have helped motivate former President Kim Il Sung to launch a nuclear program of his own." The United States removed the last of its nuclear weapons from the ROK in 1991, and there have been periodic attempts to negotiate an end to the DPRK program, but these have ultimately failed (see Wertz and Gannon for a summary). The most serious attempts were in 1994 and resulted in the ill-fated Agreed Framework and in 2006 in the Six Party Talks, both discussed in the next section. Since the ascension of Kim Jong-un, the North Koreans have moved forward aggressively both to perfect a thermonuclear device and to develop three-stage rockets capable of intercontinental range delivery of those warheads. In a series of well-publicized tests, they have failed on both counts, but it may be a matter of time until they succeed.

The problem is transformed in two ways if North Korea gains thermonuclear and missile capability. First, American soil becomes at risk: certainly Hawaii and parts of Alaska and the West Coast become theoretically reachable by a DPRK missile, and it is not entirely certain that American missile defense capabilities could destroy all incoming weapons. Questions of what to do to prevent this possibility become more salient in the process. Second, even if American targets remain out of reach, the ROK and Japan certainly are at risk with no protection except the American nuclear umbrella. Many analysts worry that this danger could force both countries to build their own nuclear weapons (both are capable of doing so), thereby running the risk of an East Asian nuclear arms race, not a happy prospect for either.

The second policy difference is over stabilization of the peninsula. After the end of the Cold War, there were active discussions in the ROK and the United States of the prospects of reunification, and in 2004, the two Koreas even fielded joint Olympic teams in some sports. That prospect has faded due both to the general deterioration of ROK-DPRK relations (as well as North Korean relations with the West) and undoubtedly because the DPRK leadership realized they would be the almost certain losers in the process. Discussions of greater interaction, even cooperation, between the two entities is now regarded in North Korea as a thinly veiled threat to bring down their regime, and periodic overtures by the South Koreans are routinely rebuffed.

The third American policy issue surrounds the human rights abuses of the North Koreans against their fellow citizens and foreign nationals (including Americans) who run afoul of the Pyongyang regime. The specific policies to which the United States objects include well-publicized political prison camps within North Korea, repression of freedom of speech by Pyongyang, and the mistreatment of North Korean refugees. All of these problems arise periodically and are either resolved or exacerbated by the particular state of American-DPRK relations at the time.

All of these issues arise and become troublesome because of the North Korean nuclear program, and doing something about that program is at the center of American disagreements regarding relations between the two countries, as well as North Korea's place in the East Asian region. During the latter part of the twentieth century, the DPRK showed some willingness to negotiate about that program to try to gain leverage in its other goals, but that policy flexibility has largely disappeared as the DPRK under Kim Jong-un has become more militant, even threatening. This change is sometimes attributed to increased influence by the North Korean military, but it is almost certainly exacerbated by the regime's realization that its nuclear weapons program is its ace card in its relations with the world. Without nuclear weapons, North Korea is a very poor, marginal country that the world would largely ignore, and it would be much more difficult for it to avoid the blandishments from the south for a reunion in which its power would disappear. Nuclear weapons are not only its ace card, they are its *only* card in the relations among countries, and the DPRK knows it. The United States and the DPRK are at absolute loggerheads about nuclear weapons, which in turn represents a quandary the solution of which is vital to any improvement in relations between the two.

U.S. Policy Options

Both the United States and the DPRK have laid down very strict and, for many purposes, intractable solutions to the problems that divide them, making efforts to resolve differences difficult without one side or another essentially giving in on positions they feel are too important for compromise. The result is that neither side has many meaningful or fruitful options for resolving the problems.

The nuclear issue is foundational. The United States will only resolve this problem on the basis of North Korean nuclear disarmament (including abandonment of their missile program) and return to compliance with the Non-Proliferation Treaty (NPT) and IAEA inspections of facilities, all of which the North Koreans agreed to in the 1990s and from which they have backed away. Given the very public statement that the DPRK program is aimed at the United States, this American position is justifiable. On the other hand, nuclear weapons play such an important role for the DPRK that it is equally intransigent on disbanding its program. Even with Chinese pressure to dial back their efforts, it is unlikely the North Koreans will back down.

The United States has attempted two different options with the DPRK since the end of the Cold War, and neither has succeeded. In the 1990s, the Clinton administration negotiated the Agreed Framework with the DPRK. The agreement was signed in 1994. Broadly speaking, it committed the North Koreans to abandoning their nuclear weapons program, in return for which the West would provide the DPRK with alternate energy sources, including two light-water nuclear reactors suitable for energy production but not bomb making. North Korean compliance was sporadic and controversial throughout the remainder of the Clinton administration. When Clinton was replaced by George W. Bush, anti-DPRK elements (notably John Bolton) called for a reassessment of the framework, concluding that the DPRK had acted perfidiously and recommending withdrawal from the agreement. After North Korea was named a member of Bush's "Axis of Evil" in his 2002 State of the Union message, the Agreed Framework was dissolved and replaced by the Six Party Talks.

The Six Party talks (the United States, DPRK, PRC, ROK, Japan, and Russia) helped re-create a confrontational tone in the relationship. Moving from bilateral to multilateral talks signaled Bush's unwillingness to talk directly to the North Koreans, but brought the other interested parties into the process. On September 19, 2005, the group issued a Joint Statement in which the North Koreans agreed to abandon their weapons program in return for food and energy assistance from the other states. Negotiated in a more adversarial atmosphere than the Agreed Framework, this agreement broke down in less than a year. Since then, U.S. relations with the DPRK have remained indirect, hostile, and adversarial. In terms of moving toward preferred U.S. policy outcomes, this approach has not been particularly productive either.

A third option is entreating the Chinese to aid in reducing DPRK intransigence. The PRC is the one country that exercises some influence over the North Koreans, and is as close to a "friend" as the DPRK has in the world. The Chinese are known to oppose the DPRK nuclear program and to be embarrassed by some of the more extreme actions and language of its neighboring state. The Chinese are, unfortunately, reluctant to take decisive action to reshape DPRK behavior.

The situation creates a quandary for the Chinese. The leadership of the PRC would prefer a more conventional regime in Pyongyang and, in the proper circumstances, might not even oppose its overthrow. The problem is that the DPRK regime guarantees a physical buffer between China and the West. China realizes that the overthrow of the Pyongyang regime could well lead to reunification, and that a unified Korea would be dominated by the ROK, a close ally of the United States. Having a potentially hostile neighbor on its border is intolerable to the Chinese and is arguably why Chinese "volunteers" joined the fight against the United States and its UN allies in the Korean War (a reaction of which the Chinese had warned prior to their intervention). In this circumstance, the Chinese view the situation as choosing between lesser evils, and in this case this has meant not placing decisive pressure on the DPRK.

What can the United States do? It has tried bilateral negotiation and co-operation (the Agreed Framework) and a more confrontational approach (the Six Party Talks), and neither the carrot nor the stick has moved the situation. During his eight years in office, President Obama pursued what he called a policy of "strategic patience," a kind of holding action seeking quietly to induce a reduction in hostilities that would reduce the level of confrontation, and that policy also did not yield positive results. Pleas to the Chinese to help have not moved the parties either.

It is not clear what can change the situation. American political elements are deeply divided as to what to do. Because of the potentially dire conse-quences of success of the DPRK nuclear weapons or missile programs, there are advocates of military action against the DPRK, but it is not clear what such actions would accomplish and what their repercussions might be in the region. (Interestingly, Obama's Secretary of Defense during the latter part of his incumbency, Ashton Carter, suggested the military option in a 2006 coauthored *Washington Post* op-ed.) There is very little sentiment for a reconciliatory approach, both because of past failures and DPRK actions regardless of whether an olive branch is offered to them or not. The status quo is equally unappealing, because the DPRK program makes the Japanese and South Koreans increasingly nervous, which could result in decisions that include their own nuclear weapons programs, with uncertain and po-tentially dire consequences as well. The result is a cauldron that continues to steep and brew, and no one quite knows how to throw away its toxic contents without making matters even worse.

CONCLUSION

China and the Democratic People's Republic of Korea are two of the most different countries in the world, and yet they share commonalities both in global standing and in American foreign policy. The differences are stark and largely demographic. China is one of the world's major powers, a rising state with the largest population and fourth-largest landmass among states, while the DPRK is a small, isolated state that, for the most part, is not a world or even regional power and would be viewed as inconsequential were it not for its one distinguishing characteristic, nuclear weapons. China has gravitas; North Korea has poverty and nukes.

But they are also similar in ways that affect their relations with the United States. As already noted, they share a land border that is one of many for China, and virtually North Korea's only physical connection to Asia. That land border has been and continues to be important, especially to the Chinese, who are loath to contemplate or accept a potentially hostile state staring at it across the frontier. That sentiment in turn creates reluctance on the part of the Chinese to assist in reining in the DPRK's aggressive military pretensions. The two countries are also among the last surviving members of the international communist experiment of the twentieth century, if in different ways. The North Koreans, along with the Cubans, are the last states to cling to both the Marxist-Leninist political and economic philosophy, although Cuba's embrace of the economic dimension may loosen with Fidel Castro's death (see chapter 6). China, meanwhile, has largely abandoned Marxist economics: it still maintains a large public sector (the SOEs) that is an economic millstone but supports the political monopoly of the Chinese Communist Party (CCP). The Leninist authoritarian political "model" remains the last major vestige of Karl Marx's nineteenth-century societal model in China.

The other thing the countries share is their relationship with the United States in the modern international system. The commonality, of course, was that they both fought—the North Koreans formally and the Chinese informally (their forces were not officially Chinese, but volunteers)—the United States in the Korean War, and this experience has continued to influence how they interact with the United States, if in very different ways.

The Korean War experience reinforced the American predilection at the time to ignore the government of the PRC as illegitimate for nearly twenty more years after the last shots were fired on the peninsula in 1953. That rupture began to be repaired in 1972 when President Nixon visited China, and it accelerated in the direction it now has in 1979. In that fateful year, President Carter restored diplomatic relations with the mainland, and Deng Xiaoping announced the Four Modernizations. These separate incidents melded in U.S.-Chinese relations, sparking a political relationship and the basis for what has become an enormous, if sometimes controversial, economic relationship. The countries have gotten past being opponents for the most part, even with some differences between them. They have become, at worst, frenemies.

The United States and the DPRK remain adversaries. The United States effectively defeated and conquered North Korea in 1951, and only the Chinese unofficial intervention prevented the overthrow of communism on the peninsula from becoming permanent. Even after the armistice ended fighting but did not include a peace treaty in 1953, the two have remained adversaries. American forces have stared across the armistice line at DPRK forces ever since, and behind the American troop (and until 1991, nuclear) barrier, the United States has provided much of the capital and encouragement that has seen the South Korean economic "miracle" unfold. North Korea, on the other hand, has peered out at the world through sullen eyes gazing through the barbed wire.

The result is a very different quality of relationship. The United States and the PRC disagree on some political, economic, and military matters, but their overall relationship is not dangerous in the meaningful prospect of a deterioration of relations that could lead to war. They are tied together too tightly by the spider's web of economic globalization for that to occur. The Americans and the Chinese spar with one another; trying to land a knock-out punch would be too bad for business to contemplate. The U.S.-DPRK relationship, on the other hand, is essentially entirely adversarial and tied to North Korea's actions as a geopolitical troublemaker. It is a true zero sum affair: one country benefits only at the other's expense. The United States wants DPRK abandonment of nuclear weapons; the DPRK sees them as its one source of leverage in the world. The United States wants peace on the Korean peninsula; the North Koreans realize the mechanism for doing so would likely be reunification and their fall from power in a reunited Korea. One gains only what the other loses. American policy with China remains largely positive and positive sum (both sides can win); U.S. policy with the DPRK is either zero sum or even negative sum: both sides would lose, to varying degrees, if the relationship devolved to another Korean conflict.

STUDY QUESTIONS

1. Discuss China as a "rising power." What does the term mean? From what is China rising and in which dimensions does it emphasize rising? How does this distinction help frame relations between the United States and China?
2. Why does the text refer to the People's Republic of China as a "frenemy"? What does the term mean? Apply it to U.S.-China relations.
3. What were the Four Modernizations? Discuss their impact, especially in the economic area. Include in your answer a discussion of the SEZs, SOEs, and the effects of Sino-American relations. Also include countervailing factors that could restrain continued Chinese growth, particularly in the energy area.
4. Sino-American relations are marked by conflict in some areas and close cooperation in others, thus framing the "frenemy" designation. What are the major points of conflict and cooperation between them? Assess the overall relationship as between friends or enemies.

5. How did the period between 1945 and 1950 create and shape U.S.-DPRK relations? Apply those events to the current level of hostilities between the two countries. Include in your answer the differences between South and North Korea.
6. What are the major points of contention between the United States and the DPRK? Why are they so contentious? Discuss.
7. Why are nuclear weapons so important to the DPRK, and why does this central importance make North Korea so intractable on the subject?
8. Why are U.S. and DPRK options for dealing with one another so intractable? Is it possible to move from zero-sum to positive-sum outcomes? How does China fit into the equation in resolving U.S.-DPRK animosities?

BIBLIOGRAPHY

Carter, Ashton B., and William J. Perry. "If Necessary, Strike and Destroy." *Washington Post*, June 22, 2006, A29.

Cha, Victor. *The Impossible State: North Korea, Past and Future.* New York: Ecco, 2013.

Cha, Victor, and David C. Kang. *Nuclear North Korea: A Debate on Engagement Strategies.* New York: Columbia University Press, 2010.

Chen, Gregory T. "China's Bold Economic Statecraft." *Current History* 114, no. 773 (September 2015): 217–23.

Christensen, Thomas J. *The China Challenge: Shaping the Choices of a Rising Power.* New York: Norton, 2015.

Cumings, Bruce. "Chinese Bullying No Match for US Pacific Power." *Current History* 113, no. 764 (September 2014): 245–51.

Demick, Barbara. *Nothing to Envy: Ordinary Lives in North Korea.* New York: Spiegel & Grau, 2010.

Economy, Elizabeth, and Michael Levi. *By All Means Necessary: How China's Resource Quest Is Changing the World.* New York: Oxford University Press, 2014.

French, Howard W. "China's Twilight Years: As Immigrants Replenish America, China's Population Is Aging and Shrinking." *The Atlantic* 317, no. 5 (June 2016): 15–17.

Garver, John W. *China's Quest: The History of the Foreign Relations of the People's Republic of China.* Oxford, UK: Oxford University Press, 2016.

International Institute for Strategic Studies (IISS). *The Military Balance 2015.* London: Routledge Journals, Taylor and Francis, 2015.

Kissinger, Henry. *On China.* Reprint. New York: Penguin, 2010.

Lankov, Andrei. "Changing North Korea: An Information Campaign Can Beat the Regime." *Foreign Affairs* 88, no. 6 (November/December 2009): 95–105.

Lanteigne, Marc. *Chinese Foreign Policy: An Introduction.* 3rd ed. New York: Routledge, 2015.

Lieberthal, Kenneth. "The China-US Relationship Goes Global." *Current History* 108, no. 719 (September 2009): 243–49.

Miller, Ken. "Coping with China's Financial Power: Beijing's Financial Foreign Policy." *Foreign Affairs* 89, no. 4 (July/August 2010): 96–109.

Myers, B. R. "North Korea's Race Problem." *Foreign Policy* (March/April 2010): 100–101.

Norris, Robert S. "North Korea's Nuclear Program, 2003." *Bulletin of the Atomic Scientists* 59, no. 2 (March/April 2003): 74–77.

Oberdorfer, Don, and Robert Carlin. *The Two Koreas: A Contemporary History*. 3rd ed. New York: Basic, 2014.

Paulson, Henry M., Jr. *Dealing with China: An Insider Unmasks the New Economic Superpower*. New York: Twelve, 2015.

Pei, Minxin. "The Dark Side of China's Rise." *Foreign Policy* (March/April 2006): 32–40.

Pollack, Jonathan D. *No Exit: North Korea, Nuclear Weapons, and International Security*. Adelphi Series. New York: Routledge, 2011.

Shambaugh, David. *China's Future*. New York: Polity, 2016.

Snow, Donald M. *Cases in International Relations*. 6th ed. New York: Pearson, 2014.

———. *The Middle East, Oil, and the U.S. National Security Policy: Intractable Conflicts, Impossible Solutions*. Lanham, MD: Rowman & Littlefield, 2016.

Sutter, Robert. *Chinese Foreign Relations: Power and Policy Since the Cold War*. Lanham, MD: Rowman & Littlefield, 2016.

Tuttle, Gray. "China's Race Problem: How Beijing Suppresses Minorities." *Foreign Affairs* 94, no. 3 (May/June 2015): 39–47.

Wertz, Daniel, and Chelsea Gannon. *A History of U.S.-DPRK Relations*. Washington, DC: National Committee on North Korea. November 2015.

CHAPTER 4

The Asian Subcontinent

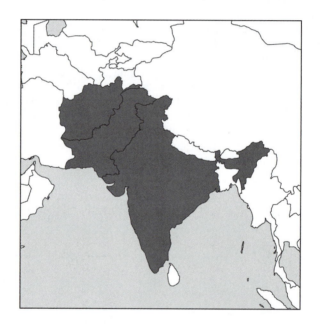

Asia is physically the largest and most highly populated continent, and, in terms of human development, it has the longest history of any continent. In terms of landmass, it is slightly larger than Africa. Roughly 60 percent of humankind calls some place in Asia home; its two largest states, China and India, account for 36 percent of humans. The three oldest civilizations in the world, the Chinese, Persian, and Indian (in that order), are on the continent. Two of the three civilizations, the Persian and Chinese, have been the subject of previous chapters in this text; India is one of the subjects of this chapter. In many important ways, Asia is the anchor of the world, and the Indian Subcontinent, jutting from the southern extremity of the landmass into the Indian Ocean, is the anchor of Asia.

India represents the third-oldest civilization in the world, dating back roughly 5,000 years. The earliest signs of the Indian civilization have been traced back to the Indus River Valley, where the world's oldest integrated irrigation system was constructed to manage scarce water resources that are still a problem today. The first influx of Aryan people arrived on the subcontinent in about 1500 BCE, and the beginnings of Indian civilization are conventionally dated to that trek.

India has been among the ripest global prizes for invading conquerors ever since. India was the ultimate destination point for Alexander the Great and his Macedonian armies, and although Alexander failed in his quest to subdue the entire region, he set a precedent that others would follow. The invasion route along which invaders traveled went through contemporary Afghanistan and Pakistan, helping to form the worldviews of the inhabitants in ways explored in the second half of the chapter.

The epochal phase began with the arrival of evangelical Muslims in the eighth century CE; they were followed by intruding Turks in the northern part of the region in the twelfth century. Rule in India was consolidated under the Turkish Moguls (or Mughals) between 1526 and 1857, a time of notable progress that included such artifacts as the Taj Mahal.

The modern era of subcontinental history began with the arrival of European colonists. The Portuguese were first and established coastal enclaves in places such as Goa in the fifteenth century. They were followed by the Dutch and the British East India Company, and the British government eventually imposed colonial sway over the entire subcontinent, which they called the British Raj, in the mid-nineteenth century. Britain ruled the area and imposed many of its values, such as the English language. Like world empires generally, the ability of comparatively small Britain to rule was undercut by the burden and exertion of the world wars. Independence movements emerged during the interwar period, and after World War II, the British recognized the inevitable and began the process of granting independence. In their haste to disengage, they also left behind some arguably intractable conditions that have plagued the region ever since.

Modern Asian subcontinental affairs began in the 1920s and 1930s. Separate independence movements had emerged in the early 1900s within both the Hindu and Muslim communities of the Raj. Many people from the subcontinent had played supporting roles in the effort during the "Great War"; returning to colonial subjugation was incompatible with their experience and led to increased vigor among those seeking to shed the British yoke. On the Hindu side was the Indian Congress, led by Mohandas Gandhi, known popularly as "Mahatma—the Great Soul." Muhammad Ali Jinnah led the Muslim League, which represented Islamic minorities scattered about the subcontinent. The goal of both sides was to force an end to British subjugation, and during the period leading to World War II, they generally succeeded in cooperating in this endeavor, with a false sense of confidence that they would also be successful in their second goal, which was to establish separate Hindu and Muslim states that could coexist peacefully.

India and Pakistan clearly form the heart of the Asian subcontinent, but the chapter also includes some consideration of a third country that is technically not part of the geographic area but is tied to it by common historical factors and, in the period since 9/11, through American national security policy toward this part of the world. Afghanistan borders Pakistan, has historically been a major part of invasion routes going south toward the subcontinent, and has numerous links and ties to Pakistan. Since the American intervention in the Afghan civil war in 2001 in pursuit of Al Qaeda, the AfPak border between them has been a significant point of contention between the two countries and with the United States, thereby warranting inclusion in this chapter as well.

A COMPLEX PROBLEM

The effort to grant freedom to the peoples of the subcontinent was negotiated by the British in 1947 under the leadership of a WWII British hero, Lord Louis Mountbatten. The British were exhausted physically and monetarily by the war effort against fascism, saw no positive future in resisting demands for independence in the empire, and thus charged Mountbatten with creating as good a partition as he could with the two sides, both of whom (along with the British) believing that interwar cooperation would somehow spill over into the dividing of Hindus and Muslims into two states, India and Pakistan. Their optimism, unfortunately, turned out to be a form of false euphoria that did not long survive the process of separation.

The negotiation of the partition faced two major obstacles, each of which was fundamental and formed a base for later disagreement among the parties. The first obstacle was finding a politically defensible partition line that would separate believers of the two religious groups without creating additional anomalies in the process. This problem was especially acute in the western part of the Raj; it had two separate and insurmountable problems. The first was that the two populations had over the centuries intermingled enough that no line could possibly create a clean division. When a line was finally agreed upon, it left millions of Hindus in Pakistan and millions of Muslims in India in minority statuses that were unacceptable to either, and the result was a massive, panicky migration along the border involving upward of twelve million people fleeing across the border in one direction or another (it was believed to have been the largest migration in history at the time). Both sides blamed the other for causing the panic and for the wretched conditions into which the fleeing people were forced. Hoped-for continued cooperation was the permanent victim of the episode. Most Hindus managed to escape Pakistan, but as many as 150 million Muslims live in India.

The second border problem was that any line in the west would have to cut across the Indus River irrigation system, the world's oldest irrigation scheme. Because precipitation is deficient (about twelve to fifteen inches per year, much of which falls in spate), agriculture on both the Indian and Pakistani sides of the partition line depends critically on Indus waters, and having a system that transverses the boundaries gives both countries the theoretical capability to interfere with the other's vital resource. When India "temporarily" cut off the flow to part of Pakistan in 1948 during harvest season, the result was the first fighting between the two countries, as well as the creation of an obsession bordering on paranoia among the Pakistanis to gain secure access to all the water Pakistan considers vital to its survival.

The second obstacle was the manner of self-determination. Part of the Raj had consisted of so-called princely states, generally fairly small and remote areas mostly ruled by hereditary rulers. In most of these cases, there was no obvious reason for them to become part of either country, and in fact, a number of them preferred independence. In the fear that allowing them to do so would simply make the process of disengagement more complicated, these areas were given the choice of acceding to either India or Pakistan but not of independence. These entities would be allowed to choose which status, but how they would choose was suggested but not mandated.

The most contentious princely state was Jammu and Kashmir, and its turmoil continues to play a major role in subcontinental affairs and to illustrate the complexities and difficulties of the region. Jammu and Kashmir (Kashmir for shorthand purposes) sit astride the northernmost part of India, adjacent to Pakistan on the west and China on the north. The population is about three-quarters Muslim, most of its commerce was with what became Pakistan, and the Muslim majority favored a plebiscite, which would almost certainly have been a vote to become part of Pakistan. The state had, however, historically been ruled by a Hindu maharajah, and thus the minority preferred that the problem be solved by government-to-government agreement, guaranteeing accession to India. While the debate over which method was raging, the monarch signed an agreement with the Indian government making Kashmir part of India. For reasons explored below, Kashmir has been a source of dissent between the two ever since.

One notable point in all these machinations is how little role the United States had in any of it. For most of U.S. history, India barely registered on the American consciousness. The United States had minimal relations with most of the world before the American Civil War, and between that national tragedy and the end of World War II, the subcontinent was under British control (the Indian Raj), making it off-limits for the United States. The process of partition similarly did not have any particular American component. American involvement in the world and the independence were virtually simultaneous "coming out parties," and it would take a while before the two regions had time to develop relations.

CASE: THE UNITED STATES AND INDIA

India is a country of enormous contrasts and complexities, regardless of the perspective from which one is viewing it. Menon describes India by analogy: "A sprawling latter-day Austro-Hungarian Empire, with a dizzying array of languages, castes and religions . . . modern India has defied pessimists who were drafting its obituary not long after its birth." Its history as a civilization stretches far back in history, and it is one of the largest and most highly populated and diverse places on earth. India is a country that could be largely ignored in a Euro-centered world where most of Asia and Africa were colonized by European masters. It cannot be ignored in a world where Asia plays an increasingly prominent, arguably critical role. India and the United States (in that order) are the world's two largest democracies, a significant commonality. That similarity has not always translated into congenial relations between the two countries.

American relations with India have gone through two distinct phases since Indian independence. The partition of the subcontinent coincided with the outbreak of the Cold War, and decolonization and the Soviet-American confrontation merged as international concerns in much of the developing world. Particularly during the 1950s, when anti-communist fervor was at its zenith in the United States, anti-communism was seen as a necessary condition for international virtue, and the failure to fundamentally oppose the Soviet bloc was seen as unacceptable. The middle ground of neutrality was seen as a de facto siding with the opposition—countries were either for or against godless communism. There was no middle ground.

The problem was that a number of developing countries chose the middle ground of neutralism. Their grounds for doing so varied, but they included the presumption that taking sides in the conflict did not serve their interests, which involved state-building and gaining developmental assistance to help close the gap between their economic conditions and those of the Cold War competitors. India emerged a leader of what was sometimes called the "neutralist bloc" (an oxymoron of sorts), and this stance enraged the American leadership during the 1950s in particular. The leading apostle of the "us-or-them" conviction was President Eisenhower's Secretary of State John Foster Dulles, whom Kinzer quotes on his view of neutralism, which Dulles described as "immoral and short-sighted." To make matters worse, the Indians adopted a statist approach to regulation of the economy that smacked enough of socialism to further alienate those obsessed with any vestiges of communism. Instead, the Americans "tilted" toward Pakistan (which had joined anti-communist defense arrangements such as the Southeast Asian Treaty Organization or SEATO) in the growing conflict between the two subcontinental powers. Relations between the United States and India during this period were not hostile, but neither were they warm and supportive.

The relationship began to change in 1991, which was a watershed in two ways. First, it was the year that signaled the end of the Cold War, as the Soviet Union collapsed and most of the overtly communist world followed suit. As a result, much of the rhetorical animosity surrounding India's neutralism and unwillingness to take sides in the American anti-Soviet coalition lost its practical meanings. Second, the Indian government adopted a series of economic reforms similar to those that had already been instituted in the West and that reflected a more capitalist approach to economic policy. In the process, India began to become part of the globalization process that dominated the 1990s and of which the United States was a leader. The result was to stimulate the Indian economy greatly and, in the process, integrate the country politically and economically into the American-dominated post–Cold War system. Relations between the two countries have warmed noticeably since.

India: A Physical and Political Sketch

India is such a large and complex place that it is impossible to describe in a summary fashion. It is the world's second most populous country with a billion and a quarter people, and with current population growth rates, it could surpass China as having the most people of any country by 2030. Its landmass is 1.269 million square miles, about one-third the size of the United States and seventh largest of any world country. It has an incredibly diverse topography: the world's tallest mountains, the Himalayas, form its northern boundary in Kashmir, and as one moves south, the land becomes less uneven, eventuating in the Ganges River Basin, one of the most densely populated places on earth. To the east the terrain includes the flood plains that are the dominant feature of neighboring Bangladesh. Slightly over half the land is arable, but despite swampy coastal plains, there are arid areas in the west bordering on Pakistan that have made water access an ongoing issue. The country has borders with Pakistan, China, Bhutan, Nepal, Myanmar (formerly Burma), and Bangladesh, virtually all of which have been the subject of disputes of varying levels of intensity with India in the past.

It is also a very diverse place of great contrasts. Jaguar, one of the world's prestige automobile makers, is owned by an Indian corporation, Tata Motor Group, but most Indians cannot afford even the most modest form of car, and Tata also produces the Nano, a small and primitive vehicle to sell to the masses. Most Indians cannot even afford such a modest vehicle, because, as Kronstadt et al. reported in 2010, "India is home to some 500–600 million living in poverty." More recent estimates reduce that figure marginally, but it remains extraordinarily high. The Indians like to brag that their middle class has 300 million, making it the largest in the world, but this claim comes in the context of a much larger community at or below the poverty level, some of which is an artifact of India's traditional caste system.

Education also provides a source of contrast. Approximately 61 percent of the population is literate, but that means that almost half a billion Indians are not. At the same time, India possesses one of the world's most prestigious universities in the area of science and technology, the Indian Institute of Technology, which provides extremely well-educated graduates for India's vibrant high technology sector and worldwide, including Silicon Valley and other scientific communities in the United States. The Indian political system struggles with the contrast between the illiterate and the elite in educational terms.

India's diversity extends to its people. The population is 72 percent Indo-Aryan and 25 percent Dravidian, but its real diversity is better captured linguistically. Hindi is the language most associated with the country, and it is spoken by about two-fifths of the population. The language of most official activities is English, and in addition to these languages, India has fourteen other "official" languages. Creating commonalities in things such as education with as many people and languages as exist is a monumental task for attempts at Indian modernization and global competitiveness.

Within this cauldron of factors, the Indians have made some progress toward joining the world economy and thus toward improving India's place in it. Technology has provided the cutting edge of this development, particularly high-technology ideas and innovations coming from places such as the Bangalore high-tech community (the country's equivalent of Silicon Valley). Many people in the West still associate India's economy with annoying telemarketers speaking stilted English, but India is increasingly at the forefront of many commercial enterprises, and unlike its competitor China, it has a relatively youthful workforce that will not become a burden on future development in the way that such problems will haunt the Chinese.

Economically, India is showing signs of emergence as a global power, but its population slows the rate at which this can be transformed into improvements in the living conditions under which Indians labor. At almost five trillion dollars, India now has the fourth-highest GDP in the world, but when that figure is computed on a per capita basis, the size of the population dampens the accomplishment: with a GDP per capita of $4,000, India only ranks 168th in the world. There is an economic miracle brewing in India, but it faces daunting obstacles that affect both its developmental efforts and its place in the world. Two stand out.

The first challenge is social and demographic. India is trying desperately to enter the contemporary world system, but it still remains a traditional society in many ways. It is still a society of contrasts that must be resolved before the Indian ascent can reach its maximum trajectory. Grinding poverty still grips large parts of the population whose lot is decided on social conventions such as the caste system that are anomalies in the modern world. The government has been unable to come to adequate grips with the dilemma of uplifting the masses from poverty while allocating adequate resources to fund the country's aspirations to cutting-edge productivity and living standards. It is true that India remains a very class-based society where some people live very well and others suffer wretched existences. One manifestation of the consequences of this disparity is that India has one of the few Maoist insurgencies still in existence. The Naxalites (named after the area of their origin) are not a threat to the integrity of country, but they cause major headaches where they are active, normally in opposition to wealthy landowners. To rise to world standards, the Indians must somehow reconcile the contrasting images of the shining modernity of Bangalore with the squalor of the Black Hole of Calcutta.

The second challenge is geographical, with two focuses. One is location. The state of India is physically wedged between two areas of geopolitical importance in the world, the oil-rich regions of the Middle East and oil-deficient East Asia, and it has an important stake in both. India's interest in the Persian Gulf arises from the fact that India is a major importer of petroleum, at about 3.72 million barrels a day (fifth in the world), and this dependency will grow as India becomes more economically active. Particularly as the United States scales back its dependence on oil from the Gulf, the competition for the petroleum from the Gulf States will intensify. China will be a major competitor for these reserves, and so will India. Additionally, as Persian Gulf oil tankers increasingly turn "left" at the Strait of Hormuz (toward East Asia) rather than "right" (toward the West), India will find itself in a strategic maritime position, since tankers heading to East

Asia must transit around the subcontinent through the Indian Ocean and the nearby Strait of Malacca. Indian primary access to the oil is certainly desirable for them, and one way to promote that primacy could be by making it tougher for East Asian states to access the resource.

There is a second geographic challenge that affects India as well. India is more water deficient than China, largely due to distributional patterns. A great deal of India's water is in the east, where the rivers bearing it flow through Bangladesh into the Bay of Bengal. Much of the major need for water, however, is in the west, and the Indus River system has been the traditional conduit for providing irrigation water. Both India and Pakistan rely on Indus waters, mostly the product of Himalayan melt water and monsoonal rainfalls, to sustain agriculture to their respective regions. In addition, the water tables in affected parts of India have been dropping, largely the result of overuse caused by excess population. As in China, water needs may eclipse petroleum in the future.

The goal of transforming India into a world-class power, an aspiration many Indians share, is daunting. Given the enormous changes that have occurred and led to the economic miracle in China, navigating the path to such status may not necessarily be beyond the reach of the Indians, although one hopes it can be accomplished without some of the more harmful effects Chinese advancement has entailed in areas such as environment degradation. Because it shares fundamental political values with the West, India could emerge as a useful counterweight to the Chinese and help stabilize the most heavily populated place in the world. Clearly, doing so is an American interest at some level of importance.

Basic U.S.-Indian Relations

The relationship between the world's largest democratic states has not been close. The distance between them is partly geographic: India's subcontinent is about as distant from the United States as any inhabited part of the globe. For geographic and historical reasons, there is not a long-standing tie between them. India is, of course, much older than the United States, and for most of the existence of the United States, the subcontinent was British "turf" and thus effectively off-limits for American purposes. As already noted, the two countries got off to an unfortunate start after Indian independence because of Cold War concerns, and since then, relations have improved somewhat but have continued to exhibit points of discord, such as Indian testing and fielding of nuclear weapons in 1998 over the strenuous objections of countries opposed to nuclear proliferation and led in that effort by the United States. Things have improved in recent years, and when Barack Obama moved into the White House, the first head of government he invited for a formal visit was Indian prime minister Manmohan Singh.

There is a strategic distance between the two countries that reflects their interests and concerns in the world. Unlike other parts of the world such as the Middle East, the United States has no pressing, obviously vital interests on the subcontinent such as access to petroleum. The United States has naval interests in the Indian Ocean (IO) that arise from the need to protect the shipment of oil to market, but those assets are not located physically on the subcontinent but instead at places such as Diego Garcia in a remote southern part of the world's third-largest ocean, and at places such as Djibouti, near the Red Sea. The United States "tilted" toward Pakistan in its competition with India during the Cold War, but that tie has been compromised by U.S.-Pakistani disagreements over what to do about Taliban and Al Qaeda elements in exile in the territorial areas of remote Pakistan. This historic lack of major interest simply reflects that the subcontinent has been remote and isolated from the mainstream of global geopolitical life. As (or if) India emerges as a major world power, the region could become considerably less marginal for the United States as well.

U.S.-Indian relations can be seen in the context of a series of relationships among the major countries of the region and the United States. This relationship is depicted in figure 4.1. The figure requires some explanation. It is organized as a four-party model depicting the major regional powers (India, Pakistan, and China) and the outside superpower, the United States. The diagram has arrows connecting each of the four with points in each direction to show the mutual directions of concerns. In parentheses are the primary issues that confront each pair of states, recognizing that they all have additional matters of concern. In turn, each of the dyadic relationships can and does spill over to others. India has reinforcing concerns with both Pakistan and China, for instance, because the status of Kashmir both affects Pakistani water concerns and Chinese concerns about control of historic invasion routes back and forth with India. This dynamic (and their shared border) has resulted in informal Sino-Pakistani alliances with mixed impacts on the United States: the initial contact between the Nixon administration and China in the early 1970s was facilitated by the Pakistanis.

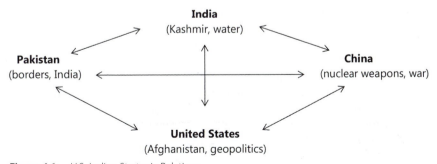

Figure 4.1. U.S.-Indian Strategic Relations

Each of the four countries is disparate in terms of its composition and interests, but each also has similarities worth reiterating. The first is size: China, India, and the United States are the three most populous countries in the world, and were Bangladesh reunited with Pakistan (which is extremely unlikely to occur), Pakistan would nudge by the United States into third place, and they would represent the four most populated countries in the world. Given matters such as potential global overpopulation and resource husbandry and ecological concerns, this sheer bulk makes them a "set" of sorts with some similar interests. One of those interests surrounds nuclear weapons, which is their other major commonality. Each of these states has a nuclear arsenal, and while their capabilities and reasons for possession may vary, they are all integral parts of the nuclear "club." The United States, the charter nuclear power, opposed the acquisition of nuclear weapons by each of the others, and in each case, the United States failed in its efforts. In some ways, the Indians' and Pakistanis', whose acquisitions occurred virtually in tandem, was the more galling, because U.S. intelligence failed to predict the event. Nuclear weapons complicate the four-sided relationship in two ways. First, they elevate the long-standing competition between China and India to a higher level (deterrence of a potential Chinese attack was one reason for the Indian program) of potential conflict. Second, the weapons were feared to make more likely an escalation of Indian-Pakistani hostilities, the volatility of which has been the major strategic factor on the subcontinent since independence, with unknown consequences. Would, for instance, a nuclear exchange between India and Pakistan somehow inexorably draw other nuclear powers into the fray as well? Such a dynamic would have seemed more likely during the Cold War, but nobody can say for certain whether escalation would occur or not—and nobody wants to find out. As will be discussed in the next section, there is also some residual concern that the Pakistani nuclear devices could become the basis for a Sunni Islamic bomb program should Iran break out of the nuclear regime to which it has committed itself.

For present purposes, the parts of figure 4.1 that are most interesting are those that impinged directly on the United States and India (the implications for the AfPak area are discussed later in the chapter). There are at least six current matters of joint concern. The United States and India share some of these interests and diverge on others, and it is important to note that most of them are more important to India than they are to the United States. These six areas are, in no particular order, Indian-American relations concerning China, conflicting interests regarding Pakistan, the future of nuclear weapons on the subcontinent, the struggle with Afghanistan, terrorism, and the environment.

The first matter of concern is China, an area of differing importance and content between the two countries. Competition between the two Asian powers is natural, since they are, by virtue of population, demographics, geography, global economic aspirations, and military power and roles the two most important countries in the region. Globalfirepower.com, for instance, combines data from the CIA and Library of Congress to compare the military strength of countries; by its measure, China is the second most powerful country in the world militarily, whereas India is fourth. Both countries feature large ground forces (infantry, tanks, and artillery, for instance) that cannot be projected easily far from their borders but which are appropriate in arming against one another. At the same time, both are rising powers with ambitious agendas within the region in economic terms. China has a head start: the Four Modernizations were proclaimed twelve years before India changed economic course in 1991, but the Indians have been furtively pursuing global competitiveness ever since.

The two countries are also geopolitical rivals by virtue of geographic juxtaposition. As mentioned, a primary source of conflict that spans the interests of both countries and Pakistan is Kashmir. The western boundary of the princely state is largely with Pakistan, with the Indus River flowing westward either directly into Pakistan or indirectly through parts of India before reaching Pakistan. The northern boundary of Kashmir is largely with China and encompasses traditional invasion routes in either direction. As part of that aspect of the competition, China occupies an area that India considers part of Kashmir, Aksai China. To attempt to put pressure on the Chinese to cede the territory to India, the Indians claim parts of the Chinese state of Tibet as part of India and provide clandestine support for Tibetan separatists.

The competition extends into the Indian Ocean. One prominent observer, Robert Kaplan, argues that a major future source of geopolitical conflict will center on the IO and southeastern Asia, an area that could logically fall under the influence of either country. Kaplan (2010) states the Indian concern in this competition: "India fears being encircled by China unless it expands its own sphere of influence. The countries' commercial and political interests are fostering competition, and even more so in the naval realm than on land." Kaplan concludes that the two countries are bound to collide in some fashion: "As India extends its influence east and west, on land and at sea, it is bumping into China."

The United States has close relations with both countries, but it has no interest either in fostering increasingly confrontational relations or in seeing one country become so dominant that it poses a serious, even an existential, problem to the other. American interests are on the periphery of any Indian-Chinese strategic access: it has historically close ties to Middle East oil producers to the west and economic ties to East Asia, including China. American interests are best served by a balance of power between the two emerging Asian giants in which American access to both is preserved and where American military—and especially naval—interests in traversing the area's waters are not endangered. The United States does not want to have to declare sides in the various aspects of the disputes between the two, preferring a rough parity where neither has an upper hand physically to be able to impair the other country. Clearly, a balance of power and influence also serves the interests of other regional states (such as Myanmar and Vietnam) that might be caught in the middle of a conflict between the Indians and the Chinese.

The issue of Pakistan continues to vex relations between the two major artifacts of partition. The acquisition, as suggested earlier, of nuclear weapons by each country in 1998 has changed the tenor of relations. After a brief clash between the two later that year made each realize that things could get out of hand and result in a potentially deadly nuclear exchange, the military confrontation between the two that has formed the underlying rationale for both countries' military efforts has been dialed back. As an example, the two foes signed an agreement creating a de facto division of Kashmir along the Line of Control that effectively legitimizes Pakistani control of the Indus system headwaters and Indian control over the strategic invasion routes. These kinds of efforts have reduced somewhat the intensity of confrontation between the two, and even some tentative signs of political cooperation have begun to emerge. When the backlash of a tsunami inundated parts of Kashmir in 2004, the countries were able to cooperate in rescue and relief matters, such as opening parts of the Line of Control to allow emergency workers to get to the suffering and destruction more easily than would have otherwise been the case.

Relations between the two countries have been intensified in recent years because of acts of terrorism, mostly but not entirely against India by Muslim extremists with alleged ties to or blessing from Pakistan. The Indians have believed that Pakistani intelligence has sponsored terrorist activities associated with Azad Kashmir (Free Kashmir) for years, including funding and running terrorist camps. There have been numerous attacks primarily against urban Indian targets, notably a massive attack against a Mumbai hotel in 2008, in which the Indians suspect Pakistani complicity, despite evidence that they were committed by Middle Eastern groups associated with organizations such as IS or Al Qaeda.

The Indian-Pakistani relationship continues to be focused on the military competition, which is a matter of Pakistani disadvantage. India, as noted, has some of the world's largest traditional ground forces, and Global Firepower ranks Pakistan eleven places lower than India at fifteenth in the world. This disparity takes on additional meaning in light of the countervailing Pakistani mission of trying to suppress Taliban and Al Qaeda activities in its northern territories adjacent to Afghanistan, a mission to which the United States wishes the Pakistanis would devote more energy. A relaxation of tensions between India and Pakistan facilitates this diversion of attention.

The American position toward the Indian-Pakistani conflict has varied across time. Until the end of the Cold War, relations were closer with authoritarian Pakistan (generally ruled by less than democratic military officers) than with democratic India, an apparent anomaly explained by Indian neutrality and Pakistani anti-communist fervor. As that factor has faded, it has become American policy to promote a more positive relationship between the two rivals. Greater stability is promoted on the grounds of reducing the likelihood of an escalation of a future conflict to nuclear exchange, an event with uncertain consequences for the rest of the world. The other motivation is to reduce military tension and the need for readiness along the border and thus to facilitate diversion of Pakistani resources to the Afghanistan frontier, which would simplify American and Afghan problems in the military campaign against the Taliban.

The third area of concern centers on Indo-Pakistani possession of nuclear weapons. It was always difficult to make the kind of apocalyptic nonproliferation arguments made against countries such as North Korea or Iran that the decision to "go nuclear" would result in the circumstance of a "madman" having a finger on the nuclear button, although the volatility of relations between India and fellow proliferator Pakistan was an argument against the decision. Anti-proliferation arguments were further compromised by India's contention that its nuclear force was really a deterrent against the Chinese, who possess a much larger arsenal than Pakistan and are a greater threat to the Indians than the Pakistanis.

India has proven a very responsible member of the nuclear club, mitigating some of the animosity with the United States that accompanied Indian testing and fielding of the weapons. As Menon points out, "India has not deliberately helped or encouraged other nations with their nuclear ambitions," and it has not engaged in any of the kind of nuclear "saber rattling" associated with countries such as the DPRK. India has, over the nearly two decades of its membership in the nuclear club, been a responsible nuclear power, a course of action with which the United States is in support, and the United States has entered into agreements with the Indians to improve India's civilian nuclear power program with American assistance. The remaining danger is an unexpected flare-up of tensions between India and Pakistan with escalatory potential, a contingency the United States seeks to dampen.

The Afghanistan War, discussed more fully in the next section, also enters into relations that span the United States, India, Pakistan, and Afghanistan itself. One aspect of that competition is over influence in Afghanistan between the Indians and the Pakistanis. From an Indian viewpoint, Afghanistan represents a barrier between India and a Russia that has historically cast a predatory eye toward India, and Afghanistan's strategic location as an invasion route made it the subject of the Great Game between the British and Russia during the nineteenth century. This competition continues between the Indians and the Pakistanis. The Pakistanis favor a weak central government in Kabul that can be influenced and manipulated by them to reduce pressure along the Pakistan-Afghan border. The Indians, on the other hand, prefer a stronger central Afghan government less controlled by the Pashtun plurality that will be more amenable to their interests than to those of the Pakistanis. As a result, Indian leaders generally desire a limit to Islamabad's influence in postwar Afghanistan. The position of the United States on post-conflict Afghanistan is closer to that of India (a strong central government) than that of Pakistan, but because the United States needs Pakistan's help in trying to seal the Afghan-Pakistan border, it has to support the Pakistanis, a disconnect the Indians understand and accept.

Terrorism has become part of the U.S.-Indian relationship as well. Terrorism is a venerable institution in this part of Asia. The practice of what has been called terrorism since the French Revolution's Reign of Terror is generally thought to have originated in Jewish resistance to the Roman occupation in the Levant, but among its early practitioners were Indians known as thuggees, from which the modern term "thugs" is derived. They were essentially thieves who preyed on visitors to the subcontinent between the fourteenth and nineteenth centuries, gaining their confidence and then engaging in criminal acts against them. These acts were not as openly political as are the actions of some terrorists, but they certainly served to frighten (terrorize) those against whom they were committed.

In more recent times, terror in one form or another has been a part of Muslim-Hindu atrocities. Beyond acts committed over Kashmir, there have been episodes within disputed territories in the Punjab, and in more recent years, by generally anonymous groups against Indian targets. Most of these have occurred in densely populated areas for the apparent purpose of maximizing human carnage. The purposes and perpetrators are generally unidentified beyond some occasional reference to Islamic fundamentalism. The apparent goal of the attacks, some of which have been directed at Pakistan as well, is to stir up trouble between the two countries as part of the general campaign to promote fundamentalist goals by causing the two countries to blame one another. If these continue to intensify and to include asserted parentage to organizations on the American anti-terrorism agenda, one can expect greater collaboration between American, Indian, and Pakistani officials dedicated to eradicating terrorism.

Finally, there is the question of the environment and climate change, an issue between the United States and both India and China. The issue is tied both to historic efforts in the area of climate control, one of the flip sides of which is economic, and especially industrial, development. The issue has arisen more dramatically with China, which has been undergoing industrialization longer than India, but it increasingly encompasses India as well.

As an international issue, the root of contention between the most developed countries and developing states such as India was presented at the time the Kyoto Protocols were signed in 1997. The Kyoto agreement created goals for the most developed states to reduce their carbon emissions from burning fossil fuels, but they excluded developing countries such as China and India on the grounds that they were not major contributors to the global problem. Since then, China has become the world's largest polluter in terms of injecting carbon emissions into the atmosphere, as noted in chapter 3, a course necessitated by the need for energy for economic activity. India is behind China in its contribution to carbon buildup in the atmosphere, but its contribution is becoming more problematical as it attempts to become more modern and prosperous, a course it must follow if it is to improve the standards of living of its people. This priority collides with environmental imperatives (which India fully understands) and creates a quandary for them.

The problem is simple to state if difficult to resolve. The position of India (and largely of China as well) is to ask why it should eschew the same kind of economic path (development through the burning of fossil fuels) that energized the development of the West. In their view, they are being asked by developed countries that were entirely profligate in their abuse of the atmosphere to deprive themselves of the same developmental advantages the West has enjoyed. Their conclusion, not entirely unreasonably, is that doing so is discriminatory and unfair to deprived elements of their populations, and it is an argument that is difficult to countermand. At the same time, the need to reduce and even eliminate excess carbon emissions is a global imperative as well.

Both sides in this debate understand the position of the other. The United States, which is a loud rhetorical proponent of reduced carbon emissions, realizes that its advocacy of lowering levels will have a particularly harsh impact on Indian development, and simultaneously argues that if India emulates Chinese levels of environmental degradation, the result could be disastrous for the ecosphere. India does not relish a stepped-up contribution to global warming, but it feels it is being asked to make sacrifices excessive to those demanding that it do so. The result is a quandary that can only probably be solved by global movement to a non-carbon-based form of world energy generation.

U.S. Policy Options

U.S.-Indian relations are anomalous, and this fact makes influence by one on the other difficult. At the interpersonal level, relations between the two peoples have always been warm and cordial. As the Kronstadt study points out, "influence of a geographically dispersed and relatively wealthy Indian-American community of some 2.7 million is reflected in Congress' largest country-specific caucus." Two Southern governors (South Carolina's Nikki Haley and former Louisiana governor Bobby Jindal) were elected and in office during the 2010s. More Indian students (around 100,000) study at American universities than anywhere else in the world, with special concentrations in the sciences and technology. These connections have helped foster cooperative relations between the two countries' scientific communities, and Indian Americans are prominent participants in the U.S. Silicon Valley process of technological innovation. India has also become a model of sorts for its approach to development in American eyes. A concerted American movement at restricting immigration could harm this relationship if it did not make provision for the highly talented and skilled to enter the country, but as long as that does not occur, the symbiotic relationship between the two countries is likely to continue.

Intergovernmental relations are not so close. American and Indian interests in the world are not identical, and there are points of friction between them. This is especially true on issues that are closely related to South Asian concerns, and these are generally much more important to the Indians than they are to the Americans. The chief American interest in the subcontinent has largely been confined to the promotion of peace and stability and continued American access to the region for economic purposes. This emphasis is largely shared by the Indians, although they have somewhat different views on how to achieve that stability. Nuclear weapons highlight the problem on the subcontinent, and gradual American acceptance of the Indian program suggests the relative balance of interests. If there is one point of disagreement, it is over who should have influence in Afghanistan, but that is primarily an Indo-Pakistani matter that does not overtly affect U.S. interests there.

The countries also have commonalities that help define the relationship. One is certainly shared political ideology and a general framework of relations reflecting their joint Anglo-Saxon style of development. Both countries also have a deep commitment to education and global advancement in science and technology. It is not a coincidence that there is a symbiosis between the extremely ambitious and best-educated Indians and the world's best higher education system in the United States. Moreover, India and the United States may not have a tradition of geopolitical cooperation, but they also have no history of animosity and violence. All these factors combine to create a relationship where two of the three most populous countries in the world do not see eye to eye all the time and in which neither has much leverage over the other a good deal of the time. The two retain a cordial relationship not dominated by geopolitical animosities or pressures in which the options for overt influence are not great.

CASE: THE UNITED STATES, PAKISTAN, AND AFGHANISTAN (AFPAK)

The two Muslim countries share a number of common characteristics and some important differences as members of the international community. Their primary importance in this chapter and volume is their location and their importance both to the subcontinent and American policy efforts in that region. Their similarities begin with three prominent shared characteristics. Both countries are Muslim, with heavy Sunni majorities: about 80 percent of Afghans are Sunnis, and 85–90 percent of Pakistanis profess Sunnism as the basis of their Muslim faith. Both have elements that either breed or are sympathetic to fundamentalist Sunni faith, and they both have some ties to Sunni extremism, such as that professed by Al Qaeda and IS.

Their second and third commonalities are related to one another. On the one hand, both countries have politically sizable Pashtun ethnic communities. The Pashtuns have long been the dominant ethnic group in Afghanistan, and before the civil war in their country, they composed the majority of the population of that country. The modern Afghan state was consolidated and declared in 1747 by Ahmed Shah Durrani, and one of the major divisions within the Pashtun community is named after Durrani; the other branch is known as Ghilzai (the larger of the two divisions, which translates as "mountain people" and which ruled Afghanistan from about 1000 to 1747). This distinction is important in understanding the Afghan civil war, since most Taliban are Ghilzai and most supporters of the government are Durrani. Pashtuns comprise about 15 percent of the Pakistani population and are the second-largest tribal component of that country.

The third commonality arises from the border between the two countries and has direct consequences for the U.S. effort in Afghanistan. The 1,519-mile AfPak frontier runs along desolate mountains and passes (including the Khyber Pass, the historic invasion route into the subcontinent from the Middle East) and is defined by something called the Durand Line. This boundary was created by British colonial administrator Sir Mortimer Durand and the Afghan emir in 1893. The line's location is virtually entirely geographically arbitrary and it cuts through traditional Pashtun lands, leaving relatives and other kinsmen in two different sovereign jurisdictions. The Pashtuns have never accepted the line and have regularly ignored it, a practice made possible by the difficulty of enforcing it. It has become an issue because Pashtun Taliban and Al Qaeda regularly move back and forth across the line to evade military contact in Afghanistan, a practice the Americans wish the Pakistanis would oppose with more vigor than they have.

An Interconnected Puzzle with Changing Pieces

One can think of the mosaic of relations between the three countries—India, Pakistan, and Afghanistan—from two vantage points. One is the inherent relationship among the three countries, and in that depiction, the primary conceptual dynamic has Pakistan sandwiched between the two others, with an eye on both but with primary focus on India. This is certainly the major vantage point from which the Pakistanis operated from partition until the end of the twentieth century. It resulted in a Pakistani obsession with its physical safety against the much more numerous Indians, whose covetous eye toward Pakistani values such as Kashmir and the Indus waters gave Pakistani politics a strong national security emphasis and enhanced the political power of the military in Pakistani politics. The United States was a handmaiden of sorts to this bent, providing assistance to the Pakistani military due to arrangements such as SEATO. India necessarily had to prepare for the possibility of conflict with Pakistan, and the geopolitics of the subcontinent were necessarily focused on the Indian-Pakistan frontier. Except for some anxiety when the Soviets occupied and tried unsuccessfully to subdue Afghanistan, the northern Pakistani frontier was of lesser interest. American interests were comparatively modest, largely limited to trying to contain Soviet interest in India and to aiding the Afghan resistance to the Soviet occupation. As a whole, America was closer in its relations with Pakistan than India (particularly during the period of major U.S. Cold War emphasis), and, except for thwarting Soviet ambitions, cared little about Afghanistan.

This framework changed with 9/11 in two ways. First, the Al Qaeda attack was planned and executed from the Afghan sanctuary that the Taliban government had granted Osama bin Laden and his followers, shifting the spotlight of Indian-AfPak attention to Afghanistan at a time when the traditional subcontinent parties were adjusting to their new relationship as nuclear rivals. Second, the response to 9/11 inserted the United States into the region as a major player with important national security interests, particularly in Afghanistan but overlapping into Pakistan as well. The first focus, of course, was the attempt to capture Al Qaeda and destroy its leadership in the months immediately after the terrorist attack on the United States. This effort failed, and the United States allowed itself to be drawn into the ongoing civil struggle for power between the Taliban and its opponents, the Northern Alliance. The United States remains part of that struggle in what is now the longest war in American history. This emphasis in turn caused the United States to develop a heightened concern about the extent to which the Pakistan government permitted de facto self-rule to much of the area along the Durand Line, areas known as the Federally Administered Tribal Areas (FATA) and the Northwest Frontier Province (NFP). Both areas, but especially the NFP (which is a Pashtun stronghold), are areas of ongoing disagreement between the United States and Pakistan, driving a wedge into their cooperation at a time when American relations with India were steadily improving. India, meanwhile, has remained aloof from the

Afghanistan conflict and enjoyed the Pakistanis' need to redirect resources away from India. Since the turn of the millennium, it is probably fair to say that American relations with India have become better than those with Pakistan, largely over the question of Pakistani diligence and controversy over U.S. raids in the FATA. Afghanistan has occupied a much greater place in the hierarchy of American interest than before.

These points of emphasis and changes in them are more nuances than signs of fundamental changes in U.S. orientation. Among the major regions of the world, the Asian subcontinent occupies, as it always has, an intermediate position in the hierarchy of American values, an important but hardly vital area to the United States certainly lower than Europe, the Middle East, and East Asia, but probably, for most purposes, higher than Latin America, Africa, or other parts of Asia. Changes in or between any of the three could alter this rough ranking. American extrication from Afghanistan would almost certainly reduce American interests there to somewhere near their pre-invasion levels, unless Afghanistan became a major launching pad for terrorism. Continued Indian economic progress could propel economic relations with the United States to a more prominent place than they are now. American extrication from Afghanistan would remove the source of major differences with the Pakistanis over the FATA, allowing U.S.-Pakistani relations to return to their more historical quality. The shape of the puzzle changes as the contours of its part assume different values.

Pakistan and Afghanistan: Physical and Political Profiles

The commonalities that they share may mean that the examination of these two countries is not a matter of comparing apples and oranges, but they are dissimilar enough to think of the exercise as a comparison of types of apples (Delicious versus Granny Smith) *or* oranges (Valencias versus Navels). The comparison can be made along both physical characteristics and their political bases and implications.

The comparison begins with issues of size. Both are larger than medium-sized countries in terms of land area. Pakistan is bigger, with an area of 307,784 square miles that ranks it thirty-sixth largest in the world and slightly less than twice the size of California or five times the size of Georgia. Afghanistan has a land area of 251,827 square miles, ranking forty-first in the world and about the same size as Texas. Both countries are generally arid with limited amounts of arable land: 26 percent of Pakistan (particularly the Indus plain) to about 12 percent for more rugged, mountainous Afghanistan. Taken together, their landmass is about 44 percent that of India.

The two countries are quite disparate in terms of population. Pakistan is the seventh most populous country in the world with just under 200 million citizens; Afghanistan, with about 32 million, ranks forty-sixth among world populations. Their combined population is about 18 percent that of India.

Both are ethnically diverse with one historically dominant nationality. For Afghanistan, Pashtuns are the dominant group, as noted, with sizable minorities of Tajiks (27 percent) and smaller numbers of other groups. The dominant languages are Afghan Persian or Dari (about 50 percent of the population) and Pashto (35 percent), both of which are official languages. In Pakistan, Punjabis are the largest ethnic group (about 45 percent of the population), followed by Pashtuns (15 percent) and Sindhi (12 percent). Punjabi is the most spoken language, by slightly less than half the population, with a variety of other languages spoken by various groups. Life is difficult in both countries: Afghans have a life expectancy of fifty years at birth, compared to sixty-seven years for Pakistanis. As noted, the vast mass in both countries are Sunni Muslim.

Both countries are poor, and both regularly are on lists of global failed states. Afghanistan is the more destitute. Its GDP stands at $54.3 billion, 101st in the world, and its per capita GDP is almost at the bottom of world rankings, at $1,100, 216th in the world. It is also annually ranked among the most corrupt countries in the world, a dubious distinction the United States has tried to improve but largely failed, since corruption has historically extended to the highest levels of government. Part of its poverty is the result of its meager physical endowments, consisting of probable unexploited reserves of some minerals, some natural gas, and virtually no petroleum. Its economic plight is illustrated by the fact that, according to the 2016 *CIA World Factbook*, its largest export was opium, followed by fruits and nuts.

Pakistan is slightly better off. Its GDP is $574 billion, good for a ranking of seventy-seventh among the world's countries. Because of its large population, however, the ranking shrinks when the economy is reduced to a per capita basis: at $3,100 GDP per capita, Pakistan is only 176th in the world. The impact on individual Pakistanis is reduced by the fact that Pakistan commits a little over three percent of its GDP to military spending, twentieth largest in the world. Its major exports are in basic commodities, textiles, and rice. Its largest trading partners are the United States and China. Unlike rival India, Pakistan has virtually no technological sector on which to anchor economic growth and prosperity. The economic plight of the country is further exemplified by the fact that large numbers of Pakistani workers are employed overseas, especially in the Middle Eastern Gulf states where, among other things, they are prominent in the armed forces.

The two countries are quite different politically. Afghanistan has a much longer and more tumultuous history than Pakistan, due in large measure to its location along east-west and north-south trading and invasion routes. It has also a physically remote, isolated terrain that separates groups and lends itself to a greater sense of autonomy from others than a more hospitable topography might provide. These factors help combine to create a virtually unique form of nationalism that has marked the Afghan people for centuries as one of the toughest, most self-reliant in the world. Different groups have been trying to subdue the Afghans for many centuries; all of them have ultimately failed. In the twentieth century, this failure befell the British and the Soviets/Russians; in the twenty-first, it appears to be afflicting the Americans as well.

Extremely combative isolationism has been the hallmark of the various Afghan clans and tribes. Within Afghan society, there is a strong sense of loyalty toward the smallest unit and a very well developed tradition of independence and autonomy that is valued above other values. It is a truism that the Afghans unite as a people only when they are besieged by hostile others, at which time they come together to expel the outsider; when there is no outside enemy, the Afghans retreat to their most parochial level, and when they fight (as they often do), it is among themselves.

This tradition has carried over to modern times and is reflected in contrasting visions of how Afghanistan should be ruled. Most Afghans, and especially rural dwellers who constitute the majority of the population, prefer a decentralized, weak central government that cannot unilaterally impose its will upon them. They prefer governance on the pattern of the traditional *loya jirgas*, periodic meetings of clan leaders where these elders make decisions regulating their interaction. Dominated by conservative non-urbanites such as the Ghilzai Pashtuns, these Afghans oppose centralization of authority in the capital of Kabul, which many of them consider virtually enemy territory. The Taliban has its strongest support among Ghilzai in the rural areas where this sentiment is most prominent.

The other element is more urban and is closer to the Durrani tradition. It is centered in the urban areas of the country and generally supports a stronger central government with Kabul as the center of the country's political power. In addition to Durrani Pashtuns, this element in the Afghan political mix includes other ethnicities such as Tajiks. This coalition formed the heart of the Northern Alliance that was attempting to overthrow the Taliban government in 2001 when the Americans arrived. The consensual leader of this coalition was a Durrani Pashtun, Hamid Karzai, who became the president of Afghanistan when the Taliban fell in late 2001 and fled into exile across the Durand Line into the Pakistani FATA (along with Al Qaeda, which escaped American pursuit in the Tora Bora mountains and established themselves in the Pakistani tribal areas). Karzai has always been a controversial figure with alleged close ties to the illicit trafficking of opium out of the country. Afghanistan is the world's top producer of the drug, and were someone to shut down this "industry," Afghanistan would have virtually no access to foreign currency.

American intervention affected this internal balance between the weak-government countryside and strong-central-government urban elements in the population in two ways. First, it aligned itself with the Northern Alliance in October 2001. The reason had little inherently to do with a preference in the civil war, but arose because, within weeks of 9/11, the United States had identified Afghanistan as the headquarters from which Al Qaeda had engineered the attacks and demanded that the Taliban remand the leadership to American custody for prosecution. When the Pashtun Taliban refused this request, the United States determined that the only way to get to bin Laden was by aiding the overthrow of the Taliban. American air and special operations forces assistance tipped the scales in the Northern Alliance's favor, and the Taliban quit the field by the end of the year.

In the process of assisting the Northern Alliance, the United States implicitly aligned itself with that element in the political struggle in Afghanistan, including support for the Karzai government. This second, nearly inadvertent outcome further alienated the Taliban and placed the United States squarely on the side of strong central government in Afghanistan, an advocacy in which it had previously had no interest one way or the other. A strong, popular central government fit the American preferred model for the developing world, so that the marriage with the Karzai government continued support against what became the Taliban insurgency to regain power. That battle continues fifteen years after the initial decisions were made, none of which anticipated the direction or duration the effort would assume.

The political formula in Pakistan has been very different. Part of the reason is that the two countries have entirely distinct histories from which their contemporary situations spring. The history of what is now Afghanistan extends back into antiquity, and its common theme has been the arrival of, resistance to, and eventual expulsion of invaders seeking either to subdue the fierce Afghan tribes or to traverse their territory on the way to other conquests. This experience bred a peculiar profile of Afghanistan and the rigor and cruelty of existence that, along with the country's relative poverty, has produced a political culture of suspicion and defensiveness.

The history of Pakistan is much shorter. Pakistanis are the descendants of Muslim waves that entered the subcontinent shortly after the founding of Islam and again in the Middle Ages; they are historic intruders, not indigenous peoples, and while they ruled from the 1500s until the establishment of the British Raj, they left behind no permanent political legacy to which the residents could turn in 1947, when partition occurred. The resulting Pakistan, halved by the Indian-aided secession of Bangladesh, was an artificial state that was the outgrowth of post–World War II geopolitics in the form of the dissolution of the British Empire. Pakistan, the name itself an acronym for the various areas comprising it (Punjab, Afghania, Kashmir,

Iran, Sindh, Turkharistan, Afghanistan, and Baluchistan) that means "pure country" in Urdu, is entirely a postwar phenomenon. Its heart was in the prewar Muslim League that envisioned a Muslim state on the subcontinent, with details to be negotiated later.

The formative events in Pakistan's development came quickly after independence and gave a military tint to the new country's imperative. As a distinct minority on the subcontinent, the Muslims were naturally defensive, and the interruption of Indus irrigation supplies in the winter of 1947–1948 and the crisis over Kashmir only reinforced Pakistanis' suspicion that their survival was the real threat they faced. The Pakistanis, in addition to the Bengalis who finally succeeded in forming Bangladesh, also have faced other potential secessionists in places such as Waziristan and fiercely independent minorities such as the Pashtuns of the FATA, many of whom dream of an independent state of Pashtunistan.

The heart of the political debate in Pakistan has thus had a different pivot than in Afghanistan, and one that has been affected by outside forces, including the United States. The basic political divide has been between rule by the military or by civilians. The exigencies of wars in 1948, 1965, and 1971 and the nuclear weapons programs of both India and Pakistan has militarized the politics of the country and created a major rift between democratizing civilians and a more authoritarian military class. For most of Pakistani history, the military has prevailed; since 2008, civilian rule has returned and survived a round of elections. Mamnoon Hussein has been president since 2013, as has Prime Minister Mohammad Nawaz Sharif.

Political tensions tend to revolve around military threats in the region and bring the United States into the debate. For much of Pakistani history, there has been a strong tie between the U.S. government and the Pakistani military that Pakistan's military leaders have translated into a political mandate. As Iqtidar puts it, "the army has been the prime conduit of American interests in the country. . . . The army took direct control when the exigencies of US wars required it to do so."

This connection has been particularly strong regarding Pakistani cooperation with the United States over Afghanistan. The Pakistanis worked with American efforts to undermine the Soviet presence in Afghanistan in the 1980s, and it has extended to American-Pakistani collaboration in the present conflict. The United States has encouraged the Pakistani armed forces to take a more proactive role in suppressing insurgent efforts in the FATA, a mission they have historically resisted, as discussed in the next section. The United States has a vested interest in shutting down or at least reducing the availability of the FATA as a sanctuary and staging ground for the Taliban (and, to a lesser extent, Al Qaeda), but Pakistani compliance with American requests has the further effect of alienating the army from FATA residents.

As Iqtidar summarized it, "Anger at the local groups that may have been affiliated with the Afghan Taliban is much less prevalent than rage directed at the Pakistani Army."

The ongoing situation is further complicated by Pakistan's ultra-secret, ruthless intelligence arm, Inter-Service Intelligence (ISI). This agency, which reportedly helped create anti-Indian insurgents in Kashmir, is also accused of being responsible for the formation of the Taliban as a means to weaken anti-Pakistani elements in Afghanistan. Its continued activities in the FATA and NFP remain part of the irritant between the government and residents of the region and the United States. The Americans are suspicious that ISI is playing both sides of the street in these areas, secretly aiding the Taliban and others while professing to be helping the United States. America is sometimes given the blame for these patterns. As one Waziristan journalist quoted by Iqtidar puts it, "We feel like our government has sold us out to the Americans to play out their fantasies of war."

Direct U.S. involvement in the FATA has another aspect that contributes to Army-civilian politics in Pakistan and adds to the growing unpopularity of the United States in Pakistan. The borderlands along the Afghan-Pakistan border have traditionally been left largely unregulated by the Pakistan government. The military has favored this arrangement because it minimizes their involvement in keeping secure an area to which their forces are not well suited—the Pakistani army is a conventional force designed to engage the Indian army in conventional combat, whereas the situation in the FATA and NFP is more unconventional (or asymmetrical), a form of warfare the Pakistanis prefer not to fight. Nonengagement also means that the Pakistanis do not have to divert military assets away from India, which they view as their core military imperative.

This orientation does not work well for American efforts in Afghanistan, since Taliban military forces and leaders routinely traverse the Durand Line to gain safe haven from American military power. The United States has responded with the use of drone and cruise missile attacks on suspected enemy sanctuaries in the remote areas of Pakistan, and this has created two major problems in the synergistic relationship between the United States and Pakistan. One problem is that there are inevitably civilian casualties in these attacks (so-called collateral damage) that inflame anti-Pakistani and anti-American sentiments in these regions. The other, and politically more consequential, is that these attacks require flying over Pakistan territory, which is a direct violation of Pakistani sovereignty. The problem is unavoidable if the United States is to continue its policy of attrition against enemy leadership, but the Pakistani government does not grant its permission for these incursions, which are particularly unpopular with the civilian political leadership and thus an issue in U.S.-Pakistani relations.

Basic U.S. Relations with AfPak

Largely due to its ongoing involvement in the war in Afghanistan, the United States finds itself in a difficult situation in the AfPak region, following policies that may be mutually exclusive and, in some instances, contradictory. In both countries, the United States seeks the evolution of the political systems toward civilian rule in a democratic, noncorrupt condition. In Afghanistan, the vehicle has been to end the Taliban insurgency and to promote a strong central government that will pursue this goal. In Pakistan, the goal is more implicit, as this country has a long-standing relationship with the military, so that pursuit of the long-term goal requires nudging the military into a more supportive role with civilian politicians.

The problem is that both goals face obstacles partially exacerbated by the policies they seek to promote and the impact of American actions on achieving those goals. In Afghanistan, it is not clear that the goals the United States espouses match up very well with the desires of the Afghan people—or at least large portions of them. The war itself is largely an internal tribal war in the Afghan tradition, where the primary protagonists are rural tribesmen, many Ghilzai Pashtuns, and more urbanized Durrani Pashtuns and tribesmen of different ethnicity. This is, and has been, a long-standing divide among Afghans, and it is not clear what effect American intervention can have in resolving it. Historically, there has been great resistance to centralizing power in Kabul, and the preference for national governance has instead resided in more informal, purposely weaker institutions such as the *loya jirgas*.

The American stake in this confrontation is directly, arguably solely, a reaction to the Taliban's refusal to turn over bin Laden and his followers after 9/11. Before that event, the Taliban received negative publicity in the United States for its treatment of women and campaign against modernity (e.g., destroying television sets and computers), but these were hardly adequate reasons for war. When bin Laden escaped into Pakistan, this restraint and disinterest were overcome by events. When the Taliban returned to Afghanistan in 2003, it was to renew their civil war; they did not bring Al Qaeda with them, according to many accounts at the time.

American military involvement in Afghanistan now spans over a decade and a half and is still ongoing, if at a very limited military level for the United States (whose major roles are training the Afghan National Army or ANA and support of ANA operations). There are two problems that impede American withdrawal as promised by President Obama. The first is that the ANA has been unsuccessful in breaking the Taliban insurgency. Part of this problem arises from a lack of support, especially in the countryside, for the government's campaign. Afghanistan has no direct democratic tradition beyond tribal *loya jirgas*, and support for democratic governance is basically limited to

urbanites who are the opposition to the Taliban. The appeals of modernization (a key part of the American plan) are similarly not embraced universally,
particularly in an atmosphere of mistrust of government on the basis of past
abuses and corruption. One can reasonably question both the relevance and
attainability of American goals given the nature of Afghan society. Moreover,
it is not entirely clear whether the United States has a sufficient interest in
promoting Westernization. The underlying basis for American presence is to
prevent the reintroduction of terrorism to that country; whether that goal is
adequate to justify continued American military presence or whether some
other option might be more appropriate is a debatable matter.

American involvement in Pakistan is more complex. It spans the Cold
War and the effective willing enlistment of the Pakistani military into the
Cold War anti-communist crusade, during which time the United States
and Pakistan were close allies and in which Pakistanis had a generally
highly favorable view of the United States. That situation has eroded because of American intrusion in the pursuit of the Taliban and terrorists in
the FATA and NFP. This campaign has alienated Pakistanis from both the
Americans and the military. As one resident of the FATA (quoted by Iqtidar)
puts it, "The Army has sold us to the Americans—our land, our people, our
hopes. We used to love the army in our area. Now it is a swear word."

The U.S. and Pakistan governments are caught in a bind where both understand the position of the other but where those positions are unpopular
in the other's capital. The United States insists on the need both to seal
the Durand Line from hostile transit by enemies of those it supports in
Afghanistan. Border patrolling is not popular among the Pakistani military—particularly to the extent that it detracts from the confrontation with
India—and American efforts have not solved the problem; instead the use
of U.S. airpower has alienated residents of the region and inflamed the
Pakistani public on grounds of violation of Pakistani airspace and territory.
The Pakistani civilian government roundly condemns the American actions
and insists they cease. These calls are largely hortatory. The Pakistanis understand why the United States carries out the attacks and even covertly
approves of them as a substitute for doing so themselves, but they censure
them anyway. The result is to fan already predominating anti-Americanism
among large segments of the country's politically active population.

From an American vantage point, the frontier between Afghanistan and
Pakistan, the Durand Line, is the key element in contemporary relations.
Closing the border to easy transit by the Taliban and terrorists lessens much
of the pressure on the Afghan government in combating its opponents, as
well as relieving the United States of much of the need and rationale for
continuing American military presence in Afghanistan. At the same time, a
less porous border would make it harder for America's adversaries to evade
American military fury. This solution, unfortunately, is easier said than

done. First, the rugged frontier is extremely difficult to patrol, and efforts to seal it are probably impossible in a literal sense. Second, Pakistan has shown neither the will nor the ability to do more than to make transit more difficult for combatants. Third, much of the crossing is by Pashtuns who have never accepted the boundary and regularly cross it as part of their normal, nonhostile business. Trying to seal the border would further alienate Afghanistan's largest ethnic group, whose support is needed if peace and stability are to be brought to Afghanistan.

U.S. Policy Options

In some ways, American options in the AfPak area are defined by American actions during the Afghan resistance and expulsion of the Soviets in the 1980s. The United States decided to support the Afghan freedom fighters (*mujahidin*) to irritate and frustrate the Soviets, not because of any inherent interest in Afghanistan per se—arguably a parallel with today. After that war, the resistance fighters split into two groups. Many of the native Afghans united to form the Taliban, who were initially viewed as reformers. Many of the foreign fighters (known as Afghanis) formed Al Qaeda, and these two groups, together and separately, have overshadowed American policy options ever since.

The Durand Line defines American AfPak options, none of which are especially good. On the northern side of the frontier, the United States continues to be an active participant against an insurgency in which it has limited interests beyond the historic connection between the Taliban and Al Qaeda. If the Taliban and Al Qaeda are in significant cahoots and the success of the Taliban would mean that the terrorists would return to Afghanistan, the United States retains an interest in what goes on there. If not, the reason for American concern over the line is reduced. The situation is less than crystalline, and thus so are the options.

Transit across the Durand Line also helps define the current malaise of U.S.-Pakistan relations. The United States is primarily unhappy with Islamabad over its inability to make the boundary impermeable and over Pakistani objections to American forays against Taliban and Al Qaeda targets in Pakistan. The Pakistanis have been less than fully cooperative with the Americans about what the Americans consider legitimate concerns: Osama bin Laden, for instance, was hiding essentially in plain sight in the Pakistani city of Abbottabad, presumably with the knowledge of ISI, before the United States raided his compound and killed him—over Pakistani objections. Once again, the transit over the Durand Line and the presence of groups the United States deems hostile in the FATA and NFP make this area important to the United States and exacerbate relations between Pakistan and America.

The Durand Line is a symbol of the underlying division between the United States and the AfPak countries. Were the United States to determine that a possible Taliban triumph would not result in a return of terrorists to an Afghan sanctuary, one policy option would be simply to end involvement in the Afghan war—as promised for 2014—and cut back sharply on relations. This option would not set well with the Afghan government, but it would reduce American concern with Pashtun movement across the border and thus take some of the pressure off the Pakistanis. The problem, of course, is that the solution of one problem might exacerbate the other. Another option would be simply to conclude that the problems into which the United States has inserted itself are much more important to them than to us, and that the soundest solution is to let them work them out. The third option, of course, is to continue what the United States has been doing, although the evidence that this solution is working is not overwhelming.

The United States is highly unlikely to exercise the withdrawal option because terrorism there has become a major part of the fabric of global terrorism. Pakistan in particular is up to its neck in this phenomenon that has infected the subcontinent. As Riedel puts it, "Pakistan is both a sponsor of terrorism . . . and a victim of jihadist terror." He continues, "Pakistan is the most important battlefield of the war against Al Qaeda and the global terrorist menace." That alone will likely keep the United States engaged in the AfPak region.

CONCLUSION

The history of U.S. relations with the subcontinent has been tumultuous, to say the least. It has vacillated and been influenced by factors that were not entirely the result of events and American interests in the area itself, but which were instead from exogenous phenomena that could be and were applied to the region. U.S. relations with India and Pakistan from partition to the end of the Cold War were largely shaped by Indian refusal and Pakistani eager embrace of Cold War allegiance, and since the Cold War has ended, the absence of that influence has allowed the United States to move closer to India at the same time that relations have become more strained with Pakistan. That change in turn was largely due to events in Afghanistan that have spilled over to Pakistan and its relations with the United States. During the 1980s, Pakistan was the staging area for American assistance to the mujahidin, and significant parts of American operations in the ongoing war have had a Pakistani component.

The American adventure in Afghanistan has also washed back upon Pakistan, with negative implications for the relationship between the two countries. The FATA and NFP are effective sanctuaries for the Taliban and some terrorists, and the Pakistanis exhibit neither much of an interest or will in uprooting them. Partly this is because the asymmetrical warfare in which the Taliban engage is a particular problem for the conventional Pakistani army. At the same time, the tribal areas have long enjoyed effective autonomy from central government control, and a concerted Pakistani campaign to "tame" those areas would meet with stiff opposition that could include a concerted campaign against the heart of Pakistan itself.

India and Pakistan have contradictory interests in Afghanistan that also have an impact on the United States. Pakistan views the relationship in Indian-Pakistani military terms, with Afghanistan providing strategic depth for Pakistan in the event of an Indian invasion of Pakistan that drives the Pakistanis out of their own territory across the Durand Line. To facilitate this exigency, the Pakistanis prefer a weak government in Afghanistan, and ISI is alleged to have "created" the Taliban to help reinforce Afghan weakness and pliability. The Indians, on the other hand, want to deny the Pakistanis this potential source of strength and thus support a strong Afghan political system. The Indian position more closely resembles America's view of Afghanistan, although there is no overt manifestation of this coincidence.

The heart of the subcontinent is the India-Pakistan axis, and Afghanistan is a sidebar to that basic dynamic. Since the turn of the millennium, however, American attention has been more closely associated with the sideshow than the main event, but that could change. The agent of change could be the spread of Islamic terrorism onto the subcontinent. In the summer of 2016, for instance, there was a rash of terrorist attacks, including one in the weekend spanning June and July 2016 when major, bloody terrorist attacks occurred more or less simultaneously against Pakistan, Bangladesh, and India. The Pakistanis have in the past been accused of terrorism in places like Kashmir (courtesy of ISI), but not of association with organizations such as IS or Al Qaeda. If this trend continues, there may be a new chapter opening in subcontinent affairs that could realign the interests of the major residents of that region and conceivably those of the United States as well.

STUDY QUESTIONS

1. Why has India been described as a country with enormous contrasts and complexities? What challenges do the differences in India pose for Indian development as a significant power in the world?
2. Indo-American relations are influenced by relations with other regional countries. Using figure 4.1 to help frame your response, explain what these interests are and how they are affected by contrary relations with other regional states.

3. Why was 1991 a pivotal year both for India and its relations with the rest of the world? Elaborate.
4. What is the future of U.S.-Indian relations? Include in your analysis how U.S. relations with both India and Pakistan have evolved in the past and how they are likely to change in the future.
5. How was the Pakistani experience in the period surrounding partition unique, and how has that experience affected its relations with India, Kashmir, and other parts of the world?
6. Why is Pakistan important to the United States? How has that relationship been affected negatively by the mutual involvement of the United States and Pakistan in Afghanistan? Elaborate.
7. Discuss the broad contours of the Afghan experience that have given it the nickname "the graveyard of empires," and how this history affects the difficulties the United States continues to experience there? What is the role of 9/11 and the civil war in Afghanistan in the initial American armed involvement there? Who are the Pashtuns? How do they fit into the puzzle?
8. What are the major issues, debates, disputes, and possible outcomes of the American military commitment in Afghanistan? What options does the United States have? What possible effects could these outcomes have on the Asian subcontinent and U.S. relations with the countries of the region?

BIBLIOGRAPHY

Ankit, Rakesh. *The Kashmir Conflict: From Empire to the Cold War, 1945–1966*. Routledge Studies in South Asian History. London: Routledge, 2016.

Bajpai, Kenti P., and Amitabh Mattoo. *Engaged Democracies: India-U.S. Relations in the 21st Century*. New Delhi: Har Anand, 2007.

Barfield, Thomas. *Afghanistan: A Cultural and Political History*. Princeton, NJ: Princeton University Press, 2010.

Biddle, Stephen, Fotini Christia, and Alexander Thier. "Defining Success in Afghanistan: What Can the United States Accept?" *Foreign Affairs* 89, no. 4 (July/August 2010): 48–60.

Cohen, Stephen Philip. "Shooting for a Century: The India-Pakistan Conundrum." *Current History* 110, no. 735 (April 2011): 162–64.

Coll, Steve. *Ghost Wars: The Secret History of the CIA, Afghanistan, and bin Laden from the Soviet Invasion until September 11, 2001*. New York: Penguin, 2004.

Ewans, Martin. *Afghanistan: A Short History of Its People and Politics*. New York: Harper Perennial, 2002.

Fair, Christina. "Pakistan's Security-Governance Challenge." *Current History* 110, no. 735 (April 2011): 136–42.

Feigenbaum, Evan A. "India's Rise, America's Interest: The Fate of the U.S.-India Relationship." *Foreign Affairs* 89, no. 2 (March/April 2010): 79–91.

Global Firepower. "Indian Military Strength." Globalfirepower.com, January 11, 2011.

Gould, Harold. *The South Asia Story: The First Sixty Years of US Relations with India and Pakistan*. London: Sage Publications, 2010.

Hajari, Nisid. *Midnight's Furies: The Deadly Logic of India's Partition*. Reprint. New York: Mariner, 2016.

Haqqani, Husain. *Pakistan between Mosque and Military*. Washington, DC: Carnegie Endowment for International Peace, 2005.

Hussein, Zahid. *Frontline Pakistan: The Struggle with Militant Islam*. New York: Columbia University Press, 2007.

Iqtidar, Humeira. "War-Weary Pakistan's Internal Divides." *Current History* 114, no. 771 (April 2015): 130–36.

Jones, Seth. *In the Graveyard of Empires: America's War in Afghanistan*. New York: Norton, 2009.

Kaplan, Robert D. "Man versus Afghanistan." *The Atlantic* 303, no. 3 (April 2010): 60–71.

———. *Monsoon: The Indian Ocean and the Future of American Power*. New York: Random House, 2010.

Kinzer, Stephen. *The Brothers: John Foster Dulles, Allen Dulles, and Their Secret World War*. New York: Times Books, 2013.

Kronstadt, Alan, Paul K. Kerr, Michael F. Martin, and Bruce Vaughn. *India-U.S. Relations*. CRS Report for Congress. Washington, DC: Congressional Research Service, October 27, 2010.

Luce, Edward. *In Spite of the Gods: The Rise of Modern India*. Reprint. New York: Anchor, 2008.

Manuel, Anja. *This Brave New World: China, India, and the United States*. New York: Simon & Schuster, 2016.

Menon, Rajan. "Pax Americana and the Rising Powers." *Current History* 108, no. 721 (November 2009): 353–60.

Mukherji, Rahul. "A Tiger Despite the Chains: The State of Reform in India." *Current History* 109, no. 726 (April 2010): 144–50.

Rashid, Ahmed. *Descent into Chaos: The United States and the Disaster in Pakistan, Afghanistan, and Central Asia*. New York: Penguin, 2009.

———. *Pakistan on the Brink: The Future of America, Pakistan, and Afghanistan*. New York: Penguin, 2013.

———. *Taliban: Militant Islam, Oil, and Fundamentalism in Central Asia*. 2nd ed. New Haven, CT: Yale University Press, 2010.

Riedel, Bruce. "Pakistan: The Critical Battleground." *Current History* 107, no. 712 (November 2008): 355–61.

Rubin, Barnett R. *Afghanistan from the Cold War through the War on Terror*. Reprint. New York: Oxford University Press, 2015.

Ruparnelia, Sanjay. *Divided We Govern: Coalition Politics in Modern India*. Oxford, UK: Oxford University Press, 2015.

Tellis, Ashley J. "Pakistan's Record on Terrorism: Conflicted Goals, Compromised Performance." *Washington Quarterly* 31, no. 2 (April 2008): 7–32.

Tomsen, Peter. "The Good War? What Went Wrong in Afghanistan—and How to Make It Right." *Foreign Affairs* 93, no. 6 (November/December 2014): 47–55.

Varadarajan, Siddarth. "Can We Deliver a New India?" *Current History* 114, no. 771 (April 2015): 123–29.

CHAPTER 5

Europe

For three hundred years beginning with the end of the Thirty Years' War in 1648 until the end of World War II in 1945, Europe sat astride the international system. It was the geopolitical center of the globe, and the European balance of power was effectively the world balance. During this long period, European countries conquered, colonized, and ruled the countries of most of the other continents, a process that began to unravel with the American Revolution and came to an effective end in the latter decades of the last century. During this 300-year ascendancy, the European continent changed politically, as new states emerged, power among the major states varied, and democratization and other political forms such as fascism challenged the monarchical domination at its beginning. Religious bloodletting between Catholics and Protestants was effectively settled in the Peace of Westphalia in 1648, only to spread to other religions and parts of the world, notably the Middle East, later.

The reign of Europe was effectively ended by the outcome of World War II. The largest war in human history literally bled its opponents dry. Precise numbers of casualties are elusive, but estimates indicate that combatant and civilian deaths from the conflict probably numbered eighty million or more; in the Soviet Union alone, that combined figure probably reached thirty million. At its end, the countries that had participated were drained of human resources and treasure. They rebuilt, but Europe, and especially its predominance, has never been reconstructed.

Postwar European political history has had two distinctive phases. The first emerged directly from the war in terms of a growing confrontation between the two states that survived the war with some power intact, the United States and the Union of Soviet Socialist Republics (USSR or Soviet Union) in the form of the Cold War. That politico-military competition dominated until the Soviet Union imploded in what current Russian leader Vladimir Putin has described as the "major geopolitical disaster of the twentieth century." Russia, as the major successor of the USSR, has struggled to recover from that disaster and to reconstitute itself as a major player in the world. That effort has brought it at odds with the United States, among other countries, and provides the rationale for making Russia one of the case studies in this chapter.

The other post-1945 dynamic that has dominated Europe has been the effort of the rest of the states of Europe to reconstitute themselves to ensure another event such as World War II can never recur. The genesis of this effort began while the war still raged in Europe. Allied planners examined what had gone wrong with the peace in 1919 that ended World War I (euphemistically called the "Great War") and concluded that the heart of European instability had been in the unbridled competition between the two major continental powers, Germany and France. Thus, a stable post-1945 peace required a solution that both could embrace and that would reduce their ability to light Europe aflame again. After the war, this desire, aided by the United States, formed the basis for the process of European integration, the major manifestation of which is the European Union (EU). That process is now over sixty years old, and it is also in a period of stress, currently exemplified by the decision of the United Kingdom to rescind its EU membership—so-called Brexit.

COMPLICATED DYNAMICS

Although their differences are far more fundamental than their similarities, Russia and the EU have similarities as well. Both are very large places. Even after its divestiture of the former republics of the Soviet Union, the Russian Federation is still the world's largest country with an area of slightly over 6.6 million square miles (1.8 times the size of the United States), whereas the EU before the exit of Great Britain was 1.7 million square miles (less than half the size of the United States). The territories that left Russia were over two million square miles, more than the EU at its pre-Brexit zenith.

Territorial issues are important in both places. Russia has been a shrinking country since the Soviet Union disbanded itself in 1991, but it retains interests in many of the USSR's former parts, either as points of interest or as possible locations for expansion. Its adventures in annexing Crimea and in eastern Ukraine since 2014 are the most recent examples; its intrusion into Georgia in 2008 is another example. Russian territorial issues work in both directions: there are areas of Russia that would like to secede (Chechnya and Dagestan in the Caucasus are prime examples), and there are clearly parts of the old empire at which the Putin regime continues to cast a covetous eye. As has been the norm in Russian history, the primary method by which the Russians seek either to keep areas from leaving or to annex others has been the use of military force, a predilection that is one of the sources of disagreement between Russia and the United States.

The territorial problem is different for the EU. Before the institutionalization of what has evolved into the EU even began with the formation of the European Coal and Steel Community (ECSC) in 1951, there was debate about the size and nature that European integration should take. The working groups in Washington that planned Europe's postwar future were divided on the issue. The Americans promoted a chauvinistic vision of a United States of Europe, a notion most of the Europeans thought too ambitious given European history and experience but one that could not be publicly disavowed, since it was clear the Americans would have to bankroll much of the process. The process began small: only six states (France, Germany, Italy, and the Benelux countries) were original members, and membership did not begin to expand until the 1960s. The British decision to remove itself from the EU roster—which may be a precursor for several other defections in the next few years—represents a reversal of that trend. It remains to be seen what this precedent means for the quantitative and qualitative nature of the EU.

Both Russia and the EU thus face uncertainties about the future and their aspirations. The problem for Russia is historical: acceptance as a great power. During the heyday of the European balance of power leading to World War I, the tsarist empire was one of the five major members of the balance (the others were Britain, France, Germany, and the Austro-Hungarian Empire), but was considered its weakest member. Like Austria-Hungary, the Russian imperial state did not survive the war, being overthrown by the Bolsheviks, surrendering to Germany, and being treated as a pariah by the victors at Versailles. The Soviet Union rose to superpower status during the Cold War, a fulfillment of the long-held Russian dream, but that accomplishment was shattered in 1991, and Russia has been reduced to a more marginal status that its people and especially its leadership strain to reverse. Russia wants to change history again; the question is whether it has the wherewithal to do so.

The central problem for the EU is also historical: building a strong, vibrant, and democratic Europe in an area where the political legacy has been one of division and dissention, not of cooperation and unity. This is a problem that was apparent to most observers and participants at the time the process of integration began and blossomed. The central task that the unifiers faced was how to rebuild Europe in such a way as to make another continent-wide bloodletting impossible, and their initial vehicle was the ECSC, which placed the coal- and steel-making capabilities of France and Germany under a common authority so that neither could independently develop the industrial capacity to build machines of war against the other. The ECSC was a spectacular success, both in achieving its stated goal and in aiding the stimulation of economic recovery. This economic success emboldened both the initial advocates of broader integration and others benefiting from the process to broaden their horizons and to seek broader and deeper forms of association—both in terms of greater numbers of participating countries (so-called broadening) and in the depth of integration (so-called deepening).

Both of these trends have contributed to the current crisis within the EU. The EU has always been an economic union at heart, and broadening of membership has brought into the European integration network a number of countries with quite different and generally weaker economic structures than the original members, a blow to homogeneity and the obligations of member states to one another. Deepening has meant that political functions formerly performed by national governments have been progressively threatened and even supplanted by powers granted to the EU headquarters in Brussels. The original designers of the European experiment recognized that the primary barrier to the expansion of their efforts was the nationalism of the various countries that joined the enterprise, and that at some point the "rubber would hit the road" between an expanding European integration and the nationalisms still deeply held by many of the citizens of the member countries. The crisis precipitated by the British referendum in June 2016 may represent the visible symbol of that conceptual confrontation.

CASE: THE UNITED STATES AND RUSSIA

Russia has always been a somewhat mysterious, forbidding place with which the United States has had a very mixed relationship. On October 1, 1939, Sir Winston Churchill described it in a radio broadcast speech the day that Nazi Germany occupied Warsaw, Poland, with Soviet blessing as "a riddle wrapped in a mystery inside an enigma." The quote was intended to capture both the difficulty in dealing with Russia and the incongruity of Soviet-Nazi collaboration (as part of the Molotov-Ribbentrop Pact named after the two countries' foreign ministers), since Hitler would use Poland as a launching pad to invade the Soviet Union less than two years later at horrible human cost. When the Soviet-Nazi condominium turned to armed hostility, the Russians changed course and became allies of the West to destroy the enemy they had previously embraced. Thirty million Soviets died in the effort.

Russia is an enormous place that embraces both Europe and Asia. It is not so much a European country as it is Eurasian. At its zenith as the Soviet Union, it covered nearly nine million square miles of territory, mostly in Asia, but its heart has always been in the quest to be a respected, and if that fails, feared member of the European international system. It has always been a comparatively underdeveloped country in economic and other terms, which has impeded gaining that status, and it has the added characteristic of national paranoia that comes from having its European psychic center on a large physical plain that has invited foreign invaders since the State of Muscovy emerged as the predecessor of modern Russia. The result has been a pattern of Russian expansionism along the length of its 12,650-mile border with fifteen other countries, most of whom rightly view the Russians with suspicion and fear.

Russia came closer to achieving its desired status in the world during the Cold War confrontation with the United States. It was a *superpower*, a very large and dangerous country with huge armed forces that included a nuclear weapons arsenal capable of destroying its chief adversary, the United States (which could also destroy it with its own nuclear weapons). The Cold War emerged gradually through mutually antagonistic acts by each of its contestants after World War II, and any illusion that the wartime cooperation they had enjoyed against fascism would continue was effectively ended by the Soviet-approved invasion of South Korea by the DPRK (see chapter 3). That competition ended when the Soviet Union ceased to exist at the end of 1991. As George Kennan, the father of the American policy of containment with which the United States faced the Soviets from 1948 forward had predicted, the Soviet state was conceptually flawed and would, if dealt with firmly, implode. Marxism-Leninism, the operating philosophy of the country, could not compete with the West. Leninism sanctioned a political repression that, while compatible with the Russian experience, could not produce a political atmosphere competitive with Western democracy, and economic Marxism demonstrated that it could not uplift a backward economy to a competitive level either.

The Russian Federation is what is left of the grand experiment of the Soviet Union. It is a shadow of the former construct, and it has left Russia in a diminished global position that its people do not embrace. Mikhail Gorbachev saw that the Soviet Union was failing when he came to power in 1985 and sought to reform the system to save it. Instead, he presided over its crumbling. Under Boris Yeltsin in the 1990s, the country attempted to democratize but instead continued to decline. Nowhere was this more evident than in military terms, the basis of Moscow's claim to international stature. As Trenin reports, "From 1988 to 1994, Moscow's armed forces shrank from five million to one million personnel." Russian spending on the military fell from $246 billion to $14 billion annually, hardly the level of support of a robust superpower. It was all part of a general decline from great power to a lesser status, and one that Russians, humiliated by that fall, could not accept. Lukyanov captures the prevailing determination: "Neither Russian elites nor ordinary Russians ever accepted the image of their country as a mere regional power."

This precipitous fall from international grace has been humiliating for the Russians, and Vladimir Putin is the almost inevitable product of that shame. Regardless of whatever else one may think about Putin or the alleged recklessness or aggressiveness of his stance toward the world (and especially the areas near Russia), his self-obsessed role is to return Russia to something like its former status—to reverse the "geopolitical disaster" of the demise of the Soviet Union. Putin enters his quest for expanded status with some advantages but with significant limitations mostly based in Russian comparative backwardness that probably requires Putin to act in ways he would not act if he operated from a position of greater strength. Anticipating what Putin will do and acting to contain his actions in ways that minimize the damage to American interests is the signal chore of the United States in dealing with this newest Russian challenge.

Russia: A Physical and Political Sketch

Russia is a formidable physical place, as even a quick glance at a world or Eurasian map quickly demonstrates. It spans two continents, from Eastern Europe to the Pacific Ocean and from the Arctic Sea to central Asia. Even in its diminished post-Soviet form, one cannot avoid being impressed with how big a place Russia is, and why it seems destined to be a major world player.

The sheer dimensions of Russia are misleading in terms of its prominence in the world. It is washed by major oceans and seas, from the Baltic and Black Seas to the Arctic and Pacific Oceans, but virtually all these exposures are in locations that are ice-locked during the winter months. The closest thing Russia has to a warm-water port (one that is not blocked by ice and thus unusable for some part of the year) is in the Black Sea, but to escape that body of water, Russian shipping (and naval forces) must traverse the Turkish Straits, which have been hostile at various points and have made securing Crimea a major Russian priority for centuries. At the same time, the vastness of Russian territory does not translate into the ability to feed itself. For climatological (too hot or too dry) and other reasons (including shortages of appropriate soils for agricultural productivity), only about 7 percent of Russian land is arable, and the result has been a need to import foodstuffs; Ukraine has served as an important source of grains and is third largest among exporters to Russia.

Russia faces other challenges as well. During the Soviet period, it was the third most populous country in the world, but the secession of the former Soviet states has reduced that population to a current level of approximately 142 million, tenth among world powers. Even that number is in decline. The fertility rate among Soviet women is only 1.61 children per woman of child-bearing age; 2.1 children per woman is considered necessary to maintain population. As a result, the population growth rate for Russia is –0.3 percent, 200th in the world. As Eberstadt pointed out in 2010, "Since the end of the Soviet era, the population of the Russian Federation has fallen by nearly 7 million, [and] life expectancy at birth looks to be lower today than it was four decades ago."

This downward trend is expected to continue, and one highly critical observer, Ukrainian anti-Russian politician Yuliya Tymoshenko, argues that by the middle of the century, it could be "below 100 million." Population shrinkage is, of course, a problem in much of the Western world, but the traditional method of solving the problem, immigration, is probably not a realistic option for the highly xenophobic Russians. Seven of nine people living in the Federation are ethnic Russians, and although the Russians seek to avoid secessionist movements among non-Russians such as Chechens, they are not likely to resort to the importation of foreigners, even from the former Soviet Union. One outgrowth of the Soviet era was russification— sending Russian nationals into acquired parts of the empire to make them more Russian—but it is unclear that bringing them back would be a source of major population enhancement.

The economic sphere has been the most volatile part of the Russian experience since the fall of communism. When Soviet control ended, there was a resulting regulatory vacuum that encompassed most aspects of life, including the economy. Especially during the 1990s, Russian "entrepreneurs" (often with Russian mafia ties) infiltrated the economy, taking over economic sectors formerly run by the state, and selling large amounts of Russian assets for personal gain. The rise of Putin and the centralization of authority helped slow this trend somewhat, but it continued into the 2000s, fueled by the rising profitability of the Russian energy sector.

Energy has been a boon to the Russian place in the world that has the potential also to become its bane, a status it has approached in the recent downturn in world oil prices. The fact that energy has become the spotlight of Russian economic revival points to an important characteristic and limitation of Russian potential. Despite draconian efforts such as forced labor to industrialize the country under communism, Russia has never become a world-class industrial power. During the Soviet era, the military had first priority on resources, and the result was that the civilian economy suffered, particularly in areas such as computers and electronics, which contributed to the decline and fall of the Soviet state (see Snow, *The Shape of the Future*, third edition for a discussion). It was often darkly joked that the Soviet Union was a gigantic "frozen banana republic with nuclear weapons" to indicate its noncompetitiveness with the rest of the developed world in other than military terms. In many ways, the Soviet Union was and Russia is a developing country, a designation that makes xenophobic Russians cringe.

The exploitation of energy has been the motor of Russian economic revival and increased foreign policy assertiveness in the last decade. Russia has formidable reserves of fossil fuel–based energy. Although the figures are not adjusted to include shale oil and gas reserves, the 2016 *CIA World Factbook* reports that Russia has the eighth-largest reserves of petroleum among world countries, at about eighty billion barrels, and the world's largest reserves of natural gas. Under Putin, Russia has maximized its exploitation of these natural resources to the point of becoming, in Thomas Friedman's terms, a classic "petrolist state"—a country where energy revenues are used to finance growing parts of the economy and to provide prosperity to people to ensure their loyalty to the regime.

Russian petroleum exploitation has certainly enhanced the country's recovery, but it has been a double-edged sword. Russia produces 10.44 million barrels a day (mbd), which is the third highest in the world, of which it exports 4.72 mbd (the second-largest amount after Saudi Arabia). This rate of exploitation, however, is probably not sustainable given Russian reserves. By comparison, for instance, Saudi Arabia produces 11.73 mbd, and it exports 6.88 mbd. While these figures are roughly comparable, reserves are not. Saudi Arabia has proven reserves of 268 billion barrels of oil, compared to Russia's eighty billion barrels. If Russia wants to remain a major oil exporter, it should reduce its production and husband those resources. It is only a matter of time until the most easily recoverable reserves will be depleted, and exploitation will become both more difficult and more expensive. The situation is not as dire for natural gas, of which Russia has the world's largest reserves.

In combination, energy production has been quite useful to Russia. It provides the Putin regime with foreign exchange wealth that it would not otherwise have, that artificially underwrites some level of citizen prosperity and support, and that provides the capital necessary for a more assertive foreign policy. In particular, it has provided considerable leverage for Russia with Western Europe, since its natural gas heats NATO and EU homes each winter, and it allows the Russians to exert some level of influence in former Soviet republics, which were also supplied by Russia before 1991 and have not successfully weaned themselves from that dependence. Part of the double-edged sword, however, is that petroleum as a source of influence has become intoxicating and has suppressed investment of petroleum revenues in other forms of long-term development that might prove useful when the oil dries up. At the same time, the American-led conversion to shale oil and gas can lead to lesser dependence on Russian sources and thus the eventual loss of leverage. An oil-based economy and foreign policy is a short-term attraction that could prove less so in the longer run.

The other limitation that dependence on oil (or any other commodity) creates is vulnerability to the vicissitudes of markets. Russia, like all other countries dependent on oil sales, has been greatly damaged by the collapse of the price of oil since 2013. Kotkin describes it thus: "Russian dollar-denominated GDP peaked in 2013 at slightly more than 2 trillion and has now dropped to about 1.2 trillion thanks to cratered oil prices and ruble exchange rates." In comparative terms, Russian GDP was quite small before the collapse of oil markets: in 2013 terms, Russia's GDP was about one-eighth that of the United States ($16.72 trillion), and that gap has only grown. Although reliable 2016 figures are unavailable, the Russian 40 percent drop in GDP has also been reflected in the economic situation of its people. In 2013, GDP per capita in Russia was about $18,000, seventy-seventh in the world and about one-third that of the United States ($52,800). A simple extrapolation of the impact of GDP retraction suggests that the Russian people are suffering and will continue to suffer until oil prices rebound, an unpredictable event.

The purpose of much of this analysis is to suggest a context with which to assess Russian foreign policy behavior in the past few years, and especially since 2013. Russia has become increasingly assertive in its policy to the point that some analysts have suggested a bellicose content that must be countered robustly through military threats and consequences. Certainly these implications have been made about Russian annexation of the Crimea and its threats against Ukraine, and there is merit in these concerns. At the same time, there are other ways to interpret these events. The Russian action in Crimea can, for instance, be seen as a defensive move to reinforce its historic desire for a warm-water port, as Treisman suggests: "Putin's seizure of Crimea appears to have been an improvised gambit, developed under pressure, that was triggered by the fear of losing Russia's strategically important naval base at Sevastopol." Its movements in eastern Ukraine may also be tied both to, as Treisman also puts it, a determination "to keep Ukraine from becoming a NATO member" and to shoring up Russia's access to Ukrainian grain. Similarly, Russian tough talk toward the West may also be a way to reinforce Russian nationalism away from the performance of the economy under Putin's stewardship.

Basic U.S.-Russian Relations

The history of relations between the world's physically largest and third-largest (in area, Canada is second) countries has been uneven, although they have been more generally adversarial than friendly. During the American Revolution, the Russian tsarist empire was indirectly aligned with the American cause as a member of the Armed Neutrality that opposed Great Britain, but the tsars were no sympathizers for American independence or political democracy. During the 1830s, Russian fur traders had penetrated as far south as San Francisco Bay (hence Russian Hill in that city), and some maintain that one of the real purposes of the Monroe Doctrine was to warn the Russians to reverse that penetration. In 1867, the Russian Empire sold Alaska to the United States (so-called Seward's Folly after American Secretary of State William H. Seward, who negotiated it), and Russia and the United States have looked warily across the Bering Strait at one another ever since. In some ways, the United States was the replacement for Russia in World War I after the Bolshevik Revolution toppled the empire and sued for peace with Germany. The ultimate cooperation between the two countries was manifested in their mutually suspicious alliance in World War II.

Then came the Cold War. Having emerged from World War II as one of two states with significant residual power, the Soviets, along with the Americans, were a logical candidate to assume major-power status. The Soviet Union was more greatly devastated than the United States by the war: most of their relatively small industrial base was destroyed in the fighting, and the Soviets replenished their losses by appropriating and moving much industry from the territories they occupied (especially their zone of Germany) to compensate. The Soviets did not, however, demobilize their armed forces the way the United States did, and their main source of strength was a large Red Army in occupation of most of Eastern Europe. The United States had the advantages of the only thriving economy in the world and nuclear weapons, an invidious comparison the Soviets erased by detonating their own atomic device in 1949.

The Cold War system evolved as the dominant feature in what was described as a *bipolar* international system. There were two major powers locked in a politico-military confrontation, they could control or influence much of the rest of the world, and they competed for influence and fealty globally, especially in the developing world emerging from decolonization. Their confrontation was fundamental and not easily resolvable: they had diametrically opposing worldviews (American capitalist democracy versus Soviet socialist economics and political authoritarianism), and both were evangelical, seeking to spread their own ideological visions and to prevent the other from doing the same. With enormous nuclear arsenals of upward of twelve to fifteen thousand warheads apiece aimed at one another, their competition seemed perpetual, with only two meaningful outcomes: either a "hot" World War III in which either might prevail but in which they both would probably lose in a fiery Armageddon of nuclear explosions; or the avoidance of such an outcome by a perpetual nonviolent conflict, a cold war. Although George Kennan and a few others had raised the possibility that the Soviet Union was such a flawed experiment it might collapse of its own internal contradictions, that possibility was never seriously considered—until it happened in 1991.

The Cold War was the geopolitical high-water mark for Russia. For the first time, the marginal major player became one of the world's two superpowers, its gross size translating into great-power status. When the Cold War ended, that geopolitical golden age disappeared with it, and Russia returned to a lesser status. When Putin talks about the "disaster" of the end of the Cold War, his reference is almost entirely a reflection of the tragedy that loss of status has meant for Russia. It may be true, as Lukyanov suggests, that the Russians have never accepted the derogatory mantle of being a regional power, but the 1990s and early 2000s represented a descent from superpower status arguably to that level.

Much of the appeal and overt purpose of Putin's tenure has been to reverse that decline and to try to return Russia to major-power status. Russian actions and American reactions to them must be at least partly conditioned by this realization and the consequences of frustrating those initiatives. Because of its sheer physical size, its location, and its retention of a large nuclear arsenal (currently about 7,000 warheads, roughly the same as the United States), Russia cannot be ignored altogether as a power. Its reach is largely limited to its own periphery through Western European dependence on Soviet natural gas and oil and its continued ability to bully the central Asian states along its borders (part of the former Soviet Union), and that probably means it is minimally a pivotal Eurasian state that has broader ambitions as a rising state with dreams and aspirations of a return to dominance in the world. The road to such an ascent is, however, rife with obstacles, including Russian demographics and the growing depletion of Soviet petroleum reserves. Its nuclear arsenal demonstrates both its promise and its limits: it is big enough to be able to cause catastrophic global effects, but Russia lacks the motivation to do so (particularly since a Russian nuclear attack would result in a counterattack that would destroy it as well) and its arsenal is both aging and, according to some reports, deteriorating.

These factors condition U.S.-Russian contemporary relations. Those relations have also followed the roller-coaster ride of Russia's experience since the Cold War. After that event, relations warmed as Boris Yeltsin and other Russian politicians attempted Westernization and democratization, but they have cooled under the Putin regime and the intervening ascendancy of Dmitry Medvedev in the late 2000s. Russian efforts to reassert what it views nostalgically as its national heritage have come into conflict with American policy preferences and interests. All the major irritants have to date been in places where the old Soviet Union was either dominant or sought dominance and which the United States had historically accepted (or at least not actively opposed). The result is a politically controversial situation for the United States: how vigorously should the United States oppose Russian actions that seek to reassert what the Russians see as part of their birthright? Current examples include Russian actions in the Crimea and Ukraine (of which the Crimea was a part before its seizure by Russia), and also Syria. All point to how the United States should respond to Russian geopolitical revivalism.

Any analysis of U.S.-Russian interactions on specific situations must begin with three parameters. The first is grounded in history, particularly since the second half of the twentieth century, of rivalry and negative relations with one another. Particularly because of the Cold War period, many Americans do not trust any Russian government, believe that anything the Russians do is suspect, think Russian motives are suspect, and thus view Russian actions and intentions suspiciously and negatively. This leads to the second parameter. Both sides tend to think the worst of the other, and there is a natural tendency to interpret events in a negative light and to advocate harsher and more adversarial policy alternatives than might otherwise be supported. Americans tend to think the Russians are generally up to no good from an American perspective, a sentiment that is reciprocated by the

Russians, who often act as though they cannot quite understand why the Americans become as exercised at their actions as the Americans appear to get. Ambivalence about the positive relationship between Putin and members of the Trump administration illustrates this dynamic, notably the controversy surrounding Russian hacking during the 2016 election campaign.

The crisis in the Crimea and Ukraine reflects this perceptual situation. From a Russian viewpoint, their actions in the two arenas are part of a reasonable Russian policy aimed at its own security. The Crimea, for instance, is a historic part of Russia and the site of the major Russian naval base in the Black Sea that, during the rule of the Soviet Union under Ukrainian Soviet leader Nikita S. Khrushchev, was ceded to Ukraine (some reports have suggested that Khrushchev was inebriated when he agreed to the change). The territory has never been an integral part of Ukraine, and most of its inhabitants are not Ukrainians. The area has historical and strategic importance to Russia. It was annexed by the Russian Empire in 1783 and has been part of Russia or the Soviet Union since. The Russians lost the Crimean War of 1853–1856 to an alliance of European states and Ottoman Turkey but retained control of the peninsula. It only became an issue after the end of the Cold War, when Ukraine was one of the defectors from the defunct Soviet Union and took Crimea with it. A prostrate Russia could do little about this secession, but tensions have existed ever since over the security of the naval base at Sevastopol.

On March 1, 2014, President Putin ordered an unexpected invasion and occupation of Crimea, an action the Ukrainians were unprepared to resist either militarily or politically, since the Ukrainian government itself was in crisis. There was universal condemnation in the West of this event as an unprovoked and illegal aggression by Russia of the territory of another sovereign state, and this sentiment was particularly pronounced in the United States, where there was great pressure on the Obama administration to "do something" about it, including the possibility of military threats or actions. The Russians seemed surprised at the vehemence of Western objections, because they felt they were simply restoring Russian territory and protecting their vital security interests in the naval base. Whether, as Treisman suggests, the action was part of some geopolitical plan by the Russians or the act of a "gambler" in the Kremlin in the form of Putin is not clear, but it was almost certainly an act by the Russian leader to reassure the Russian population and to warn the West that Russia was indeed more than a simple regional power. By this standard, in Lukyanov's estimation, the action, when taken in tandem with Russian assertiveness in Syria, was evidence that "Russia has made clear its intention to restore its status as a major international player."

Its subsequent actions in eastern Ukraine bolster this projection, adding two further elements to it. The first was the problem of a sizable Russian population (both ethnically and linguistically) in the eastern part of the country. Protecting Russian minority populations outside Russia is a problem inherited from the Soviet days and represents what the Russians consider a basic obligation to protect Russian communities in the "near abroad" (areas contiguous to Russia). The problem is partially a legacy of the Soviet period because one of the aims of the Soviet regime was to "russify" non-Russian areas of the USSR by emigration of Russians to these areas, both to inculcate Russian/Marxist values and to aid in controlling potentially disaffected areas and peoples. When the Soviet Union dissolved, many of these émigrés were left behind and were potentially subject to discrimination and recrimination by disaffected majorities in the newly independent areas. These kinds of concerns were voiced when Russia invaded Georgia in 2008, and they returned in 2014, when political turmoil in Ukraine splintered ethnic Ukrainians, who formed a large majority in the central and western part of the country, from ethnic Russians, who formed a majority in parts of the east. Putin has consistently maintained that the actions of military groups in Ukraine have been motivated by an intent to protect those ethnic Russians from hostile elements in the country, an intention expressed particularly vehemently in calls for secession of parts of the east and their annexation by Russia. To the West, these policies smack of imperialism and expansionism; to many Russians, they are merely acts to protect countrymen in the near abroad.

The other added element was geopolitical. Ukraine shares location on the northern European plain with Russia, the classic east-west invasion route into the country. Given past experiences with Napoleon's French armies and Hitler's Nazis and even the Poles in the 1920s, it is hardly a surprise that Russia would desire to have a strong sphere of influence between itself and Western European enemies, and part of the reason both for adding states such as Ukraine and Belarus to the Soviet empire and for maintaining its satellite empire of Warsaw Pact associates during the Cold War was to ensure that the next attempted invasion of Russia would be contested on the soil of one of its western neighbors, not in Russia itself. When Ukraine began its flirtation with the West in terms such as Western-style democratization and association, even membership, in the EU and NATO, it committed, in Laruelle's terms, a "crime": it "violated an implicit agreement, according to which Russia accepted an independent Ukraine provided it did not lead to an anti-Russia policy or Western encroachment." In addition, the Ukrainian regime was a center of "organized extortion and corruption," and that constituted an additional crime, in Laruelle's terms: Ukraine was "badly governed" and regularly "experienced Maidans [anti-government demonstrations]." Neither was acceptable to Putin.

This combination of factors apparently accumulated to cause Putin to decide to intervene unofficially (if transparently) in the instability of Ukrainian politics, sending Russian "volunteers" and military equipment into eastern Ukraine to assist Ukrainian citizens of Russian ethnicity to rebel and try to secede from Ukraine and presumably join Russia. It was, in conventional terms, a typically Russian action: strengthening Russian territorial security by expanding to create a *cordon sanitaire* between Russia and those it believes wish it harm, and acting to protect the Russian diaspora from suppression by the countries in which they live. In this light, actions in the Crimea may seem crude and internationally offensive, but they are also classically Russian.

Russian intervention in the Syrian civil war is also a classic Russian action, although one motivated and explainable in terms more geopolitical than directly nationalistic. The relationship between Russia/USSR and Syria goes back to 1971, when the Soviets negotiated rights to a naval base in Tartus, which is the only Russian military facility in the eastern Mediterranean and the only naval repair and replenishment facility it has in the region. It is, in a sense, Russia's naval foothold in the Mediterranean Sea and its only really solid connection in the Middle East since the fall of the Soviet Union. Moreover, the naval base is located along the northern coast of Syria, which is the province of Syria from which the Alawite minority that rules Syria comes. This helps create a synergy between the Russian and Syrian governments that helps explain why the Putin administration has come to the aid of the beleaguered government of Bashar al-Assad, who is an Alawite. Should the Assad government be overthrown by any of its assorted opponents, it would almost certainly be replaced by a non-Alawite alternative that would be less sympathetic to the Russians and more likely to evict them from Tartus. Being kicked out of Syria would also be a blow to Russian national pride, revealing the limits on Russian pretensions of a return to the ranks of significant world powers.

What is notable about Russian motives in all this is how little they have to do intrinsically with the Syrians or their welfare, except for that of Assad and his supporters. The Russians have engaged in a brutal campaign of aerial bombardment of the various opposition groups to Assad and have done everything they can to protect him from predators who, by some accounts, are gradually wearing down resistance to regime change. The Russians and the American-led coalition have applauded Russian participation in attacking IS targets, but they have come into disagreement with Russian attacks on anti-Assad non-IS elements of the resistance to the point that cooperation has been strained and some Americans have questioned the strategic partnership. This position is somewhat curious, since it should have been clear from the beginning that Russia can only come out ahead (keeping their naval base) if Assad remains in power. Moreover, Russia's actions are openly geopolitical. As Lukyanov argues, "The Syrian intervention was aimed not only at strengthening Assad's position but also forcing the United States to deal with Moscow on a more equal footing."

U.S. Policy Options

The United States and Russia will, in all likelihood, always be rivals, not close friends or allies. They are two very large countries with different geographical and ideological interests and imperatives, and both aspire to the most prominent positions on the world stage, a situation each implicitly wants to deny or impede for the other. For Russia, this aspiration is to reverse the geopolitical decline it experienced with the demise of the Soviet Union. For the United States, it is to influence any Russian revival along more peaceful, orthodox lines.

Russia enters this competitive foreign policy interaction with significant disadvantages. It has significantly rebuilt its military power in its quest to return to major-power status, but it has done so by using oil revenues (its major source of wealth) at the expense of other priorities. It faces a demographic challenge, as its population is shrinking, and its oil-based economy cannot sustain the kind of growth necessary to be more than a pivotal or rising regional power. What it has going for it is a leader in Vladimir Putin who is, as Treisman puts it so well, a "gambler" willing to take chances to enhance Russian power and prestige in the face of formidable odds.

How should the United States deal with the more troublesome manifestations of Russian foreign policy actions? During the recently concluded Obama administration's first term, the answer was the infamous "reset" of those relations from a negative to a positive base. It did not work largely because the amicable relations the United States proposed were more restrictive of Russian resurgence than Putin was willing to accept. His actions in places such as the Crimea, Ukraine, and Syria are evidence of that unacceptability. So what is the alternative?

Answering that question requires two determinations. One is why the Russians are acting as they are. Russia is clearly in an expansionist mode. What is not certain is why they are acting in the specific ways they are and how ambitious their aspirations are. One interpretation is that they are simply being Russian, pushing outward from their borders to bolster their defenses. With the exception of actions in Syria, most of their actions have been in the near abroad of former Soviet states that either present geopolitical problems (Crimea) or where former satellites threaten actions that could endanger Russian security (Ukraine). If that is all they plan to do, what does that mean for U.S. policy? Certainly, the United States should oppose open or semicovert aggression—the Ukraine case—but what form should that opposition take?

This leads to the second determination, which is what the United States should do in the face of what it views as threatening, obnoxious Russian behavior. To this point, reactions have been measured and limited to condemnations and some economic sanctions, which appears to be all America's

European allies are willing to support, and these have not been sufficient to alter Russian behavior fundamentally. It is not clear where one goes from here. Military threats are almost surely incredible: no one believes the United States (and certainly not its NATO allies) would risk major war over territory that is historically part of the Russian sphere of influence, and it is not clear that more limited commitments such as military aid will make much difference unless it is so extensive as to be provocative. Ties between Trump and members of his administration to Putin may help forge closer bonds with Russia; they also may fail to do so.

CASE: THE UNITED STATES AND THE EUROPEAN UNION

The European Union is a direct outgrowth of global, and especially European, reaction to World War II and the determination to avoid a third European-based world conflagration. The United States shared this sentiment, and through collaboration with its principal European allies during the war, helped design and advocate various ways to achieve that goal. In a very real sense, the United States was the midwife of the ultimate expression of that process, the EU. The two entities have been close collaborators ever since.

Unlike the other territories that are profiled here, the EU is not a state. Rather, it is a collection of states in Europe that have united on an increasing number of grounds, both economically and politically, for their common good. The most notable achievements of the EU have been in the economic area, and especially in the earlier days of the enterprise when the membership was more homogeneous. Progress in the political areas has been more contentious, because the citizens of all the member countries still retain nationalistic loyalties that they are unwilling to see diluted in the name of greater power to the union. There is, and always has been, a kind of dynamic tension within the union among those who wish to see a tighter, more inclusive union and those who wish to retain more autonomy for the constituent states, an expression of residual nationalistic feelings. In recent years, these tensions have been expressed most evidently in both dimensions of the EU: economic divisions in the sovereign debt crisis of the early 2010s, and political dissent over attempts by the EU bureaucracy in Brussels to extend union authority at the expense of the individual states in a variety of areas. The most prominent in the mid-2010s has been connected to the issue of large-scale immigration from the Middle East and the new European Border and Coast Guard Agency that was created on December 15, 2015, and which centralizes union-wide authority over who enters the EU. Both elements are present in the current major crisis of the EU, the referendum vote in Great Britain (so-called Brexit) by which the British have begun the process of withdrawal from the EU. As will be noted, this issue is complicated by other, more historical considerations that have attended British membership since it entered the integration process in 1973 as a member of the European Common Market.

Because the EU is not a "normal" state, its description must be approached somewhat differently as well. Part of the burden is historical, through a series of gradually more greatly integrating steps that have moved an initial group of six basically contiguous and homogeneous states whose purpose was to regulate coal and steel production to the current membership of twenty-eight European states (before the subtraction of Britain) that spans the continent and represents very different political experiences and histories. The other part of the burden is conceptual in terms of the kind of union that has evolved through a series of sequentially more entangling and comprehensive steps in the economic, and to a lesser extent, political realms. The examination is complicated by the intertwining of both political and economic motives and actions.

The narrative begins with the physical evolution of the process, which began in 1950. At the suggestion of Jean Monnet, often considered the "father" of the movement, French foreign minister Robert Schuman proposed pooling French and German coal and steel resources, a direct response to the universal desire to prevent another European war by depriving the two major continental powers of the ability independently to produce the steel on which war-making machines were totally dependent. In 1951, the Schuman Plan was negotiated among what became the core six members of the European integration movement in the form of the European Coal and Steel Community (ECSC). The organization began operation in 1952 and was so wildly successful and popular that it spawned a subsequent meeting to expand this politically motivated initiative into the beginnings of an economic association spanning continental borders. The Treaty of Rome was signed in 1957; it created two additional institutions among the six countries. One was the European Atomic Energy Community (EURATOM), which expanded the kinds of controls instituted for ECSC to atomic energy. The second, and ultimately more significant, was the formation of the European Economic Community (EEC). The EEC incorporated both ECSC and EURATOM into an expanded enterprise that included the European Common Market. The movement to the EU was born in Rome.

The creation of the EEC put in motion the process of economic and, on its heels, political integration. In economic terms, that process can consist of three sequential steps. The first is the formation of a *free-trade area*, a mechanism by which the members reduce or eliminate all boundaries to trade among them. The most common form is the elimination of tariffs between the member countries. The second form is a *customs union*, by which the members of the economic association agree to institute common economic barriers on all goods and services coming into the area in addition to eliminating trade barriers among them. When both of these steps are taken, the result is a *common market*.

The Treaty of Rome created a common market, but it was not an arrangement initially attractive to everyone in Europe. The notable absentee from all the negotiations to that point was Great Britain. The British saw the EEC negatively in two ways. First, it would tie the British Isles closely to the continent; it had been British policy for hundreds of years to remain as aloof from continental affairs as they could. Second, Britain had what it considered a "special relationship" both with the old British colonies that were part of the British Commonwealth and the United States, and were not convinced that these relations could survive intact if it associated itself with the new arrangement.

Britain's initial response to the Rome Treaty was to create a rival organization, the European Free Trade Association (EFTA). Formed in 1960, EFTA was strictly a free-trade area, as its name implied. The "outer seven" members of EFTA were Austria, Denmark, Norway, Portugal, Sweden, Switzerland, and the United Kingdom. EFTA was not an effective rival to the EEC, which quickly enjoyed enormous success as its provisions stimulated enormous economic growth due to stimulated economic interaction within the EEC area. Part of the reason was that the absence of a customs union arrangement meant goods and services could be imported indirectly into member countries by sending goods into one country with a low tariff and then taking advantage of the absence of a tariff among the states to allow their importation into another country with a higher tariff toward the sender.

EFTA did not succeed as a rival to the EEC. Most of its members, led by Great Britain and Denmark in 1963, migrated to the EEC. Of the original seven, only Norway and Switzerland have remained within the shell of EFTA, along with two additional states, Iceland and Liechtenstein. The EFTA experience did, however, leave some residual resentment among EEC enthusiasts, since the open purpose of the organization was to undercut the EEC. It is notable that, in the aftermath of Brexit, other countries prominently mentioned as possibly joining the process of defection are former members of EFTA such as Denmark and Sweden.

The next steps in the process are economic and political union, which means the creation of area-wide institutions and regulations that, in their strongest form, are enforced by institutions of the union and not by the individual states. The process of reaction to the EU has its seeds in this last step. Enthusiasts of the union have generally seen a gradually greater commitment to the EU at the expense of loyalty to the constituent parts as the necessary steps to complete the integration of Europe into something like a single entity. Since the early spectacular success of the EEC starting in the late 1950s, the implicit logic has been that economic success will cause a transfer of loyalty from the older, more parochial political forms, since union provides greater economic benefits than the older patterns. For some time, this logic appeared to be successful in nurturing and sustaining support for "Europe" on the continent. In recent years, the economically driven momentum has appeared to slow and even to attract opposition. Part of the reason is that the economic momentum has slowed. Part of it is the result of decisions made by the union in terms of membership expansion and the attempt to transfer more authority from national governments and to consolidate those powers in Brussels. Another, and possibly the most potent, reason is the resurgence and resiliency of traditional nationalism.

The EU: A Physical and Political Sketch

By any measure, the territory included in the European Union represents a consequential economic and political force in the world. With Great Britain still included as a member, its land area is 1,702,000 square miles, slightly less than half the physical size of the United States. The loss of Britain reduces that figure by 150,000 square miles to about 1.55 million square miles. Similarly, the population of the twenty-eight-member EU is about 509 million people, larger than any countries in the world except China and India. Even subtracting Great Britain's roughly sixty-four million people does not change its relative status, reducing the population under the EU banner to about 455 million.

It is in the economic sphere that the loss of the British makes a difference. The GDP of the EU including Britain stands at $15.83 trillion, second largest in the world after the United States. Subtracting the British GDP of $2.38 trillion (ninth largest among global countries) leaves the EU with a GDP of $13.45 trillion, almost the same as China's. EU GDP per capita stands at $34,500 (forty-first in the world), whereas the British rate is $37,300 (thirty-fourth), meaning some dilution when the British contributions are removed. As the details of Brexit began to be negotiated in the second half of 2016, what effect the divorce would have either on the EU or British economies was, of course, speculative, but since the British economy was an integral part of the overall European system, rending the two apart has to have consequences. These could be particularly negative for the short term in Britain, whose goods and services are suddenly outside the customs union and thus must enter the continent with external tariffs attached (their size will be a central part of the negotiation).

The politics of the EU are more complicated and are caught up in differing visions of what different people and groups want the EU to become. There have been two broad schools of thought on the subject. The most pro-EU advocates want it to evolve to being a state or something very close to it. Following from earlier visions from planning during World War II, the preference is for a federal form of political organization wherein the member states of the EU become something like the states of the United States, except with more autonomy in areas such as cultural preservation and language than is enjoyed by American states. This preference arises in some large measure from the dictates of economic integration.

In 1993, for instance, the Maastricht Treaty created a monetary union that empowered the EU with broad powers in fiscal and monetary policy in areas such as the issuance and regulation of currency. When a common market is combined with a monetary union, the result is an *economic union*, the ultimate form of economic integration. It has been a rude awakening, as captured by Muller. "In the early 1990s, the people of Europe woke up to the fact that new procedures adopted in Brussels meant that member state governments no longer had anything like a veto over policies—they simply could be outvoted. Moreover, the introduction of the euro seemed to signal the beginning of a qualitatively different stage of integration."

These changes rekindled or ignited controversy within and about the EU among those who do not embrace completely the idea of a single "Europe." Before the adoption of the monetary union, most of the progress of the union was in the economic realm, with limited assaults on the sovereignty of the member states. Politically, the political bodies of the union like the Commission (the bureaucracy) or the European Parliament were limited by the Council of Ministers, the members of which were the major states of the EU, and the council members had an effective veto over community actions. The result was an organization that was effectively *confederal* (decision powers controlled by the constituent members, which delegated some authority to the central mechanisms), not unlike the arrangement under the American Articles of Confederation or the Confederacy during the American Civil War. While such arrangements preserve the power and autonomy of the member units, they are unwieldy in terms of making and implementing EU-wide policies and regulations.

The apparent dictates of monetary union, in the minds of its proponents, required the EU to become politically more of a federal, or even unitary, political system. The ability of dissenting countries to be outvoted was the result of reforms that made it effectively impossible for one or a few countries to block initiatives in the council, thereby removing sources of autonomy for people with different cultural or political views to enforce their differences from the majority. Delanty, in a review of McNamara's *The Politics of Everyday Europe*, argues that this has created problems of crisis proportions that is "a sorry tale of a continent . . . facing the catastrophic consequences of a common currency that has divided Europe into debtor and creditor states. . . . [T]he EU is now faced with a problem possibly greater than it was created to solve: How to overcome the stranglehold of currency union in the absence of fiscal unity and the policies it necessarily presupposed."

The requirements of the monetary union brought the political differences to a head. Economic policies, and especially matters as fundamental as the issuance and regulation of a common currency, require a political body that is empowered by and can act in the name of the entire unit it services—in this case all members of the EU. To implement and strengthen monetary policy dictates required strengthening EU-wide bodies such as the commission and the parliament, and this effort created a negative reaction among those states that were less enthused about an all-encompassing EU. The euro was adopted in 1999, and not all members—most notably the British—agreed to accept it as their currency. In 2002–2003, an effort was made to develop an EU-wide constitution that would consolidate the union politically, but it was quietly dropped after original ECSC members France and the Netherlands voted against it in national referenda. The fallback from this defeat was the convening of a union-wide conference in Lisbon in December 2007, which produced a treaty among the members that defines their ongoing relations and the evolution of the union. Known as the Treaty of Lisbon, it went into effect on December 1, 2009. Its smooth implementation has been interrupted by a series of other crises that now define the political agenda and problems of the EU and that ultimately affect U.S. policy toward it.

The evolution of the euro is clearly at the center of this controversy and has been since it was introduced. The problem has two dimensions. One is participation: only nineteen of the twenty-eight states in the EU before British withdrawal had accepted the currency as their own. In addition to Britain, the holdouts include Bulgaria, Croatia (the most recent member), the Czech Republic, Denmark, Hungary, Poland, Romania, and Sweden. It is probably not coincidental that this list contains former EFTA members and former communist states, both of which value their autonomy. Most of the dissenters were concerned over the loss of economic control, which is the second problem. Increasing membership (discussed in the next section) has meant more economic diversity among members, prominently a division between affluent and less wealthy states, and there has been a growing tendency of the richer and more powerful states (Germany is the prototype) to use monetary union as a way to try to force economic reforms on the poorer states. Greece is the prototype.

Another emblem of the increased political power of the central union has been in the area of immigration and border control, an issue familiar to Americans from the 2016 election campaign. Border control within the EU follows the principles of the economic union: there is a common policy that regulates admission into the EU area, but once someone has been admitted, their movement within the EU area is unrestricted. With these principles in place, immigration control everywhere is a matter of policy administration at the borders between the EU and the rest of the world. Historically, this has been the province of individual states, but in order to create more uniformity, Brussels has acted to create an EU capability to perform this function, increasingly at the expense of state regulation. In 2005, the EU created something called Frontex (a French acronym for "external borders") to assist governments in performing this task, and this initiative was broadened and intensified with the creation of the European Border and Coast Guard Agency in 2015 to, in the words of a December 15, 2015, European Commission press release, "manage our external borders." The implementing agreement creating this authority came into force on June 22, 2016, in the midst of the immigration crisis over Middle East refugees fleeing their region and more or less coincident with Brexit.

The current crisis within the EU arises significantly from the collision of economic and political imperatives, and especially the expansion of EU-wide control over functions traditionally controlled by the member states and which many citizens in the member countries view as their national prerogatives. When adherence to the evolving union primarily resulted in economic benefits and spreading prosperity without fundamental political impacts on being French or German or Dutch, there was virtual universal support for the union, even its expansion. The honeymoon, however, ended for many when it became clear that the continued expansion of the union threatened the national status of the constituent units. Nationalism and continued integration collided, and in many countries, nationalism has proven to be a very resilient, even predominating, value.

U.S.-EU Relations

The relations between the United States and the European Union have been basically very mutually supportive. This should come as no surprise, given four factors. The first, of course, is American early parentage of the integration concept and process as a way to pacify European politics. The second is that the members of the union as it has grown are basically allies and friends of the United States (the original six plus Britain, prominently) and countries that the United States wanted to see become committed to a peaceful, democratic, and harmonious Europe. Third, by spreading its domain to encompass virtually the entire continent, it has relieved the United States of the need to expend its own resources on residual European problems, for instance, the integration of the formerly communist states of Eastern Europe or the Mediterranean states into the greater prosperity. Fourth, there is considerable synergism and mutuality of membership between the EU and NATO, America's first peacetime military alliance.

Both the United States and the EU want the relationship to remain convivial and mutually reinforcing in both politico-economic and security terms. A strong United States committed to the defense of the overlapping NATO/EU area relieves the Europeans of the need for heavy defense spending, a luxury that became controversial during the 2016 presidential campaign in the United States. A vibrant EU with which the members are happy because they are prosperous relieves the United States of major responsibility for maintaining the alliance in the face of outside pressures (like those currently posed by Russia) and because they allow the United States to focus more fully on other, more contentious parts of the world, notably the Middle East.

Wideners versus Deepeners

The two entities do differ on some issues, one of which is fundamental in terms of the evolution of the EU, and others that are more specific. The underlying disagreement is the future direction of the EU; it is a concern that reflects the basic European dialog on the subject. In essence, there are two basic opinions on the future direction of the EU. On the one hand, there are those individuals and countries who believe the EU should concentrate its efforts on including as many countries in Europe as possible within the EU network of countries. They are known as the *wideners*, since they seek to widen membership as much as possible, a kind of horizontal approach to the future. The wideners have enjoyed considerable success in a series of so-called rounds of membership increases, as depicted in table 5.1.

This progression has been both geographic and political. Round 1, of course, consisted of the original six members of the ECSC and the EEC. Round 2 was significant because Great Britain joined the fold along with

Table 5.1. EU Membership Expansion by Rounds

	Round 1	*Round 2*	*Round 3*	*Round 4*	*Round 5*	*Round 6*
	1958	**1973**	**1981**	**1995**	**2004**	**2007**
	Belgium	Denmark	Greece	Austria	Cyprus	Bulgaria
	France	Ireland		Finland	Czech	Romania
	Germany	U.K.	**1986**	Sweden	Republic	
	Italy		Spain		Estonia	**2013**
	Luxembourg		Portugal		Hungary	Croatia
	Netherlands				Latvia	
					Lithuania	
					Malta	
					Poland	
					Slovakia	
					Slovenia	
Total	6	3	3	3	10	3

Source: Wikipedia.

Denmark and Ireland. The Irish case was significant because their economy was less developed than that of the others. Round 3 incorporated the first of the Mediterranean states. All three new members shared relatively young democratic forms of governance. Round 4 completed the inclusion of former EFTA states. Round 5 consisted of two separate inclusions, the net effect of which was to incorporate a number of formerly communist states (excluding notable examples such as Ukraine) and two Mediterranean island countries, Cyprus and Malta. Croatia completed this round by joining in 2013. A number of other countries remain in the queue for possible membership, notably Turkey and Macedonia.

The original membership was homogeneous: long-standing democracies with very healthy economies. As rounds have unfolded, both these characteristics have been relaxed. Round 3, for instance, required a dilution of the duration of commitment to democracy and started the process of allowing countries with less robust economies and in need of developmental assistance into the union. This latter inclusion in particular has created tensions and crises in the EU, as some states either cannot or will not adhere to the economic policies demanded by the strongest members.

Widening has reached an impasse of sorts. One of the underlying purposes of widening was to focus EU energies on membership rather than on creating more complex, entangling forms of union, a process known as *deepening*. Those countries, led prominently by Great Britain, have preferred a looser form of political integration that preserves as much national independence as possible and have been the major champions of new membership, a position the United States largely supports. For the wideners, the current problem is that it is not clear where useful member expansion can occur. The physical area of Europe outside the EU is largely former Soviet states near the Russian border and security priorities of the Russians. The Baltic States (Estonia, Latvia, and Lithuania) have already joined, and Ukrainian flirtation with membership application is part of the source of Russian-Ukrainian confrontation.

The other advocacy is that of the deepeners. Represented symbolically in the institutions of the union in Brussels, their emphasis has been on moving the EU to a more complete, federal status politically by moving increasing numbers of functions into the union and thus beyond the control of the individual states. The implementation of monetary union and its consequences for the less-developed members and EU reaction to the immigrant crisis facing Europe are the two most prominent examples of opposition to deepening; one of the underlying reasons for Brexit has been a negative response to the perception that British sovereignty is being undermined by "Brussels."

The United States and the EU also disagree on a number of specific items in the current environment. None of these are fundamental or have any explosive potential, but each creates some disagreements among friends. A sample of these problems includes economic crises within the EU that can affect the United States, immigrants and terrorists in both jurisdictions, financial contributions to European defense within NATO, and Brexit and its potential to spread to other parts of the union.

Sovereign Debt Crisis

One consequence of widening has been to admit countries into the EU that have less vibrant economies than the original members, making the meshing of national economies more difficult. One prominent example of this disparity is in the amount of debt that different countries accumulate and their ability to service and repay it. Sovereign debt is an intimidating term for debt issued (borrowing) by a country, and such debt is a common feature of governments worldwide. The question is when such debt becomes excessive, and there is no consensus on when that point is reached, as the debate in the United States illustrates.

The problem became acute in Greece, which has one of the lower GDPs per capita in the EU ($23,600) and a large debt that it is questionably capable of servicing. Richer member countries such as Germany ($39,500 GDP per capita) insist that Greece engage in austerity measures to provide funds for debt servicing and retirement, but such austerity could only come at the expense of transfers of funds to citizens, who object to the process and demonstrate their displeasure loudly when the EU seeks to impose restrictions on the country. In this case, the negative consequences of widening to poorer states and the coercive pretensions of deepening clash. The issue with Greece is not entirely resolved several years after it first emerged and could spread to other countries such as Cyprus, Spain, and Italy. The United States wants this crisis resolved to avoid EU destabilization, but its own debt controversies restrict its moral or practical ability to affect it much.

Immigrants and Terrorists

The spate of terrorist attacks in Europe in 2015–2016 has highlighted two differences in U.S.-EU policies. The Europeans have a distinct problem because of their dependence on immigrants. As Bonoli explains, "There are few countries on the aging continent that can avoid population decline without resorting to massive immigration." He adds, "If Europe wants to avoid population decline, it has no other option than to accept massive immigration. This is not speculation. It is already happening." The problem is that many European countries have not integrated their immigrant communities into their national lives, and many immigrants live in ghetto-like conditions that breed radicalism. The refugee crisis from Syria magnifies this problem, and in Muller's contention, has "led to an unprecedented politicization of the EU" because of its sheer extent and attempts to stanch the flow. A major result has been the epidemic of terrorist activity that has exploded on the continent and for which the EU has not developed an effective response other than in areas such as the European Border and Coast Guard Agency.

The immigrant problem has effects not unlike some alleged in the United States. Muller explains that "in highly open societies like those of Austria and the Netherlands, the not-so-well-off have become particularly hostile to European integration" because, as Bonoli points out, "the losers in these processes are essentially lower-middle-class individuals and families." Many people in these affected categories voted for Brexit.

The United States shares the concern Europe has with terrorism, but has been at odds with the EU over how to cope with it, particularly in the area of terrorist identification, monitoring, and suppression. American officials have long felt that efforts in EU countries (Belgium is a frequently cited example) have been lax, and particularly that the Europeans have not cooperated with intelligence and other efforts by the United States sufficiently to protect themselves and to reduce the possibility that European-born terrorist efforts will somehow spill over onto U.S. soil.

Defense Burden Sharing

It has long been the case that the United States has borne a disproportionate responsibility for European defense. This condition goes back to the formation both of NATO and the EU in the immediate aftermath of World War II. The United States underwrote and supplied more of the needs of NATO because Europe could not afford to while it was rebuilding from the war and was faced by a huge Red Army in the Soviet zone of Europe, and the economic integration process had as an implicit objective strengthening economies both to be resistant to communist blandishments and to become strong enough to pick up more of the burden themselves.

As long as the Cold War raged, there was little disagreement with the idea that the United States would shoulder much of the burden, but that has changed. The threat has greatly diminished, and Europe is economically more prosperous than it once was. Europeans argue that their continued prosperity is hinged on low defense spending, especially against a distant threat. Some Americans—notably presidential candidate Donald J. Trump—questioned the absence of a European commitment to its own defense and suggested during the 2016 campaign that the United States should rethink its own level of support in the absence of a larger European commitment. At some level, this disagreement is likely to remain part of the dialogue between the two entities in the future, to some extent dependent on the actions of potential adversaries such as the Russians.

Brexit—and Beyond?

The EU has been in a difficult stage of transition for some time, as the integration process has reached critical points on both the economic and political fronts that have created a sense of misgiving, apprehension, and even opposition to its further expansion, and even to continued participation in the union. It has, in Muller's terms, reached "what is now called a 'constraining dissensus' about the future of European integration that citizens may not really like the Europe that is being brought closer to them." Integration does not clearly create a better life and prosperity around which to expand support. Instead, economic integration may threaten the well-being of some groups, and political integration threatens nationalistic integrity, a feeling that is deeper and more enduring than the champions of union have believed. It happened first in Britain; it may not stop there.

It is not really surprising that dissention would turn to secession first in Great Britain. The British, after all, were not original members of the union movement for a reason, and that was British nationalism, one of the central tenets of which was not being truly a part of Europe. It had been British policy for centuries to remain unattached to Europe and its power politics, acting as the "balancer" in Europe—remaining aloof behind the English Channel and only throwing its weight into the breach when European affairs got out of hand. This tradition made the United Kingdom a "broadener" as a way to deflect attempts to deepen the powers of the EU, and helps explain why the British did not join the currency union as well.

There is more. The pro-Brexit vote came primarily from parts of England and Wales that were not benefiting positively from the deepening union, whereas the affluent, urban area surrounding London, as well as Scotland and Northern Ireland, where many people consider themselves conquered people, voted to remain within the union. The Brexit vote may, coincidentally, strengthen sentiment in both places to leave the United Kingdom. The people who voted to leave the union match the more general profile of those who have not benefited from deeper union elsewhere.

The issue of immigration and refugees was the emotional core of much of the Brexit phenomenon. As Luedtke points out, "European integration cannot be separated, institutionally or politically, from issues of immigration." The reason, of course, is that individual countries under the rules accepted in the Lisbon Treaty have lost considerable control over who does and does not enter their countries. Thus, Luedtke argues, "Arab refugees . . . are a common EU-wide problem, since those who enter can move internally with relative ease." With the spate of terrorist attacks by Islamic terrorists, he adds that "Europeanization has redefined what it means to be a foreigner and has made it easier to circulate freely inside the EU," putting an emotional edge on other misgivings many British subjects had over remaining part of the union.

The fallout of the British vote will continue to take shape during the two-year period of separation. Part of the uncertainty is over the extent of fissure, particularly the possibility that the EU will seek to punish their departed member economically for its act by imposing high duties on British goods and services crossing over or under the English Channel. Part of the reaction will be in the United Kingdom itself, where either the Scots or the Northern Irish or both may seek to leave the country as a way to regain membership. At the same time, there are other members who are not entirely satisfied with the affairs of the union, and may find the British action the stimulus they need to follow a similar course. Countries such as Sweden, Denmark, the Netherlands, and Greece were mentioned in the immediate aftermath of Brexit as candidates. Whatever ensues, the EU will not emerge from this separation the same as it was before. European integration may be stronger or weaker, but it will be different.

U.S. Policy Options

Because relations with individual European countries and their collective mechanisms, the EU and NATO, are bedrocks of American relations with its traditionally closest international friends, its options in dealing with affairs within the EU area are constrained. Because the EU membership correlates so closely with that of NATO, the United States cannot take punitive action against the countries of the EU without harming its ability to deal with the original objective of NATO, constraining an expansionist Soviet Union. Russia is no longer the Soviet Union, and Western Europe is no longer the prostrate entity it was in the latter 1940s, but Russia remains troublesome and Europe's help is needed in the effort to contain Russian resurgence, at least in the short term before negative factors kick in for the Russians. Taking negative sanctions to punish the paucity of European contributions to NATO finances or operations, as was suggested in the 2016 election campaign, would appear to be a classic example of the old enjoinder not "to cut off your nose to spite your face."

Similarly, it is hard to imagine economic actions against the EU. The EU is too strong economically for any meaningful form of sanctions to be applied against it as a whole, and punitive actions would probably only hurt the weaker countries of the union, either exacerbating their crises such as sovereign debt (e.g., Greece) or strengthening forces of disunion, imitating Brexit. The United States was initially fairly quiet about its reaction to the

British withdrawal, but it does not want to see the unraveling of the EU which, on balance, it strongly supports as a bulwark of stability and barrier to forceful change from the east. The United States is more supportive of the economic aspects of integration than the more nettlesome political aspects, but it remains supportive of the phenomenon it helped create. The EU is one of the crowning achievements of postwar foreign policy for both the United States and for EU members, and it is hard to see how opposition to it could serve any useful purposes.

The United States and both the EU and its members are at some odds over issues such as Brexit and terrorism and immigration policies, but the tools available for the United States to affect those areas of disagreement are largely limited to diplomatic persuasion. The United States, for instance, has for several years advocated much more intimate cooperation with the EU and its most vulnerable members in the sharing of intelligence on terrorist activities, but national governments tend to be very covetous of their intelligence assets, and thus professions of cooperation tend to be more rhetorical than real. In the wake of a spate of 2016 terrorist attacks in EU countries, that may change, but not entirely because of U.S. diplomatic efforts. Similarly, as immigration and refugee problems have, in Luedtke's term, become "deeply Europeanized," there may be some greater propensity toward cooperation in that area as well.

The differences between the United States and the EU are at the peripheries of their relationship, not at the core. The United States and Western Europe forged a bond during World War II and its aftermath to form a peaceful and prosperous half a continent, and they succeeded almost completely. When the Iron Curtain fell at the end of the Cold War, it was in both American and EU interests to extend an inviting hand to the formerly communist countries of the erstwhile Soviet bloc, and the EU and NATO, with American blessing and help, have been successful in their mutual efforts to envelop those countries into the peace and prosperity of the EU area. There are isolated areas where the process is incomplete; most of these are in the peripheries of Russia, where there is still resistance. Russia largely remains the enigma that it always has been, the one area where U.S.-EU/NATO policy has not totally succeeded in creating peace, stability, and prosperity.

The problem is that Russia does not fit well with Europe. It is physically so big, populous, and traditionally militarily powerful that it cannot be a peer with other European states. Moreover, Russia is not culturally or historically a part of the European experience comparable to that of other states. Over the past few centuries, Russia has aspired to being a European great power, but its differences ethnically, economically, and politically have never permitted that to occur. During the Cold War, Russia as the Soviet Union achieved the status of a superpower and conquered half the continent, but it did so as an outsider, not as an acolyte. Today, a shrunken Soviet

Union as Russia still stands on the outside, politically not quite democratic, economically a petrolist, developing state, and still a sullen power seeking respect and acceptance as one of the world's most powerful states.

Europe and the United States have been unsuccessful in figuring out how to make Russia part of the European prosperity. As Charap and Shapiro put it, "The inherent flaw in this expansion was that NATO and the EU could never fully integrate Russia." Russia will only join the European or Transatlantic associations as a special, favored participant, a status that the major states of Europe such as Germany refuse to accord it, and this creates a chasm between Russia and the rest of Europe that neither seems able or willing to resolve. As a result, Charap and Shapiro conclude that "the key question for European security remains what to do about the relationship with Russia."

Russian resurgence in places such as Ukraine currently accentuate this dilemma. Most ethnic Ukrainians living in that country have a more kindred feeling toward the EU and NATO than they do with Russia and would, in the absence of Russian objection, join the integration movement. Because Ukraine is part of the historic invasion route to Russia, the Russians are unwilling to let that happen if it can be avoided. The Europeans, who are physically on the scene, have been unwilling to press the Russians for concessions, and the Americans have followed suit. The result, according to Wilson (October 2014), is that "the Ukrainian crisis has shown how ineffective European soft power is, and how distant from the region the United States has become."

One can make too much of these differences and of Brexit-inspired turmoil within the EU. Relations with Russia are neither as good nor as bad as they could be, and the EU will likely muddle through its current crisis. From an American standpoint, it is too bad that relations with other parts of the world are not as close and stable as they are with Europe.

CONCLUSION

Europe represents the greatest triumph of American foreign policy since World War II. The United States, through instruments such as the Marshall Plan, was a crucial partner in rebuilding the continent from its war-torn aftermath and aided in its recovery through championing the integration movement. The prosperity and peace that are basic parts of European life are not American creations, but the United States has been a useful partner in nurturing those European determinations and actions. The successful conclusion of the Cold War only adds to the synergism between North America and Europe.

Europe remains, of course, a work in progress in two ways highlighted in this chapter. The most problematical aspect of the European landscape remains post-Soviet Russia. In some ways, the ideal solution would have been the integration of the Russian Federation into EU/NATO, but that has not proven feasible. Russia will only accept a special status within any European arrangement, and the Europeans are unwilling to accord it that status, because doing so would diminish their own place in the order of European things. Russia has proven unwilling to accept integration on Western terms, and Europe will not accept Russia on Russian terms. Russia is simply sui generis within the European system.

The other aspect is the future of the EU in light of centrifugal and centripetal forces on the union. Brexit represents the frustration of those who are not enchanted by a deeper political union—the centrifugal force—and it remains for events to unfold exactly how that process will eventuate. The EU will not disappear without British participation, but the centripetal forces of greater union will almost certainly be compromised, at least in the short run. The United States will be an intensely interested observer of events that transpire both with Russia and within the EU.

STUDY QUESTIONS

1. Discuss the tenor and evolution of U.S.-Russian/Soviet relations historically through the end of the Cold War. How would you typify how the two countries have gotten along historically? What significance does this have for current relations?
2. How would you typify Russia as a power, using the categories of superpower, pivotal power, and rising power as terms of reference? How has that power evolved, and is Russia content with its current status? Is that evolution important in understanding Russian foreign policy? How?
3. Recent U.S.-Russian policy interactions have centered on crises in the Crimea, Ukraine, and Syria. Discuss each. How do they fit into an understanding of the bases of Russian foreign policy and national aspirations?
4. What should American policy toward a resurgent, ambitious Russia be? What motivates the Russians? What can the United States realistically do to influence that policy?
5. Discuss the genesis and evolution of the European Union movement. How did it begin, and why? What was the U.S. role in this process?
6. What are the economic and political dimensions of European integration? How are they related to one another? How and why do they

come into conflict? Discuss in terms of the advocacies of "widening" and "deepening."

7. How does Brexit illustrate the tensions and conflicts within the EU? Should it have been a surprise that the first act of disunion came in the United Kingdom? What are the possible ramifications of the British action both for the United Kingdom and for the European Union itself? Discuss.

8. What are American preferences about the evolution of the EU and the problems it has encountered? What options does the United States have to try to bring the EU more in line with those preferences? How does this problem relate to U.S. relations with Russia?

BIBLIOGRAPHY

Bache, Ian, and Stephen George. *Politics in the European Union.* 2nd ed. Oxford, UK: Oxford University Press, 2006.

Bonoli, Giuliano. "Europe's Social Safety Net under Pressure." *Current History* 115, no. 779 (March 2016): 102–7.

Brickerton, Chris. *The European Union: A Citizen's Guide.* New York: Pelican, 2016.

Charap, Samuel, and Jeremy Shapiro. "How to Avoid a New Cold War." *Current History* 113, no. 765 (October 2014): 265–71.

DaVargo, Julie, and Clifford A. Grammich. *Dire Demographics: Population Trends in the Russian Federation.* Santa Monica, CA: RAND, 2007.

Dawisha, Karen. *Putin's Kleptocracy: Who Owns Russia?* Reprint. New York: Simon & Schuster, 2014.

Delanty, Gerard. "The EU's Indistinct Identity." *Current History* 115, no. 779 (March 2016): 117–19.

Dinan, Desmond. *Europe Recast: A History of the European Union.* Boulder, CO: Lynne Rienner, 2014.

Eberstadt, Nicholas. "The Enigma of Russian Mortality." *Current History* 109, no. 729 (October 2010): 288–94.

Friedman, Thomas L. "The First Law of Petropolitics." *Foreign Policy* (May/June 2006): 28–36.

Gorbachev, Mikhail. *The New Russia.* New York: Polity, 2016.

Gros, Daniel. "The Dogs That Didn't Bark: The EU and the Financial Crisis." *Current History* 108, no. 716 (March 2009): 105–9.

Kennan, George F., and John J. Mearsheimer. *American Diplomacy Sixtieth Anniversary Expanded Edition.* Walgreen Foundation Lectures. Chicago: University of Chicago Press, 2012.

Kotkin, Stephen. "Russia's Perpetual Geopolitics." *Foreign Affairs* 95, no. 3 (May/June 2016): 2–9.

Laqueur, Walter. "Moscow's Modernization Dilemma: Is Russia Charting a New Foreign Policy?" *Foreign Affairs* 89, no. 6 (November/December 2010): 153–60.

Laruelle, Marlene. "Russian Nationalism and Ukraine." *Current History* 113, no. 765): 272–77.

Luedtke, Adam. "'Crisis' and Reality in European Immigration Policy." *Current History* 114, no. 770 (March 2015): 89–94.

Lukyanov, Fyodor. "Putin's Foreign Policy: The Quest to Restore Russia's Rightful Place." *Foreign Affairs* 95, no. 3 (May/June 2016): 30–37.

McCormick, John. *European Union Politics*. London: Palgrave Macmillan, 2015.

McNamara, Kathleen R. *The Politics of Everyday Europe: Constructing Authority in the European Union*. Oxford, UK: Oxford University Press, 2015.

Moravcsik, Andrew. "Europe, the Second Superpower." *Current History* 109, no. 725 (March 2010): 91–98.

Muller, Jan-Werner. "The EU's Democratic Deficit and the Public Sphere." *Current History* 115, no. 779 (March 2016): 83–88.

Nalbandov, Robert. *Not By Bread Alone: Russian Foreign Policy under Putin*. Washington, DC: Potomac, 2016.

Pomerantsev, Peter. *Nothing Is True and Everything Is Possible: The Surreal Heart of the New Russia*. New York: PublicAffairs, 2014.

Snow, Donald M. *The Shape of the Future*. 3rd ed. Armonk, NY: Sharpe, 1999.

Soros, George. *The Tragedy of the European Union: Disintegration or Revival*. New York: PublicAffairs, 2014.

Treisman, Daniel. "Why Putin Took Crimea: The Gambler in the Kremlin." *Foreign Affairs* 95, no. 3 (May/June 2016): 47–54.

Trenin, Dmitri. "The Revival of the Russian Military: How Moscow Reloaded." *Foreign Affairs* 95, no. 3 (May/June 2016): 23–29.

Tsygankov, Andrei. *Russia's Foreign Policy: Change and Continuity in National Identity*. 4th ed. Lanham, MD: Rowman & Littlefield, 2016.

Tymoshenko, Yuliya. "Continuing Russia." *Foreign Affairs* 86, no. 3 (May/June 2007): 69–82.

Watts, Duncan. *The European Union*. Edinburgh: Edinburgh University Press, 2010.

Wilson, Andrew. "The High Stakes of the Ukraine Crisis." *Current History* 113, no. 765 (October 2014): 259–64.

———. *Ukraine Crisis: What It Means for the West*. New Haven, CT: Yale University Press, 2014.

CHAPTER 6
Latin America

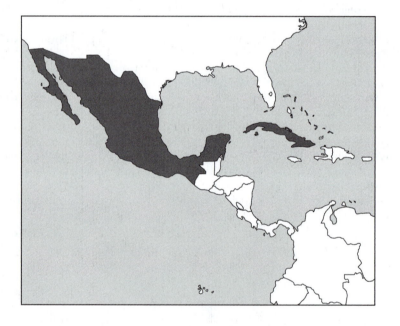

The Western Hemisphere is composed of two continents (North and South America) and a number of nearby islands, from Canadian islands in the Arctic and Greenland in the north to the islands in the Caribbean Sea and some small islands between the southern tip of South America and Antarctica. The heart of North America has historically been Canada and the United States, the second- and third-largest countries in the world in landmass, and since the negotiation of the North American Free Trade Agreement (NAFTA), Mexico has generally been thought of geographically North American, even if it is culturally and historically closer to the south. Although it is somewhat arbitrary, the territory south of Mexico to the Panamanian-Colombian border and most of the Caribbean islands are lumped into North America as well. In its most expansive definition, North America is the world's third-largest continent physically, with the fourth-largest continental population after Asia, Africa, and Europe, and is comprised of twenty-three independent countries.

South America constitutes the rest of the hemisphere. It extends from the Colombian-Panamanian land bridge between the continents to Tierra del Fuego and Cape Horn, and consists of twelve independent states. It is the fourth-largest in landmass and the fifth most populous continent. South America is physically dominated by its largest state, Brazil, which contains over half of South America's population.

The term "Latin America" is generally associated with those countries, basically all of which are south of the U.S.-Mexico border, who share an Iberian background, having been conquered or acquired by either Spain or Portugal in the period after Columbus inadvertently landed in the Caribbean on his quest to find an express route to India in 1492. The natives the conquerors encountered were mostly Indians from different tribes and backgrounds (some of which, like the Aztecs, were quite advanced), and the colonizers brought with them the Spanish and Portuguese languages and Catholicism. The colonial period extended from the sixteenth into the twentieth centuries. The experience of some of the states in Central America and the Caribbean were different, but by and large, these characteristics distinguished what became the countries of Latin America.

Most of the development in Latin America occurred in isolation from the experience of the countries north of Mexico. The United States and Canada were both born from British and French colonization, reflected their English backgrounds (if rejecting British control), and they had relatively little contact with their co-hemispheric cousins to the south. There were, of course, exceptions. Mexico claimed parts of California settled by Spanish missionaries and other territories in the southwestern United States, and Mexico and the United States fought a war in 1846 to draw a distinct line between the two countries. In the Caribbean, there was occasional interest in some of the islands, notably Cuba. One of the largely forgotten episodes of U.S. history was the 1854 issuance of the Ostend Manifesto (named after the Belgian town in which it was proclaimed) stating the desirability of annexing Cuba to the United States. The basis of this advocacy was to add an additional slave-holding state to the union (Cuba shared with the United States the practice of human chattel slavery) to balance control of the U.S. Congress. The suggestion was, obviously, rejected, but it does show at least some interruption in the general neglect of Latin America by the United States.

COPING WITH THE COLOSSUS OF THE NORTH

It is difficult to typify the relations between the United States and a region of well over a half-billion people living in over twenty sovereign states of different levels of development, politics, and interests. In conventional terms, Latin America is divided into three distinct subareas. The largest and, in geopolitical and economic terms, most important is the South American continent and its twelve independent states (as well as French Guiana and Suriname). It is distinctive because it contains two of the physically largest countries in the world, Brazil (fifth) and Argentina (eighth), and the world's fifth most populous country (Brazil). In addition, the countries of South America are generally more developed than those of the other subareas and have significant natural resources that are in global demand. The second subarea is Central America. It is generally defined as the territory between the southern U.S. border and the Panamanian-Colombian frontier. Most of the states of this region are comparatively small and poor, and Mexico towers over them in size and importance to the United States. The third subarea is the Caribbean, which consists of a long chain of islands stretching from the Bahamas and Cuba to the north to the southern end of the Antilles off the Colombian coast. The islands are a mixed bag politically, including some that are still colonies (the American Virgin Islands, for instance), and they are uniformly poor, mostly reliant on the tourist trade from North America and Europe.

The importance and traditional levels of interest of the United States in Latin America are basically related to the physical proximity of various areas and countries to the United States. American relations have been extensive with Central America because of the long Mexican-American border that has served as a conduit for entrance into the United States for legal and illegal immigrants into the country from Mexico and countries farther south. In addition, Central America has provided the overland route for drugs transiting from South America into the United States. Particularly since the completion of the Panama Canal in 1914, the United States has had a geostrategic interest in protecting control of and access to the Canal Zone, an interest it has enforced with military interventions in various Central American countries. The most recent interference was in Nicaragua during the Reagan administration, when the Marxist Sandinista government appeared to pose a threat to control of access to the canal.

Central America and the Caribbean share political instability in a number of countries. Because of proximity (Cuba) or access to the Panama Canal, the states of Hispaniola (Haiti and the Dominican Republic) have been a matter of American physical interest, and the status of Puerto Rican independence or statehood is also a concern. The heart of U.S. policy toward the Caribbean is concentrated, of course, on Cuba.

South America has been less important than the other areas, but it is the Western Hemispheric area that often considers itself the most threatened by the United States. The concern arises because of American economic and political dominance of the hemisphere, and is popularly depicted as the relationship with the "Colossus of the North." The heart of the concern is economic and is manifested in a fear that the United States, with its enormous productive base, will flood South American markets with American goods and services that will undercut and destroy nascent industries in those countries. The result has been a history of protectionist measures such as tariffs under the rubric of "trade substitution" that have protected the South American economy from the United States but that have simultaneously isolated Latin America from many of the dangers and opportunities of the outside world.

The fear of Yankee domination is a recurring theme in Latin America that is more justified in some areas than others. During the twentieth century, the United States intervened fairly frequently in different Central American and Caribbean locations, but that has largely receded as a concern since the end of the Cold War: the only American physical incursion since 1991 was its 1994 occupation of Haiti, and it is not an exaggeration to say that U.S.–Latin American relations are, for the most part, on a kind of back-burner status. One result is to make it difficult to choose countries on which to concentrate attention in a volume such as this.

The choices made here are admittedly arbitrary and reflect the most spectacular and controversial relations between the United States and the countries to its south. Mexico is the more obvious choice: it is a comparatively large, populous, and developing state that forms the southern land boundary of the United States. The porosity of that border and advocacies of making it less so was a major campaign issue in the 2016 election, and ongoing relations between the two countries are likely to be the most—or close to it—important dealings the United States has with Latin America in upcoming years. Cuba has been chosen because it is also very obviously high on the American policy agenda due to the reopening of relations between Cuba and the United States in 2015 and the death of Fidel Castro on

November 25, 2016. How much of an opening these events will provide in the evolution of dealings between the island and the North American mainland is a matter of speculation with Donald Trump as president.

CASE: THE UNITED STATES AND MEXICO

The United and States and Mexico are next-door neighbors, and their proximity helps define the relationship between them. Like most neighbors, they get along most of the time and over most matters, but there are things about each that the other does not like and that can become the basis of disagreement, sometimes heated. Their long common border is 1,933 miles in length. They have different basic languages and cultures, and different historical experiences. Many of their common experiences have been at the expense of one another and generally decided to American advantage. Both peoples are Americans (they both are from the Americas), but only one calls itself American.

The focus of their interactions is what divides them—the border. It is by no means the longest border for the United States; the Canadian-American demarcation, including Alaska, is nearly three times as long at 5,558 miles. It is, however, the most contentious boundary. It *is* the longest boundary in the world between a highly developed country and a developing country; this means there is added incentive for those in the poorer country to come to the more affluent. This border fact has fueled an effort to stanch the flow of people seeking to enter the United States without permission across the border in the form of a fence or other obstruction that could run the entire length of common boundary. Currently, about 700 miles of the border are controlled by a physical barrier, and President Trump has promised to expand it. There have been modest actions taken at obvious crossing points to check the flow across the U.S.-Canada frontier, but nothing even close to what has been proposed for the southern border.

Border issues are at the heart of the contemporary U.S.-Mexican relationship. To understand the nature of this issue, one must view it from two vantage points. One of these is the function that borders fulfill. The other is the question of what transit is to be regulated by the barriers and boundaries that exist. Each is important in assessing what kind of a problem the United States and Mexico have and how they can approach and try to solve it.

Nevins makes a useful distinction in terms of the functions of borders, arguing that they can have two basic purposes that, unfortunately, can conflict with one another. The first function is as *a line of control,* an idea introduced regarding Kashmir in chapter 4. In this conceptualization, the primary purpose of boundaries is exclusionary, to regulate and exclude the entrance of undesired people and things onto one's territory. This screening and blocking function is the common conceptualization most people conjure in contemporary terms, whether it is "illegal" immigrants entering the United States or undocumented Middle Eastern refugees entering the EU, but it can and does extend to other commodities as well. In the Mexican-American debate, for instance, it includes the movement of drugs north across the boundary to American customers, and weapons (usually bought with drug money) heading south into Mexico. In both directions, the net effect is to contribute to crime in the receiving venue and is thus a problem each would like eliminated—at least for itself.

The other function of a boundary is as a *gateway*, a mechanism to promote the flow of desirable people and things across that same boundary, normally in either direction. With the current emphasis on the negative aspects of border exchanges in the political arena, this function has become less prominent in political discussions. This function, however, is important for some major purposes, such as the promotion of trade between countries and the attraction of desirable immigrants, such as people with needed skills in areas such as science and technology.

These two functions can conflict with one another, as they have in contemporary American (and European) discussions. The United States is a polyglot country for whom immigration has provided a relatively useful and youthful flow of new citizens in a situation where the population is otherwise aging. Immigration provides a hedge against the kind of economic stagnation so dangerous to many European countries and China, who have more difficulty replenishing their pool of youthful, productive workers than the United States has historically experienced. As the controversy over sealing the U.S.-Mexican border suggests, the gateway can lead to demands for a more effective line of control to keep out undesirable immigrants. At the same time, there is a dynamic tension between inviting and impeding the flow of goods and services across the border. Most Americans accept the value of importation of things entering the country that they desire (tropical fruit from Central America, for instance), but would like to be able to thwart drug dealers bringing their contraband across the same boundary.

The other border question is for what a border serves as a barrier or a gateway, a matter that will occupy the policy section of the chapter. In the current debate, the question regarding U.S.-Mexican relations centers on three issues in roughly descending and not entirely compatible terms. The first and most visible is immigrants and centers on the flow of undocumented, "illegal" Mexican and Central American people crossing the border in search of a better life. The second concern is with drugs coming into the United States and the problems this transit has for both countries (feeding American addictions, destabilizing the Mexican political system). The third is the possibility that terrorists will use the Mexican-American border to enter the United States to carry out terrorist attacks (a problem that contrasts with the same problem on the Canadian border).

Mexico: A Physical and Political Sketch

Mexico has one of the oldest civilizations in the Western Hemisphere, and one that predates organized social activity in North America by centuries. The first artifacts of social life in contemporary Mexico go back to around 1500 BCE, and numerous civilizations, the most famous of which are the Mayan and Aztec, have thrived there. The first Indian civilizations were active between 300 and 900 CE. The Toltec empire thrived until about 1200 CE, and they were supplanted by the Aztecs, who built Mexico City (Tenochtitlan) and ruled when the Spanish under Hernando Cortez arrived in 1521. The Spanish colonized Mexico and replaced the traditional civilization with the Spanish model. All this occurred about a century before the first English colonies were established in North America in Virginia (1607) and Massachusetts (1620). Until the American Revolution, North America north of the Isthmus of Panama was effectively divided among England, France, and Spain, a division that, among other things, led to different patterns of development and progress between Canada, the United States, and Mexico.

Mexico is a country that physically and developmentally stands on the cusp between the traditionally defined developed world of the most advanced national economies and the developing world of less economically advanced countries. A symbol of its status is its inclusion in the Group of 20 economic powers (see Snow, *Cases in International Relations*, sixth edition for a discussion) when that group transcended the historic mantle of the Group of Seven most developed economies. One can easily argue that if Mexico was not physically contiguous with the United States, it might be considered a rising power, a designation that might be fitting for its status in Latin America.

Mexico is a substantial place by most measures. It is the fourteenth-largest country in the world in physical territory with an area of slightly over three-quarters of a million square miles, which is slightly less than three times the size of Texas, and this also makes it fifth in area in the Western Hemisphere after Canada, the United States, Brazil, and Argentina. In addition to the United States, it has land borders with Guatemala and Belize. With a population of over 120 million, it is the world's twelfth most populous and the hemisphere's third behind the United States and Brazil.

Mexico stands statistically on the world developmental cusp as well. At a little under $2 trillion, Mexico has the eleventh-largest economy in the world, although much of it has come from the stimulus of the controversial NAFTA connection. As Gonzalez (2011) explains, the bulk of Mexican industry (really its distinguishing characteristic) is its concentration in assembling products from non-Mexican parts for importation into the United States. Automobiles are a significant example that creates political controversy: many of the parts are sent to Mexico for assembly to evade American customs restrictions under NAFTA, assembly in Mexico rather than the United States avoids higher labor costs in the United States, and a concentration on putting together products from foreign sources does relatively little to enhance Mexican structural development. The result is a fairly fragile economy. This fragility is also evident in the Mexican petroleum industry: Mexico exports about one and half million barrels a day (mbd) of oil, ninth in the world (mostly to the United States), but its reserves (estimated at 10.26 billion barrels) are eighteenth, meaning the Mexicans face a diminishing potential not unlike that of Russia.

Development in the country has been uneven. Its GDP does not translate into a high per capita: at $15,600, it ranks only eighty-eighth in the world. Although it has a low unemployment rate (4.9 percent), over half the population (52.3 percent) live below the poverty line. Two phenomena indicate the effect of that poverty. First, more Mexicans migrate from the country despite efforts by the Americans to exclude them, and this is particularly true among rural, agricultural segments of the population than others. Second, a major source of income for many poor Mexicans is remittances sent to family in Mexico from workers—both documented and undocumented—in the United States. An effective program of deportation by the Americans would reduce that source of income and make living conditions even worse in Mexico than they already are for many Mexicans.

The situation in Mexico is exacerbated by the political impact of governmental corruption, the major source of which is the impact of wealth controlled by the drug cartels. The Mexican political system has a long and often unstable tradition. Mexico achieved independence from Spain in 1821 after a prolonged civil war and has been independent ever since, despite the efforts of France's Louis Napoleon to recolonize it in the 1860s. A second revolutionary event occurred in 1911, bringing to power the Institutional Revolutionary Party (PRI), which ruled until nearly the end of the century.

Intermingling between the PRI and the drug lords who have gradually accumulated wealth and power led to the epochal election of Vicente Fox, the candidate of the National Action Party (PAN) in 2000, on a platform to reform government and suppress drug interests. Felipe Calderon succeeded Fox in 2006 (Mexican presidents are limited to a single six-year term); he engaged in a highly publicized but ultimately unsuccessful effort to bring down the cartels. When Calderon's term ran out, the rising importance of the drug cartels led Mexican voters to return to the PRI, whose leader, Enrique Peña Nieto, has vowed a renewed and intensified campaign to reduce the influence of the drug cartels and drug-related violence. The most spectacular success of this program was the eventual capture (a second time) of the notorious drug dealer El Chapo (Joaquín Guzmán) and his trial in the United States in 2017 on numerous drug-related charges.

From an internal Mexican vantage point, dealing with the flow of drugs northward to the United States is, along with more general questions of economic development, the greatest crisis the country faces. Drug money has corrupted the political system fundamentally, and drug cartel violence (often carried out with weapons bought in the United States and smuggled more or less openly southward) destabilizes everyday Mexican life. The United States believes the basis of its problems with Mexico is illegal immigration; Mexicans tend to see it more as the corrosive effects of enormous amounts of money from American drug addicts flowing into their country.

Basic U.S.-Mexican Relations

The "border issue" has been at the heart of U.S.-Mexican relations since the two countries achieved independence and began to move into territory that was not unambiguously part of one country. The first overt manifestation of this collision occurred with the Louisiana Purchase from France by the United States in 1803, because there was ambiguity exactly how far west the Louisiana Territory extended and the places where the two countries might have conflicting claims. The issue came initially to a head over Texas, whose North American immigrants declared the state independent from Mexico and established the Texas Republic in 1837. The border between Texas and Mexico became a matter of contention in the early 1840s (whether the boundary ran along the Rio Grande or the Nueces River) and became a proximate cause of the Mexican War in 1846. The Treaty of Guadalupe Hidalgo of 1848 settled that dispute to American advantage, and the southern border between the two was further consolidated when the Gadsden Purchase of 1854 added parts of southern New Mexico and Arizona to the United States. In the aftermath, Americans took over remaining disputed southwestern lands (including California) to help consolidate the present continental U.S. boundary, a demarcation with which Mexico has never been entirely pleased but which it is powerless to change. The net result is a border dispute that exists on both sides of the frontier.

The relationship between the two countries has always been uneven. The United States has always been the larger, more powerful of the two countries. Some of this difference is attributable to the developmental models each followed given their different colonial legacies—the United States evolving from the more entrepreneurial traditions of northern Europe and Mexico from the more traditional, hacienda-based Spanish model. The designation of the United States as Colossus of the North has always been strongest in Central America (it was originally associated with U.S. policies toward Nicaragua and Panama at the turn of the twentieth century regarding construction of the Panama Canal), and it is felt as far north as Mexico.

In some important ways, the border question is an umbrella for the adversarial side of Mexican-American relations rather than the issue per se. The border is important because of the things that happen at and across the border, and solutions such as sealing the border with an impenetrable barrier are directed at those activities in which the border plays a role. Thus, related questions of immigration and trade are really about who and what comes across the border, and it becomes a border issue in the sense of determining what people and goods should or should not be allowed to penetrate the frontier. The drug issue is fundamentally about the problem of American use of narcotic drugs and the effects on the Mexican economy and political system of the money deriving from that trade. The issue of terrorists entering the country comes closest to being a "pure" border issue, in the sense that there is no controversy over the policy goal—keeping out those who would do the United States harm—but about how best to avoid that penetration.

It is worth noting that these same concerns are not a prominent part of U.S. relations with its other neighbor, Canada. The United States does not seek to exclude Canadians from entering the country, and there are no discussions of deporting those Canadians who live here, including those who may have simply crossed the mostly unguarded border without official permission. The only U.S.-Canadian drug "problem" is the controversy of Canadian medicinal drugs crossing the border at considerably lower costs than American-produced counterparts. There is a potential disagreement over the possibility that a porous border with Canada could be used by terrorists to enter the United States. This porosity is an unavoidable fact, for which the Canadians attempt to compensate by making it more difficult to enter Canada in the first place, thereby reducing or eliminating the number of potential terrorists who can get to the border.

Immigration

These two questions are not always treated in the same breath, but the effects, especially in gateway–line-of-control terms, are quite similar. Immigration affects the flow of who does and does not enter the country, in this case from Mexico and its southern neighbors in Central America. The question has centered on the millions of unauthorized immigrants who have entered the United States and who create an alleged economic and other menace to the population. The spate of international trade agreements of the latter 1990s and early 2000s, and especially NAFTA in the U.S.-Mexico relationship, has more recently become an issue. The two have been tied together in contemporary politics by their negative impact on American jobs.

The immigration phenomenon has been by far the more prominent. In important ways, it is nothing new nor is it unique to U.S.-Mexican relations. Mexican workers have entered the United States on a temporary basis as seasonal agricultural workers harvesting crops in places such as California for well over a century. Invited, temporary migrants are, in a sense, a vital link in the food chain, and their virtue is that they will do hard labor for lower wages than American citizens will perform the same jobs—if citizens are available at all for those wages. These temporary invited immigrants remain a part of the temporary workforce and are relatively noncontroversial. The more controversial elements are Latin Americans who come across the border without permission and who may or may not plan to return to their native lands.

Most of these people are *economic* immigrants whose motives include making a better living for themselves and often to remand part of their earnings back to family in Mexico and elsewhere (many of these immigrants come from Guatemala and Honduras). Their virtue is that they are willing to perform the so-called 3D jobs: dirty, difficult, and dangerous, and they will do so for lower wages than American citizens. This dynamic is true for most immigrants worldwide. The controversies surrounding them in the American debate are that they allegedly do not pay taxes, drain social services monies reserved for American citizens, and commit a disproportionate volume of crime than do American citizens. These accusations are all debatable. Illegal immigrants cannot pay income taxes, because doing so would identify them to authorities, for instance, but they pay user taxes such as sales tax. The accusation of criminality is even more questionable. There is indeed a class of *criminal immigrants* who penetrate the boundary to engage in criminal behavior that has nothing to do with the activities of most immigrants.

Much of the controversy over illegal immigrants surrounds the sheer number of them in the United States. By definition, unauthorized immigrants do not identify themselves to those keeping statistics, but their number is conventionally estimated in political accounts at around eleven million. What is less well understood is why they are here, and the answer is that, at least inadvertently, they are here because of American economic policies. As Rozental says, "Few of our American friends like to recognize these realities driving immigration: an increasingly globalized economy, the social and economic factors to join families and friends who have already settled in the United States, a constant shortage of labor for certain jobs, because Americans will not take them, and the growing demands for immigrants to enter the service sector."

To this list, one can add what I have elsewhere called NAFTA's "dirty little secret" (see Snow, *Cases in International Relations*). When NAFTA came into force in the early 1990s, it had the immediate effects of stimulating the American economy (and thus the need for workers) and suppressing the Mexican economy. This was particularly true in agriculture, and especially among small peasant corn farmers, as the reduction of barriers to trade allowed American corn (which is subsidized by the American government, thereby increasing the price disparity) to flood the Mexican market, thereby putting millions out of work and susceptible to the temptations of crossing the border. Krikorian summarizes the shortcoming: "Agricultural modernization *always* sets people on the move by consolidating small farms into larger, more productive operations. The problem with NAFTA was that neither country did anything meaningful to make sure the excess Mexican peasantry moved to Mexican cities, not to ours." One way to do so, infrequently raised, would be to reduce American corn subsidies so that Mexican producers could become more competitive and thus less likely to migrate across the border. During the period between the implementation of NAFTA and the early 2000s, the undocumented immigrant number went from an estimated 4.2 million to its current dimensions.

There is an additional NAFTA-related source of controversy regarding trade that has emerged in growing American disenchantment with the free trade emphasis of globalization (discussed in chapter 10 of Snow and Haney, *U.S. Foreign Policy*, fifth edition). Because NAFTA is indeed a free trade area that does not include a common external tariff, other countries attempting to avoid American trade barriers to penetrate the market can take advantage of indirect importation by shipping goods (including parts) to Mexico, which has much smaller tariffs on the same goods. The products are then assembled in Mexico and shipped to the United States at prices that undercut the reasons for which the original barriers were created.

What to do about the importation avoidance problem is wrapped up in nascent discussions about free trade and is a derivative, not a fundamental part, of the U.S. trade policy debate. What to do about the problem of immigration is a more immediate foreign as well as domestic policy issue. Proposed solutions have tended to emphasize line-of-control approaches and sometimes draconian measures. The "popular" advocacies have included rounding up and deporting the estimated eleven million undocumented workers (probably a logistically impossible task) and then sealing the boundary with something like an impenetrable fence. All these plans, however, face difficulties on both sides of the border.

The first objection is that these plans are impracticable. President Donald J. Trump advocated extending the fence that now separates 700 miles of Mexico from the United States to create a physical line of control across all 1,933 miles during the 2016 campaign, but is that solution practical or affordable, and will it work? Depending on the capabilities the barrier had in terms of things like electronic monitoring, it would cost literally billions of dollars, but would it be effective? There are skeptics: former New Mexico governor Bill Richardson once famously said, "If we build a ten-foot fence, someone will build an 11-foot ladder." Moreover, if breaching the line is important enough to those who do it, they will probably find a way to thwart it. One is reminded of the Sixth Corollary to Murphy's Law: "Nothing is foolproof, because fools are so ingenious." Moreover, the symbolism of such a project would be significant, serving as an analogy with China's Great Wall, which was erected to protect the Han from outside barbarians. The Great Wall has the virtue of doubling as a tourist attraction; it is hard to imagine the border fence having that appeal. Even if one could erect a barrier that could exclude new undocumented immigrants from crossing into the United States, that still does nothing to deal with whatever problems the existing eleven million create.

The second is that unauthorized immigrants fulfill an economic function that would be difficult to replace. There are two basic reasons there are so many undocumented Mexicans and other Central Americans in the United States. One is that the opportunities for an improved quality of life draw people from impoverished conditions in their home countries to the relatively greater affluence than they can attain in the United States. As long as that is true, there will be economic migrants seeking to enter the country, and sometimes succeeding. The other reason is that these immigrants serve a real economic function that it would be difficult to perform in their absence. To reiterate, the undocumented workers do jobs that American citizens will not do: the 3-D jobs. Removing the immigrants will not, for example, open the floodgates for American citizens seeking jobs as roofers or "landscape architects." Moreover, their illegal status also means they can be compensated at below market wages, since they have no legal recourse to discrimination that does not jeopardize their residence. Making living conditions better in Latin America and wages for menial jobs that can attract American workers may well be more attractive than an enhanced line of control. Andreas adds that American employers are also to blame, suggesting the cure is "tighter requirements and tougher employer penalties," adding that unless these kinds of measures are enacted and enforced, "popular calls to 'seal' the border are little more than distracting political theater."

The third, and most relevant as a foreign policy matter, is Mexican disdain for these plans. Building the fence would be a significant barrier to the movement of legitimate goods and services across the frontier as established as a goal of NAFTA. Mexico, understandably, is somewhat offended by these proposals, which strike them as discriminatory and demeaning at a time when cooperation is needed between the two countries in other areas, such as drugs and terrorists.

The Drug Problem

The transit of illegal drugs across the Mexican-American border is a shared problem for the two countries, if for different reasons. It is clearly a line-of-control problem for both, and one that interacts with immigration and barriers to regulate the movement of both people and things across the frontier. In the case of drugs, the object is the interruption of illicit substances for the American narcotics market for the United States; for Mexico, it is the return of enormous amounts of money and weapons to Mexico from the sale of the drugs. For both, it is the actual or potential impact of criminality associated with those in the drug "business."

It is neither a particularly new nor strictly a border problem. It has centered on the transit of cocaine from South America (the Andes region) and has been ongoing at least since the aftermath of the American Civil War, which created opium and morphine addictions among many of the wounded; this was reinforced after each of the world wars. Cocaine demands go back to the late nineteenth century when, according to Gonzalez (2009), cocaine was used both for smoking and "as a cure-all." Coca, the leaves of which are refined into cocaine, was also widely used to flavor soft drinks: at one time, the "coca" in Coca-Cola was to be taken literally.

Mexicans have been involved in the business of getting illicit drugs into the United States for a long time, and especially since the flood of cocaine and cocaine-derived products became popular in the latter part of the twentieth century. The transit of cocaine through Central America and across the U.S.-Mexican border was only one way in which these drugs reached the United States until presidents Reagan and George H. W. Bush initiated their versions of the "war on drugs" in the 1980s. This campaign had limited lasting effect on the drug problem in the United States, but it dramatically affected the drug-selling "business." Efforts by the U.S. Air Force, Coast Guard, and Navy greatly choked off transportation of drugs by water through the Caribbean and in the air by small planes, leaving overland shipment as the remaining mode for drug running. Bush's efforts in particular were aimed at the Colombian drug lords and their cartels and essentially destroyed them. Mexican drug lords stepped into the breach and established their own cartels. The result was to concentrate the drug supply problem in Mexico.

It has also created a lucrative, destabilizing business. Although the figures are somewhat dated, Shifter (2007) estimated that "70 to 90 percent" of the illegal drugs, worth (according to O'Neil) $15–25 billion in profits, annually flow across the Mexican border, and more recent figures are probably greater than that. This growth has facilitated drug cartel operations across the United States and has produced enormous profits that allow the Mexican cartels to corrupt the political system: one reason the PRI was voted out of office in 2000 was alleged ties to the cartels, and one of the reasons for their return was promises to defeat the cartels. Moreover, some of these profits go into armaments bought from American gun dealers that mean the cartels usually outgun their Mexican government counterparts.

The drug cartels become part of the border problem because one way to reduce the U.S. drug problem is to reduce available supplies of drugs by U.S. border agents. This task is extremely difficult because drugs are not bulky and can be hidden in the enormous legitimate traffic that moves across the border. One estimate, for instance, is that all the drugs that come into the United States from Mexico in a year could fit into eighteen tractor-trailer trucks.

The drug problem poisons Mexican politics and relations with the United States. The Mexican political system is permeated with drug cartel money; that has corrupted much of the political system, and there are cartel-controlled areas that are virtually lawless as a result. The potential for destabilization of the Mexican system is not inconsequential and would, if it occurred, create enormous future difficulties for both countries. Moreover, the two countries engage in a kind of "blame game" with one another over the problem. The United States blames the Mexicans for not taking adequate steps to help the United States reduce its drug problem by reducing the supplies coming into the country. The Mexicans, in turn, argue that the real problem is American addiction to the drugs, and that if the United States would act decisively to reduce demand, the problem—including the influence of the cartels—would shrink. Moreover, they also blame the Americans for taking inadequate steps to reduce the ease with which the cartels can buy and transship sophisticated weapons out of the United States, thereby making their own efforts even more difficult. This problem is difficult, complicated, and important, but it has taken secondary importance to the immigration "problem" and even, in the future, to terrorists using the Mexican border to enter this country.

Terrorists

The least discussed border problem between the two countries is the possibility that terrorists could attempt to penetrate the frontier at vulnerable places (of which there are currently many) to enter the United States and commit terrorist acts here. It is relatively more difficult to penetrate the Mexican frontier than the Canadian border, because much more of it is patrolled, mostly for reasons unrelated to terrorism, than it is to walk across the Canadian-American border at most places from the Great Lakes to the Pacific. On the other hand, it is relatively easier to get onto Mexican than Canadian soil in the first place.

This national security concern ranks at the bottom of U.S.-Mexican relations (although not overall American national security worries) for the simple fact that it has yet to be a major problem: there have been no terrorist events in the United States publicly attributed to foreigners entering the country through Mexico. It is, however, conceivable that sometime in the future, such an effort will occur (if such attempts have not already been tried and quietly thwarted), in which case it will be added to the list of concerns surrounding line-of-control issues surrounding the border.

U.S. Policy Options

Mexican-American relations are strained by the border issues and the kinds of problems associated with them. The United States entreats the Mexicans to assist with the major problems a porous border creates, but the Mexican government is either unwilling or unable to deal with most of these. Border security is considerably more relaxed in Mexico than it is in the United States, restricting the ability of Mexico to slow or stanch either the flow of illegal immigrants or drugs across the border. Regarding immigrants, the Mexicans turn American arguments around. First, they point out that statistics do not support the notion that *Mexican* nationals are at the heart of the problem. Recent U.S. statistics show that in recent years there has been a net inflow of Mexicans back into Mexico, and that the vast percentage of undocumented people coming across the border are from Central America, notably Guatemala, Honduras, and Nicaragua.

Moreover, the Mexicans point out that American actions, such as reducing or doing away with corn subsidies that put Mexican peasant farmers out of work, would do more good than the draconian line-of-control solutions currently being advocated. Mexico also has strong positions about the drug trade. They argue that the whole complex of problems both countries face is the result of an apparently insatiable appetite that Americans have for illegal narcotics. If that part of the problem were to come under control, there would be much less demand for Mexican-supplied drugs, much less excess money in the hands of the drug cartels, much less interference and corruption of the Mexican system that drug money allows, less violence and instability caused by American-purchased, drug money–supplied levels of weaponry along the border, and a stronger, more viable Mexican political system that could interact with the United States as an international partner and neighbor.

Unfortunately, the approach to mutual problems has not been entirely cooperative from either side. The United States wants the immigrants and drugs to stay out of American territory, but it ignores or brushes aside Mexican objections to the U.S. construction of the problem. Is, for instance, the real solution to the immigration problem building a barrier to keep people out, or is it creating conditions where either people do not want or need to immigrate such as nurturing prosperity or so there are not ready—if illegal—jobs waiting for those who enter? Or is it both? Regarding drugs, is the problem the power and strength of the cartels and their pollution of the Mexican political system, or is it the number of American junkies who create a ready market for the drugs? Or, once again, is it both? In this latter regard, the pursuit and capture of El Chapo and his remanding to an American prison system from which he cannot escape may be a model of sorts for what cooperative efforts recognizing one another's interest may be and a harbinger for the future.

There is also an elephant in the room of Mexican-American relations. Dealing with the ongoing situation and differences is certainly a concern of the United States, but it is a medium-level priority. The elephant, however, is the possibility of a massive destabilization of the Mexican system that the Mexican government cannot contain. The possibility of a Marxist revolution was a concern before the end of the Cold War, with the Yucatan and Chiapas regions as likely points of origin. The Marxist element in that formula has disappeared, but destabilization, probably involving the drug cartels, remains a possibility. The consequences of such a destabilization could make the current concern with boundaries pale by comparison. Until or unless something like such a destabilization occurs, the elephant will remain contained and relations between the two neighbors will likely bump along.

CASE: THE UNITED STATES AND CUBA

There are few, if any, countries in the world with which the United States has more of a love-hate relationship than Cuba. Other than the two countries with which the United States shares a land border, Cuba is physically closer to the United States than any other state, located slightly over ninety miles from the Florida Keys across the Florida Straits. Since the early days of the American Republic, some Americans have cast a covetous eye on the island, which is slightly larger than Pennsylvania, from the Ostend Manifesto forward through the rest of the nineteenth century, a yearning dampened by Cuban independence in 1898 and American recognition of Cuba as a sovereign state in 1902.

Cuban independence was one outcome of the war between Spain and the United States. The immediate precipitant of that war was the sinking of the USS *Maine* in Havana Harbor, and it has never been conclusively determined that Cuban nationalists seeking to enlist American support in their struggle did not have a part in that event.

The pendulum between ardor and hatred has been swinging back and forth ever since. Although the United States did not move to annex Cuba after it established its independence from Spain, U.S. citizens and corporate entities did engage in significant economic imperialism on the island, gaining control of much of Cuban production concentrated in sugar culture. After World War II, the American mafia moved into Havana, building hotels and casinos and transforming the island into a vacation playground for wealthy Americans, much to the chagrin of religious Cubans and others who deeply resented this indirect form of colonization, which was personified for many Cubans in the dictatorial rule of Fulgencio Batista. He ruled the island from 1940 to 1944 and again from 1952 to 1959, and was allied with the Americans, and particularly with mafia elements in the tourist trade. The corruption of his rule was a symbol leading to the formation of the July 26 Movement in 1956 under a then-obscure Cuban lawyer by the name of Fidel Castro. In 1959, Batista's regime crumbled and the upstart revolutionaries marched into Havana and established their domain. Love quickly turned to hate.

The initial reaction to the success of Castro's revolution was mixed in the United States. Staunch anti-communists such as Secretary of State John Foster Dulles suspected that Castro at least harbored communist sentiments, and it was their hope that they could manage somehow to contain his tendencies and behavior within acceptable limits in terms of U.S. strategic and economic interests. Others believed that Castro was a liberator and heroic figure. As he consolidated power and, in some ways most significantly, began expropriating American property on the island in the name of the state, the worst of Dulles's suspicion was confirmed.

With Castro's predilections established and the demands for reimbursement for expropriated property growing among affected Americans, the United States severed diplomatic relations with the island on January 3, 1961. In the waning days of the Eisenhower administration, Dulles and his brother, Allen, director of the CIA, hatched plots against the Cuban regime, the most famous of which was the unsuccessful landing of anti-Castro "rebels" sponsored by the CIA at the Bay of Pigs on April 17, 1961, a fiasco that ended with their surrender to Cuban authorities three days later. In addition, a series of assassination plots were developed during the early 1960s that failed in their mission. Disaffected Cubans fled the island, some with regime blessing, and many ended up in South Florida, where they have formed a vocal source of opposition to any relations between the countries ever since.

Relations between the two countries effectively went into the deep freeze for over a half-century after the 1961 rupture of relations. With comprehensive sanctions in the form of an embargo of the island in place, there has been no commerce with Cuba, and a travel ban made it impossible for most Americans to visit the island. A steady stream of refugees has managed to traverse the Florida Straits and to land in Florida, where the Cuban exile community embraces them. The exiles have, for most of the intervening years, had a virtual stranglehold on U.S.-Cuban policy, and their bitter anti-Castroite feelings have ensured that any contact has been minimal. Cuba has become the subject of American concern almost in entirely negative contexts: the Cuban missile crisis of 1962 and the emotional return of Elian Gonzalez to the custody of his Cuban father living on the island in 2000, for instance.

The breach between the two countries is both emotional and economic. From an American viewpoint, much of the emotion has always surrounded the fact that, once in office, Castro declared himself a communist. That revelation and the subsequent development of a strong relationship with the USSR left many Americans who had viewed Castro as a reformist to the corrupt dictator Batista deeply disillusioned with the Cuban regime. As Castro extended his hold and began to try to export communism in the region, this emotion gained a reinforcing national security component, as Havana's initiatives threatened countries with access to the Panama Canal, America's most important strategic interest in the region. From a Cuban viewpoint, ridding their island of American influence meant reducing the neocolonialism that American influence and control implied. The Guantanamo Bay Naval Base remains the sore subject in the emotions affecting the two countries on both fronts.

Two related economic issues framed the divorce between Havana and Washington. When the Castro government came to power, one of its first acts was to expropriate the extensive land holdings (sugar cane plantations are a notable example) of absentee American landholders, which the Cubans saw as an instrument of economic colonialism and poverty among the Cuban masses. The Cubans refused to offer prompt and full compensation for these holdings, and the United States replied by seizing Cuban assets in the United States and declaring an embargo on all American economic dealings with the island in return. The order to do so was first implemented in 1960, before relations were severed, and was made permanent in 1962. The flip side, compensation and rescinding the embargo, remain major sources of disruption between the two countries.

The isolation of the two countries from one another has never been entirely accepted by everyone in the United States. Particularly since the fall of the Soviet Union, fencing off Cuba because it is a communist state has seemed an anachronism to many, and the lack of contact has also made it more difficult for the United States to encourage political and economic change in Cuba. At the same time, many other countries aligned with the United States have opposed the embargo and American actions to force their compliance as strong-armed intrusions on their sovereignty. As a result, countries such as Canada have engaged in profitable interactions with Castro-led Cuba, while the United States has shut itself off from Cuba largely because of the hatred of the regime by Cuban exiles. The major "engine" of political opposition to dealing with Cuba while Castros remain in power (or until, as some euphemistically put it, the "biological solution"—the death of Fidel in November 2016 at age ninety and of Raúl at some later time—changes the structure of Cuban politics) has been the exile community concentrated in South Florida but also powerful in other states with exile communities, such as New Jersey.

The pendulum swung back on July 20, 2015, when long months of negotiations between the Obama administration and the regime of Raúl Castro produced an agreement restoring relations between the two countries, including reopening embassies in the two countries shuttered for fifty-four years. The move outraged those Cubans resolutely opposed to the Castro dictatorship, but they were unable to prevent it, and there has been implementing action in areas such as travel to and from the island that suggests the likelihood of a growing connection between Cuba and the United States.

Cuba: A Physical and Political Sketch

Cuba has a long and colorful history. Christopher Columbus visited the island in 1492 as part of his accidental discovery of the New World. He encountered the Taino, an Indian tribe of small and dwindling numbers. When the Spanish returned in the 1510s to colonize, they discovered too few natives to perform the labor they planned and quickly began to import African slaves to provide chattel labor in the cultivation of sugar cane and later tobacco crops. The practice of slavery on the island endured until 1879 after the first, unsuccessful Cuban war of independence (in which many slaves participated). Resistance to Spanish rule continued until the end of the century, when American intervention in the wake of the controversial sinking of the *Maine* led to the Spanish-American War of 1898 and the subsequent eviction of the Spanish from the island.

The period immediately after that war helped define subsequent U.S.-Cuban relations in two ways. The Americans remained in occupation of the island until 1902, when their withdrawal was a major symbol of real Cuban independence. That departure, however, was preceded by the American imposition of the infamous Platt Amendment of 1901, which put two "stipulations" (Suddath's term) on Cuban independence. One of these was, in Staten's words, to grant "the United States the right to intervene in Cuba for the 'preservation of Cuban independence,'" a direct limit on Cuban sovereignty, since the United States reserved the option of deciding when intervention was needed. The Platt Amendment remained in force until President Franklin D. Roosevelt rescinded it as part of his "good neighbor" policy in 1934. The other defining condition was the establishment of the Guantanamo Bay Naval Base in 1903 on the southeastern corner of Cuba. When the agreement was negotiated (or imposed, depending on one's point of view), it granted the United States the right to retain "Gitmo" in perpetuity, with cancellation of the agreement only by mutual consent of the two countries. Needless to say, the Cubans would like to rescind the arrangement, which the Americans refuse to do for reasons discussed later in the chapter. American occupation of the facility remains a reminder of the unequal relationship between the two countries.

The U.S.-Cuban relationship is asymmetrical at least partially because of the enormous physical differences between the two countries. Cuba is the largest island in the Caribbean, with an area of 42,803 square miles, which makes it slightly smaller than the state of Pennsylvania and the 106th-largest country in the world. Cubans sometimes describe this 759-mile (northwest to southeast) by 135-mile (north to south) island as the "Pearl of the Antilles" for its natural beauty. Of this area, a little over three-tenths is arable and has historically supported tropical growth, notably the cultivation of sugar cane and after its introduction to the island, tobacco. The country occupies the entire island, so Cuba has no international boundaries. Gitmo represents the exception: its eighteen-mile perimeter is strictly off-limits to Cuban citizens (except those employed by the Americans) and officials, and both sides of the fence surrounding the base are heavily patrolled, leaving it the virtual semblance of a boundary. Cubans, as might be expected, denounce the perpetual relationship as a violation of Cuban sovereignty.

Part of Cuba's importance derives from its strategic location as one of the major gateways or obstacles to transit between the Atlantic Ocean to its north and east and the Caribbean Sea to its west and south. Two of the most strategically located waterways between the two wash on the shores of Cuba: the Straits of Florida between Cuba and the United States, and the Windward Passage between Cuba and Hispaniola (the island shared by the Dominican Republic and Haiti). Both are important. The Straits of Florida are the waters that Cuban exiles fleeing the island have had to traverse to reach South Florida. The Windward Passage is the most direct route between the Atlantic and the Panama Canal, protection of the access to which is the major American national security priority in the Caribbean area and one that was under threat from the Cubans during the Cold War. The passage also washes on Guantanamo, adding to the importance to the United States of maintaining the naval facility.

With a population estimated at 11,047,251 in July 2014, Cuba is the 78th most populous country in the world. Its population is well educated, with a literacy rate of 98 percent, and its citizens have a life expectancy of over 78 years, compared to 79.5 years for Americans. These positive characteristics, however, are offset by negative factors. The population growth rate for Cuba is negative, largely due to a net migration rate out of the country of -3.64 percent. People may live a relatively long time on the island but are not entirely happy with the quality of life. Economically, Cuba has a GDP of $121 billion, which is the 68th largest in the world, and per capita GDP of $10,200 is 117th among the states of the world. The Cuban economy has been unstable since the demise of the Soviet Union in 1991 ended Soviet support for the Cuban regime, estimated at between four and six billion dollars annually. To try to stabilize the economic situation, the regime has engaged in some attempts to loosen control and allow very limited private economic activity, and the reestablishment of relations with the United States is at least partially designed to stimulate American tourism.

The political situation is, and has been for over a half-century, the major problem for the island and its relations with the United States. Since the revolution succeeded in 1959, the country has been ruled with an iron hand by one of the two Castro brothers. The regime's founder, Fidel, ruled until 2008, when he turned over the presidency to his brother Raúl. The heart of the exile community's wrath is directed toward the Castro regime personally: many exiles, for instance, were wealthy, upper-class Cubans who fled to the United States after Castro ordered the expropriation of their wealth upon coming to power. In return, the Castro regime has hurled invective consistently at the Americans and has engaged in hostile acts such as agreeing to host the emplacement of Soviet nuclear-tipped missiles on the island in 1962, an action that precipitated the Cuban Missile Crisis. In return, it has been political suicide in Florida—and to a lesser extent nationally—not to condemn the Cuban regime and to perpetuate the embargo against the regime. This atmosphere of political recrimination has contributed enormously to the policy gulf between the two neighbors. Anti-Castroite exiles hope the situation will improve when the "biological solution" has occurred, but on the island itself, the shape and content of succession is not clearly established. Much of the future of Cuban politics and Cuban-American relations depends on how that succession turns out.

Basic U.S.-Cuban Relations

Given the history of animosity between Cuba and the United States for nearly six decades, the restoration of relations between the two countries represented a basic sea change in their relations. It is not unfair to say that since 1960, policy has consisted of glaring at one another across the Straits of Florida and occasionally condemning the other for one reason or another. A new era is about to unfold; nobody really knows what will happen.

Prior to the reopening of relations between the island and the Colossus of the North, U.S.-Cuban relations can be thought of as consisting of three distinct stages, including the unfolding contemporary stage. The experience of the two previous stages helps to establish the parameters within which those relations can evolve. The first two stages, predictably, are divided by the rise and rule of Castro, and the third begins but presumably will not end with a Castro in the Cuban presidency.

Relations before Castro

As the earlier discussion suggests, American interest, sometimes bordering on fascination, with Cuba spans the history of the United States. The third American president, Thomas Jefferson, was the first American leader to show an interest in annexing Cuba as a potential state, and this possibility has recurred periodically since. Much of the time, American attention was diverted to other priorities such as the settling of the American West, but Cuba never disappeared from the American radar altogether. After a conditioned Cuban independence (limited by the Platt Amendment) was sanctioned at the turn of the twentieth century, the annexation of Cuba was replaced by economic penetration and control, including corrupting influence such as the activities of the American mafia before Castro came to power.

The historical theme that arose from this experience was a kind of condescending paternalism that was almost certainly more revered by Americans than it was by most Cubans. Americans might look upon this process as beneficial, uplifting, and well intended, but Cubans almost certainly saw it as demeaning, corrupting, and exploitative as well. The lives of average Cubans might have been improved somewhat, but most of the benefits accrued to the American overlords, and many Catholic Cubans in Havana and other resort areas were offended at the quality of mafia-controlled night life designed for wealthy American tourists, notably gambling and the open operation of brothels. The activities of the American mob extended to official corruption in the government (an accusation frequently leveled at Batista), and the Cuban rural population was effectively reduced to the status of sharecroppers on their own land. By the middle 1950s, the situation for Cubans had deteriorated to the point that when Castro appeared on the scene and promised change, there was a ready audience for his appeals. Because he suppressed the Marxist content of his beliefs, his reforming message also appealed to Americans, many of whom saw the July 26 movement as a positive sign and Castro as a liberator of his people.

The Castro revolution was, in a very real sense, a rejection of American paternalism and exploitation. After his successful march on Havana in 1959, where the Cuban army essentially dissolved in the face of his advancing guerrilla forces, Castro rapidly consolidated power and instituted numerous Marxist-based reforms, including the expropriation of the property both of Americans and also wealthy, often professional Cuban members of the indigenous elite. Americans who lost their property responded by demanding payment for the value of their property, claims the Cuban government ignored and continues not to honor. Government seizure of property is an accepted right and practice under international law, but international legal conventions insist on providing just compensation for expropriated properties. The Americans were simply kicked out of Cuba, their pockets empty.

Wealthy displaced Cubans received the same treatment and responded by fleeing the country to the welcoming shores of South Florida. Both groups blamed Castro and hated him for their losses. The two groups have formed the heart of the anti-Castro movement ever since and have, until recently, had a virtual veto over U.S. policy toward Cuba. For this group, the precondition for any improvement in U.S.-Cuban relations has been the removal of the Castro brothers and their socialist policies from the Cuban political scene.

Relations under Castro

Since 1960, U.S. policy toward Cuba can be described succinctly: get rid of Castro by any means possible, and isolate and ignore the island and its problems until that has occurred. The corollary to that basic position has been that the Castro regime must be replaced by democratization on the island, including creating economic and political conditions that will permit Cuban refugees who choose to do so to return to Cuba with the opportunity to resume their pre-Castroite lives.

This American position arose from the circumstances of the Castro takeover. Many Americans were simply blindsided by the new regime's communization of the island, because they had not anticipated it and had instead believed him to be a liberal reformer toppling a hated dictator. Communization turned the Cuban economy upside down, to the chagrin and disadvantage of wealthy, generally conservative American investors, but it also had strategic implications with direct national security issues, particularly as Cuba joined the communist bloc and became a virtual dependent of the Soviet Union.

An evangelical, ideologically opposed regime in the Western Hemisphere violated U.S. hemispheric policy in place since the enunciation of the Monroe Doctrine of 1823 in three intolerable ways. First, it meant that Cuba could potentially be used as a naval platform to harass commerce moving through the Panama Canal. Second, the island could (and for a time did) serve as a launching pad from which Castro and his Soviet sponsors could launch efforts to destabilize, undercut, and replace American-influenced regimes in Central America with hostile Marxist regimes that could threaten Panama and the Canal Zone. Individually and in tandem, these problems directly threatened the core of U.S. hemispheric security policy, the sanctity of the Panama Canal and accesses to it. From a geopolitical perspective, this threat overrode all other objections to Castro because, as Eriksen points out, "Stability, not democracy, is the watchword in the Pentagon and the Miami-based US Southern Command" toward Cuba.

The third strategic difficulty was the possibility that Cuba could be used by the Soviet Union as a nearby launching pad for military efforts against the American mainland. This is exactly what happened in 1962. At the time, the Soviets were far behind the United States in deployed nuclear strategic weapons, and sought to narrow that gap by sneaking intermediate-range nuclear-tipped rockets into Cuba, from which they could menace most of the American east coast. When the United States discovered preparations for the missiles and the presence of Soviet ships headed for Cuba with the first rockets onboard, the result was a confrontation: the explosive Cuban Missile Crisis. For thirteen days, the world waited with bated breath to see if Nikita Khrushchev would bend to the American demand not to complete the emplacement or face the direst of consequences. In the end, the Soviets backed down and the crisis passed (the definitive accounts are Allison and Zelikow and Kennedy and Schlesinger). It is generally acknowledged to have been the closest the two countries came to nuclear war, and it is arguable that the roots of the end of the Cold War were sown in the sober analysis of what might have happened (see Snow 1987).

Disposing of the Cuban dictator and his regime has proven easier said than done—witness their longevity. The earliest attempt was the Bay of Pigs, a plot devised and organized by Allen Dulles and his colleagues in the CIA and carried out, much to his later chagrin, by President Kennedy in 1961 shortly after his inauguration (see Kinzer). In subsequent years, the CIA joined forces with the American mafia (whom Castro also kicked out of Cuba without compensation) to try to assassinate the Cuban leader in a series of attempts worthy of the Keystone Kops. Suddath describes a "years-long series of increasingly far-fetched attempts on Castro's life" as part of something called Operation Mongoose. "Between 1961 and 1963," she says, "there were at least five plots to kill, maim, or humiliate the Cuban leader using everything from exploding seashells to shoes dusted with chemicals to make his beard fall out." While these kinds of efforts became less frequent (especially after Kennedy's assassination), this fanatically anti-Castro approach survived and prospered for years thereafter. As Sweig (2007) puts it, "For decades, a vocal minority of hardline exiles—some of whom directly or indirectly advocated violence or terrorism to overthrow Castro—have had a lock on Washington's Cuba policy."

Beyond efforts to physically remove Castro from the scene, the heart of U.S. Cuban policy has been to make life on Cuba as economically miserable as possible in the hope that doing so would cause the Cubans on the island somehow to demand and accomplish his overthrow. The major instrument of this policy has been economic sanctions in the form of a comprehensive economic embargo of the island that the United States has endeavored—with mixed success—to get other countries to join. The intent was to isolate Cuba from the outside world through economic and other restrictions that extended to areas such as communications and travel. Originally, these punitive actions were justified in terms such as just compensation for those who had property seized by the Castro regime, but had gradually evolved as the basis of an overall strategy to force regime change.

These policies have become increasingly controversial. Attempts to kill the officials of foreign governments are, of course, illegal, and invite reprisals against one's own leaders, and the isolation of the Cuban economy has been attacked as well as a policy that could not be sustained against any other country (Iran is a partial exception), and that has endured only because of the power of the exile community. That power cannot be overstated: a contrast regarding the immigration policies of the United States toward the citizens of the two countries featured in this chapter reveals a very hostile attitude toward undocumented Mexican immigrants compared to the virtual embrace of Cubans who navigate the Florida Straits and wade ashore in Florida. That balance of power may, however, be changing.

Contemporary Post-Recognition Relations

The relationship between Cuba and the United States since the two countries agreed to resume diplomatic ties is both fundamentally changed and not changed at all. The basic change is in bilateral atmospherics: the United States (and many Americans) do not like the Castro brothers or the communist regime they created any more today than they did before, but representatives of the two countries meet openly, both have reopened embassies in the other's capital, the president of the United States has conducted a state visit to Havana, and travel and tourism to Havana permit and even encourage people-to-people interchange, including communications between families divided by the reaction to Castro's takeover. The human landscape is changing.

Policy differences have not changed, although the new atmosphere and the death of Fidel Castro may encourage the kind of dialogue in which progress can be made. With the Soviet Union gone and communism an anachronistic holdout in only a few places, Cuba no longer poses any particular threat to the United States, an improvement from the Cold War era. The United States continues to condemn both the authoritarianism and socialist economics of the Castro regime, but behind the scenes has attempted, and will continue to attempt, to cajole both political democratization and the introduction of aspects of capitalist economics. As long as Raúl Castro remains in power, it is unlikely that there will be overt, dramatic Cuban reforms that can be interpreted as concessions or capitulation to the Americans, but slow reform and change will likely continue quietly, a phenomenon the United States will probably equally quietly applaud.

There are two major policy schisms that are holdovers from the "era of bad feelings." The most important is the status and continuation of the economic embargo, the resolution of which will require concessions on each side to resolve satisfactorily for all concerned. The other is the continuing status of Guantanamo Bay Naval Base, a sore point mostly for the Cubans whose importance to the United States is primarily its value as a place to detain enemy combatants in the war on terror.

In substantive terms, the embargo is by far the more consequential and is at the heart of the controversy over U.S. policy toward Cuba. In essence, the embargo damages the Cuban economy and thus the standards of living of Cubans. As long as the embargo is in place, relations between the two countries cannot be fully "normal." The embargo was imposed to force change in Cuba, including both political and economic liberalization and indemnification of Cubans and Americans whose property was seized and not compensated for by the regime.

The question about the embargo from an American perspective is whether it has worked, and there are two basic positions. The first, expressed by Haass, is that "the American policy of isolating Cuba has failed." The evidence for this assertion is that it has failed to move Cuba in the directions for which it was created after over fifty years of enforcement. Cubans may have suffered from the embargo, but Cuba has not changed much. Embargo supporters vehemently oppose any relaxation or abrogation of the embargo on the grounds that leverage would be lost in the embargo's absence, that doing so would effectively reward what they consider the Castro regime's bad behavior, and that it would remove any incentive for the regime to reform. These two positions have tended to cleave along liberal-conservative lines, and at least until recently, the exile community has been able to block relaxation of the policy.

The result is a quandary for the United States. Cuba suffers from the embargo and the United States does not incur major costs, so that the Cubans are more anxious to see the policy rescinded than are Americans. The key element is how to break the logjam. The Americans hold the stronger hand, because this country enforces the embargo without suffering its consequences, except in minor, symbolic ways such as easy legal access to Cuban cigars. The proud Cubans are wary of appearing to buckle under to the Americans and especially the exiles, both of which remain symbols of why there was a 1959 revolution. Who gives first?

Those who oppose change argue that Cuban reform is the precondition to relaxing or lifting the embargo. But there is a catch, as Shifter (2010) points out: "Lifting the embargo remains politically unrealistic absent significant reform on Cuba's part . . . [and] there is no indication the Cuban President Raúl Castro intends to adopt any such changes any time soon." But there is a conundrum involved. Haass explains, "Current law requires that Cuba becomes a functioning democracy before sanctions can be lifted. But it is precisely engagement that is far more likely to reform Cuba." The reestablishment of relations may prove a first step in that engagement.

The other major issue is Gitmo. In one sense, the base has lost much of its significance in national security terms: Cuba no longer menaces oceanic movement to and from the Panama Canal, and strategically, all Gitmo does is make it harder for the Cubans to reinstitute such practices in the future. Substantially, the only real function of Gitmo is as a place not on American soil to hold foreign terrorists whose detention on American territory would bring waves of domestic political recrimination. If the detention situation is voided, as President Obama promised but failed to do, that rationale would disappear as well, leaving the naval base largely an anachronism about which negotiations for the United States to renegotiate its status would seem possible as a way to improve overall relations.

In the absence of a strategic imperative for the naval base, negotiating change could improve U.S.-Cuban relations considerably at a low cost. The Cubans are humiliated by Gitmo's existence, the fact that it was essentially imposed upon them as a reminder of their weak status, and its use essentially as a Devil's Island–style penal colony. Any concession would probably be welcome, with shutting down the base and reverting it to Cuban sovereignty as their preferred outcome, but with lesser forms of change negotiable. The question is whether maintaining Gitmo is too high a price to pay for greasing the path to normalization.

U.S. Policy Options

The U.S.-Cuban standoff has, in some ways, been a model of ensuring that policy does not change and that efforts to resolve differences are not seriously addressed. The two countries have serious differences based on the consequences of the Cuban revolution of 1959. Since they broke relations in 1960, there were no open, formal contacts between the two until 2015, although Switzerland had provided good offices that allowed the two to talk informally at low levels since 1977. Both sides have taken positions that they have fully known the other side would not accept: democratization and economic reforms in Cuba that the regime finds humiliating and a repudiation of their rule, and economic sanctions on Cuba at the insistence of the Cuban exile community and the American political right.

These positions have been highly public, and to compromise on them would require the conceding side to engage in actions that would be seen as a public "defeat" for whoever took them. Since neither side will do this, the result (which is also the purpose of taking the position) is to make progress impossible. This has been the mode of the nonrelationship until 2015, when the two parties agreed to relatively small concessions that permitted the restoration of relations. Incremental chipping away at the negative façade is the only way in which progress can be achieved. Prior to

2015, nobody seriously tried. How much has changed and thus what may be possible remains a matter of disagreement.

Going forward, the question is whether a conciliatory approach will become the norm and allow incremental improvement in the relationship. For the United States, this means showing a willingness to loosen economic restrictions gradually in return for Cuban agreement to meet some American demands in areas such as imprisonment of political dissidents and making it easier for Cuban citizens to engage in market economic activities such as opening small businesses (restaurants in Havana to service the tourist trade offer an example). If such activities are to result in real improvement, they need to be gradual enough so that neither side appears to be giving too much to the historically hated other side. The failure to do so could bring negative reactions in both countries that would undermine the effort.

One remarkable thing about the process is how little overt, emotional opposition there was to it in Washington, especially in the lead-up to a very vituperative 2016 presidential election campaign. The old coalition in the United States that had persuaded the George W. Bush administration to pass even more restrictive acts against Cuba in the 2000s was unsuccessful in preventing or making the case effectively against improved relations in 2015. Indeed, there was very little overt partisan outcry, especially from the exile community, and one can only ask why—an important consideration in assessing the likelihood of further progress toward greater normalization in a new administration. Is the reason demographic—the gradual replacement of the original exile community with a newer generation born and raised in the United States who has never known their relatives on the island? Has the recognition that Cuba no longer poses any realistic threat to the United States taken hold? Have the Americans clamoring for compensation for expropriated Cuban holdings died or given up? In Havana, did the recognition that the biological solution clock is ticking cause the Castro brothers to mellow or try to create a new context in Cuban-U.S. relations after they depart? At the most extreme, can Cuba and the United States be friends again after over a half century of being adversaries?

CONCLUSION

One geographic blessing the United States has enjoyed is that it is surrounded by neighboring countries that are too small or weak to pose a threat to it or that do not bear enough animus to make life more difficult for the United States. The flip side of that virtue, however, is that being one of those neighbors means you live in the sometimes hostile shadow of a country for which the nickname "Colossus of the North" is not meant as a term of endearment. At one time or another, the United States has cast covetous eyes at numerous neighbors and has engaged in hostile and even condescending actions that would not have been possible against a more powerful opponent. Both of the neighbors discussed in this chapter have been victims of American wrath at one time or another. Their ability to fend off American blandishments has been different.

Of the two neighbors, Mexico is the larger and more geopolitically consequential, but it is also less than half the size of the United States by standard measures such as territory and population and is far less powerful militarily. In addition, it shares a 1,933-mile border with the Americans, a line drawn geographically to its disadvantage as the result of often violent encounters during the nineteenth century that ended with Mexico being forced grudgingly to cede ground to the United States. The location of the border is no longer a matter of active dispute between the two countries, but it remains a matter of symbolic contention between them nonetheless. The human flow across the border, the transport of illegal drugs in one direction and weapons in the other, and the prospect that terrorists might slip across the frontier from Mexico to America are all concerns of the United States that create tensions between the two that are disproportionately and, in Mexican eyes, unfairly directed toward them.

The immigration question highlights the asymmetry of relations. One way to look at the problem is in terms of supply and demand. If there were adequate economic opportunities in Mexico and Central America, for instance, economic migration would be far less of a problem. Moreover, part of the attraction for going north arises from the fact that the immigrants indeed can find employment, often with American employers who knowingly break American laws to hire and retain them. There are places for them in the United States because they will do work—the 3-D jobs—that Americans will not. Looked upon this way, the problem is not so much the porosity of the Mexican border as it is in correcting conditions to the south that drive workers north and to decrease their incentive to try by making jobs less plentiful. Similarly, one answer to illicit drugs coming across the border is to attack demand for them. In the American political dialogue, the answer to both is how to build an impermeable wall along the border.

Cuba has also suffered indignity at the hands of the United States. The yearning eyes of the Americans have frequently peeked over the Florida Straits, from the period before the American Civil War through the formal declaration of Cuban independence, about annexing the island to the United States. That became impractical in 1903, but was replaced by a degrading American economic imperialism that left many Cubans the virtual lieges of American absentee landholders. The result was that Cuba was an economic, if not officially a political, dependent of the United States.

For all its other sins, the Castro revolution did create autonomy for the island from the colossus. Communism may not have created prosperity for

Cubans, but it removed the long shadow of the United States from their affairs. Their thirty-year alliance with the Soviet Union created tensions and precluded the emergence of renewed relations with the Americans, but being under the Soviet wing also protected Cuba from American domination. The price was a deep resentment by the Americans and exiled Cubans victimized by communization. The demise of the Soviet Union left them potentially vulnerable once again, but it also removed some of the basis of animus that is reflected in the reinstatement of relations.

For the rest of the Western Hemisphere, the presence and embrace of the Americans has been and continues to be a mixed bag, and the resulting ambiguity is especially evident for those located most closely to the United States. It is a simple and unavoidable fact that the United States is the biggest and most powerful country in the neighborhood, and trying to establish an equal footing with it is a constant, frustrating struggle.

STUDY QUESTIONS

1. The Mexican-American relationship has been described as revolving around borders. What does that depiction mean? What are the functions of borders? How does the U.S.-Mexico relationship fit into those categories? Identify the major issues between the countries in these terms.

2. What is the problem of undocumented immigrants from Mexico and Central America in both American and Mexican terms? Is the border issue the cause or a symptom of the problem? Discuss and assess the innuendos and possible solutions to the problem. Is it more of a line-of-control or gateway problem? Why?

3. The flow of illicit drugs across the Mexican border into the United States is a major problem for both countries but for different reasons. Discuss the problem from both countries' perspectives. What are the possible solutions? How does the capture and imprisonment of El Chapo serve as an example of this problem as a bilateral foreign policy issue?

4. The border is the symbol of the tensions and disagreements in U.S.-Mexican relations, if not necessarily the cause of those problems. What options are available to the United States to deal with those problems? Is the proposed fence along the entire 1,933-mile length of the border (a line-of-control solution) the answer? What alternatives are available? Discuss.

5. Trace and typify the early history of U.S. relations with Cuba, up to and including its role in Cuban independence and limitations on that independence. What is the nature of the U.S.-Cuban relationship that arises from the history? Explain.

6. Why are the economic embargo and the future status of Guantanamo Bay Naval Base the two most important issues facing Cuba and the United States? What is the basis for, nature of, and consequence of the embargo on Cuba? Why is "Gitmo" such a sore subject for the Cubans? Discuss.

7. How has American domestic politics affected the nature of U.S.-Cuban relations under the Castro brothers? How has it affected the tone and sometimes bizarre nature of those relations?

8. How have circumstances changed the environment of U.S.-Cuban relations? What is different about Gitmo? The basis of advocacy of the embargo? The support base for punitive measures toward Cuba? Discuss each.

BIBLIOGRAPHY

Allison, Graham T., and Philip Zelikow. *The Essence of Decision: Explaining the Cuban Missile Crisis.* 2nd ed. New York: Longman, 1999.

Andreas, Peter. *Border Games: Policing the U.S.-Mexico Divide.* Ithaca, NY: Cornell University Press, 2009.

Beezley, William, and Michael Meyer, eds. *The Oxford History of Mexico.* New York: Oxford University Press, 2010.

Bonner, Robert C. "The New Cocaine Cowboys: How to Defeat Mexico's Drug Cartels." *Foreign Affairs* 89, no. 4 (July/August 2010): 35–47.

Camp, Roderic Ai. *Politics in Mexico: Consolidation or Decline?* 6th ed. New York: Oxford University Press, 2013.

Carbonal, Nestor. "Think Again: Engaging Cuba." *Foreign Policy* (online), April 10, 2009.

Carpenter, Ted Galen. *The Fire Next Door: Mexico's Drug Violence and the Danger to America.* Washington, DC: Cato Institute Press, 2012.

Cooke, Julia. *The Other Side of Paradise: Life in the New Cuba.* Berkeley, CA: Seal, 2014.

De Palma, Anthony. *The Man Who Invented Fidel: Castro, Cuba, and Herbert L. Matthews of the* New York Times. New York: PublicAffairs, 2006.

Dominguez, Esteban Morales, and Gary Prevost. *U.S.-Cuban Relations: A Critical History.* Lexington, MA: Lexington, 2008.

Edmonds-Poli, Emily, and David A. Shirk. *Contemporary Mexican Politics.* 3rd ed. Lanham, MD: Rowman & Littlefield, 2013.

English, T. J. *Havana Nocturne: How the Mob Owned Cuba . . . and Then Lost It to the Revolution.* New York: Morrow, 2009.

Eriksen, Daniel P. "After Fidel, Oh Brother. . . ." *Current History* 106, no. 697 (February 2007): 91–94.

Finan, William W., Jr. "Has the Cuban Moment Arrived?" *Current History* 109, no. 715 (February 2009): 93–94.

Ganster, Paul, and David E. Lorey. *The Mexican Border Today: Conflict and Cooperation in Historical Perspective.* Lanham, MD: Rowman & Littlefield, 2015.

Gonzalez, Francisco. "Drug Violence Isn't Mexico's Only Problem." *Current History* 110, no. 733 (February 2011): 68–74.

———. "Mexico's Drug Wars Get Brutal." *Current History* 108, no. 715 (February 2009): 72–76.

Grillo, Ioan. *El Narco: Inside Mexico's Criminal Insurgency.* New York: Bloomsbury, 2011.

Haass, Richard N. "Forget about Fidel." *Newsweek* (online), March 7, 2009.

Haney, Patrick J., and Walt Vanderbush. *The Cuban Embargo: Domestic Politics of American Foreign Policy.* Pitt Latin American Series. Pittsburgh: University of Pittsburgh Press, 2005.

Hober, Stephen, Herbert S. Klein, Noel Maurer, and Kevin Middlebrook. *Mexico since 1980.* Cambridge, UK: Cambridge University Press, 2008.

Kennedy, Robert F., and Arthur Schlesinger Jr. *The Thirteen Days: A Memoir of the Cuban Missile Crisis.* New York: Norton, 1999.

Kinzer, Stephen. *The Brothers: John Foster Dulles, Allen Dulles, and Their Secret World War.* New York: Times Books, 2013.

Krikorian, Mark. "Bordering on CAFTA: More Trade, Less Immigration." *National Review* (online), July 28, 2005.

Lowenthal, Abraham. "Obama and the Americas: Promise, Disappointment, Opportunity." *Foreign Affairs* 89, no. 4 (July/August 2010): 110–24.

Nevins, Joseph. *Gatekeepers and Beyond: The War on "Illegals" and the Remaking of the U.S.-Mexico Boundary.* 2nd ed. New York: Routledge, 2010.

O'Neil, Shannon. "The Real War in Mexico: How Democracy Can Defeat the Drug Cartels." *Foreign Affairs* 88, no. 4 (July/August 2009): 63–77.

Payan, Terry. *The Three U.S.-Mexican Border Wars: Drugs, Immigration, and National Security.* Westport, CT: Praeger Security International, 2006.

Rozental, Andrés. "The Other Side of Immigration." *Current History* 106, no. 697 (February 2007): 89–90.

Shifter, Michael. "Latin America's Drug Problem." *Current History* 106, no. 697 (February 2007): 58–63.

———. "Obama and Latin America: New Beginnings, Old Frictions." *Current History* 109, no. 724 (February 2010): 67–73.

Snow, Donald M. *Cases in International Relations.* 6th ed. New York: Pearson, 2015.

———. *The Necessary Peace: Nuclear Weapons and Superpower Relations.* Lexington, MA: Lexington, 1987.

Staten, Clifford L. *The History of Cuba.* 2nd ed. Greenwood Histories of the Modern Nations. Westport, CT: Greenwood, 2015.

St. John, Rachel. *Line in the Sand: A History of the Western U.S.-Mexican Border.* America in the World. Princeton, NJ: Princeton University Press, 2011.

Suddath, Claire. "A Brief History of U.S.-Cuba Relations." *Time,* April 15, 2009.

Sweig, Julia. "Castro's Last Victory." *Foreign Affairs* 86, no. 1 (January/February 2007): 39–56.

———. *Cuba: What Everyone Needs to Know.* 3rd ed. New York: Oxford University Press, 2016.

CHAPTER 7

Africa

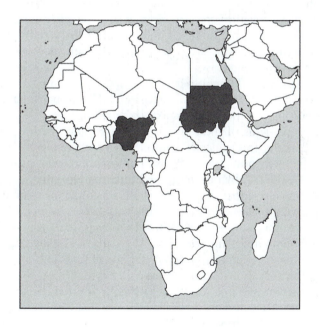

A frica is, in many important ways, the enigma of the world's populated continents. It occupies 20.4 percent of the world's landmass,
second among inhabited continents to Asia at 21.2 percent. It is the only
continent other than Asia with a population of over a billion people
(1,156,434,405 in 2015, almost one-sixth of the world's total). That population is the fastest growing of any part of the world: Africa's population
has grown fivefold since 1960, compared to a global increase of 2.8 times.
By further contrast, the population of Europe has grown a comparatively
paltry 1.36 times its 1960 total.

Africa is also one of the most demographically and politically diverse
parts of the world. There are fifty-four independent countries on the continent compared to a little more than a dozen in North America, depending
on how North America is defined. Virtually all African countries were parts
of the European colonial empires built during the seventeenth to twentieth
centuries and achieved their independence in the last half century as part of
the general decolonization of the world that occurred after the end of World
War II. The process of national self-determination is not complete: South
Sudan, one of the countries featured in this chapter, successfully seceded
from Sudan in 2011, and it is not likely to be the last state in Africa to seek
an independent path. Many other states display the same basic characteristic that led to South Sudanese separatism: multinationalism along tribal/
ethnic, linguistic, historical, and especially religious lines.

Despite these kinds of indicators of its importance, Africa remains the
most marginalized and neglected continent on the globe. Most of its countries are desperately poor, often deprived of natural resources and educated
populations, and in obvious need of humanitarian and developmental
assistance that is in global short supply. Oil is its most prominent resource,
but it is a mixed blessing in most of the countries in which it is located,
because the competition over its control by subnational groups often leads
to considerable conflict and violence. The Biafran War of 1967–1970 in
Nigeria and the competition between the Sudan and South Sudan in the
twenty-first century, both discussed here, are evidence. At the same time,
Africa has become notable for its negatives. It is, after all, the continent
on which both AIDS and the Ebola virus were first discovered, and it has
become the secondary home of increasing terrorism in the form of Islamic
terrorist organizations operating in Saharan Africa and further south in
parts of central Africa. These sources of instability and insecurity are both
supranational (the presence of IS and Al Qaeda variants) and more local,
from Boko Haram in Nigeria to the Lord's Resistance Army in eastern Africa.
As Dowden puts it, "Hell has seized parts of the continent in recent times."
That hell shows little sign of leaving.

Africa is such a large and diverse area that most generalizations have so
many exceptions as to be of limited helpfulness. Generically, people divide

the continent along three geographic lines that have distinctive topographies, peoples, and problems. Northern, or Saharan, Africa touches on the Mediterranean Sea on the north and extends southward through the Sahara Desert area. Most of its countries are Islamic, and both they and the desert are gradually moving southward, bring their religion and culture and problems with them. In the general Sahel region, they collide with central Africa, which is physically distinguished by greater levels of vegetation and large amounts of water, and is populated by people who are more generically African and more diverse ethnically, religiously, and in almost all other ways. Central Africa is further subdivided into eastern and western areas, each with its distinctive characteristics and problems. In southern Africa, the rain forests and lowlands of central Africa give way to savannah lands where there is greater available land for farming and animal husbandry. It is also where rare gems such as diamonds and strategic minerals such as titanium are found, and it is the area with the largest European population of any part of the continent.

Africa is also the continent that has been most often globally ignored, and the United States is no exception to this observation. Nobody in the State Department or elsewhere within the government would admit it in so many words, but Africa is the true backwater of American foreign policy. From a strictly geopolitical vantage point, there are relatively few vital or even very important American interests engaged in most African states. The exceptions to that rule are countries that have important natural resources (like Nigerian oil), strategic location (such as South Africa or Djibouti), or places that have had extraordinary levels of the worst kinds of violence (like Rwanda or Sudan). Many other countries have had serious troubles that occasionally engage American attention such as the western African countries where the Ebola epidemic was most severe, but these involvements are either limited geographically or of a lower general order of priority compared to issues in other parts of the world that demand U.S. attention.

In a place as large and diverse as Africa, it is probably impossible to choose a pair of countries to explore in their relations with the United States that would meet anybody's definition of "representativeness" in the sense of being prototypical examples of relations with the continent's countries. The two countries chosen are the Sudans—the Republic of Sudan and its offshoot, South Sudan—and Nigeria. The Sudanese case is chosen because it contains so many of the problems of the continent writ large—multiple ethnicities and religions, multiple civil conflicts such as Darfur and the war that eventuated in the secession of South Sudan, even the pernicious impact of discovering and exploiting petroleum on ongoing political dynamics. Nigeria shares most of these characteristics, to which can be added the impact of terrorist activity in its territory. Nigeria is the most populous country in Africa and has its largest petroleum industry, making it the most consequential black majority state on the continent and the country that probably receives the most attention by the outside world. That much of that attention currently arises from the crisis with Boko Haram speaks to the quality of Africa as a foreign policy concern for the United States and most of the rest of the world.

AFRICA AS GEOPOLITICAL MAELSTROM

The most basic problem that pervades Africa is the artificiality of most of its states. Almost all of them—with the partial exception of some of the Saharan states and a few east African states—have little historical rationale for existing within their current boundaries. Rather, most of them resemble the boundaries given them by the European colonialists from whom they received independence mostly in the hasty manner with which most de-colonization was accomplished, and the colonialists generally had no idea who—what groups with what natural ties or animosities—lived within the units they aggregated as colonies. "African states," as Dowden summarizes, "were formed by foreigners, lines drawn by Europeans on maps of places they often had never been to." When the final partition of the African interior was made in the late nineteenth century in Berlin, for instance, the participants lacked accurate topographical maps of the area they were carving into colonies, much less any demographic characteristics. It was not deemed important then; it is now.

The basic characteristic of African countries is their *multinationalism*. In *National Security*, sixth edition, I have defined this quality as "the situation where there are multiple groups in a country to which the members proclaim greater loyalty than they do to the state." In Africa, that primary loyalty has normally been tribal and ethnic, where people think of themselves as members of their tribal grouping before they think of themselves as nationals of the country in which they live. The resulting divisions are complex and pervasive: there are, for instance, more than 2,000 languages reflecting different cultures on the continent and spread among its fifty-four countries. These loyalties preceded the colonial experience, and in almost no cases was there any attempt by European colonialists to overcome this parochialism and to instill a primary loyalty focus on the larger unit to which they would eventually grant independence. Since the primary purpose of colonies was to exploit them and to turn a profit (which usually did not occur), nurturing intertribal cooperation could only have negative outcomes such as bringing colonial subjects together jointly to throw out the invaders. Having subjects who disliked one another as much as—or even more than—they disliked the overlords simply made colonial administration easier than it might be should loyalties be transferred to the unit that would eventually be granted sovereignty.

Ethnic differences tended to overlay other differences. In parts of Africa, for instance, an early and perverse European-inspired practice was to enlist coastal tribes to go inland and capture members of other tribes for sale to slave traders. The profits could and often were used to purchase weaponry that aided the continuing slave trade and to shift the balance of power toward those who colluded with the European traders. South Sudan was, for instance, one of the prime sources of slaves obtained in this manner.

Another overlaying influence was religion, a factor that continues to exacerbate instability in a large number of African countries, including both contained in this chapter. In general terms, there are three different constellations of religions in competition in different countries. Native animists of one variety or another often represent the pre-European majority and persist in generally less developed areas of many countries. The colonial intrusion brought with it Christian missionaries and thus both Protestant and Catholic faithful. More recently, Islamic forces have infiltrated from the Middle East and North Africa, moving steadily southward into eastern and central African countries. Conflict between Muslim and non-Muslim forces overlaps with ethnic differences in a number of countries, prominently including both Sudan/South Sudan and Nigeria.

In addition, the colonial experience, although humiliating in all its African guises, was different depending on which colonial ruler was exercising it. Colonial rule was generally harsh and exploitive wherever it existed, but some colonizers were at least slightly better both about educating and "civilizing" the indigenous populations than others, making the process of assimilation more or less difficult for, say, subjects in a British or French colony than natives living in a Portuguese or Belgian dependency. Nowhere, it should be noted, did the colonizers prepare the population for the transition to successful self-rule, since such preparation would have implicitly imparted skills that might have proven useful in organizing the expulsion of the European overlords.

All these kinds of factors are staples in the African fabric. There is not a single state on the continent that is not multinational to some extent, and the result is at least some nationalist deficit in each country that impedes a united support for the government or the country itself. In some places the divisions are deeper than in others, but they exist everywhere and form the potential for unrest. In its worst form, in places such as the Darfur region of Sudan or Rwanda, the results can be tragic and bloody enough that the outside world cannot ignore them and acts to mitigate the disaster, sometimes half-heartedly. Religious evangelism, particularly by Muslim acolytes, is a common factor in much ongoing instability, as Muslim conversion—often by the sword—moves relentlessly southward. One of its expressions is in the rise of Islamic fundamentalist terrorism in a number of African countries. Economic and political development remains a precarious work in progress in many places, and the clash among population groups for the often meager fruits of that process is an underlying current, especially when its source—such as petroleum or mineral wealth—is regionally and thus ethnically distinct.

The discussion that follows features two states of Africa where these dynamics are particularly evident. Sudan/South Sudan suffered from a long and bloody process of attempted assimilation followed by active efforts of separatism that resulted in the fracture of the country into two entities in 2011. The Republic of Sudan, the larger remnant, is almost entirely Muslim, and its attempts to force its language and religious beliefs on the animists and Christians of its southern region, South Sudan, was a major factor in the successful secession of the latter from the former. Oil discoveries and the competition for the wealth they produce animated the conflict. Even separation has not entirely solved the problems of either, and more or less active civil wars continue against both by the peoples who form the population of each. Nigerian instability is ethno-religious as well and has been an ongoing problem since the Biafra Civil War of 1967–1970, a conflict, symbolically enough, largely created by the attempted secession of that part of Nigeria where the oil is found (largely the Niger Delta) from the rest of the country.

CASE: THE UNITED STATES AND SUDAN/SOUTH SUDAN

On a continent in which artificial states are the norm, Sudan, at least as constituted before the 2011 secession of the south, is one of the more blatant examples of a country for which there is little reason to exist in its boundaries. The idea of a place called Sudan was a product of European colonialism extended to Africa. It began with a joint Turkish-Egyptian invasion in 1821 that was primarily concerned with the dual imperatives of spreading Islam southward into Africa and protecting the sources and flow of the Nile River. The latter represented a strategic concern. Egypt's historic claim to status was as a granary for the region given life by Nile waters. The White Nile rises from Lake Victoria in Uganda, the Blue Nile in Ethiopia, and both flow into Sudan, meeting in Khartoum, Sudan, and then flowing into Egypt and eventually the Mediterranean Sea. When Great Britain entered and colonized Egypt, protection of the Nile caused it to enter what became Sudan.

The original Sudan mainly consisted of the area around the capital of Khartoum, which was predominantly Muslim and effectively controlled by three local tribes that eventually gained control of the whole of what became Sudan. All this evolution goes back to the 1821 invasion, and as Teny-Dhurgon puts it, "Sudan in its present boundaries did not exist" before then. The entity created included both the Muslim north of Sudan and what is now South Sudan, which was culturally, ethnically, and linguistically distinct from the rest but was part of the area through which the White Nile flowed.

When Sudan achieved independence in 1956, there were thus two distinct parts of a new country that was very diverse anyway. As Natsios reports, the original population contained 597 distinct tribes that spoke 133 different languages. The population is also distinguished by religion, which became the strong basis for separation. According to pre-secession *CIA World Factbook* figures, about 40 percent of the population was Muslim and was concentrated in the northern areas that remained part of Sudan after 2011. That population, most of which considers itself Arab, was also fractured. Because of the dominance of the three tribes around Khartoum governing the country, there were uprisings against Khartoum within other Muslim regions as well. The most notorious was the uprising in the western area of Darfur near the Chadian frontier, where an estimated 400,000 Darfuris were killed by "rebel" forces known as the *Janjaweed* in the 1990s and early 2000s (a fragile ceasefire has been in place since 2007 in the region). In the south, almost all of the population (57 percent of the non-Arabs) considers itself African, but is divided into numerous tribes, the two largest of which are the Dinka and Nuer, both of which were prominent in the fighting leading to secession and to post-secession instability and violence in the new country.

The state of Sudan has been more or less constantly at war with itself since 1956. It has had two separate emphases. The struggle between north and south that eventuated in the secession of South Sudan is the oldest. A civil war, mostly caused by the attempt of the rulers from the Islamic north to impose Islamic law, language, and lifestyle on the non-Muslim south, broke out the year independence was granted. This conflict is known as the First Civil War; it lasted until 1972, when a negotiated settlement granted substantial autonomy from Islamic domination to the dissenters centered in Juba in the south. This arrangement lasted until 1983, when a new, militantly Islamist regime came to power in Khartoum and began to enforce Islamic values—notably sharia law—nationwide. The south went into rebellion again, and the Second Civil War lasted until 2005, when the Comprehensive Peace Agreement (CPA) that opened the path to secession was negotiated with international assistance. This conflict occurred largely outside international public scrutiny; its most visible symbol was the so-called Lost Boys of Sudan, southern tribal members forced to flee the violence and to wander Africa until the 2005 CPA allowed them to return. Although statistics are not terribly precise, as many as 2.4 million were killed and another four million displaced in the two wars. The end of this process was the establishment of the state of South Sudan, which solved some north-south problems but left others behind.

The other emphasis of Sudanese instability has been among Muslims in the Islamic-dominated north. The ruling elite tribes based around Khartoum tend to be fundamentalist and evangelical in their orientation to a degree of intensity not shared by all Muslims in the north (now effectively the Republic of Sudan). The most notable intra-Muslim clash has been in the province of Darfur in the southwest part of current Sudan, where the attempts to apply fundamentalist Islam were resisted by the Darfuris and resulted in a virtual reign of terror by government-sponsored "militias" (the *Janjaweed*) to defeat their insurgency. There were abundant well-documented atrocities committed against the Darfuris that resulted in international efforts to settle the dispute and to protect the besieged natives of Darfur from further government atrocities. As many as 300,000 people were killed in the active phases of this conflict, which raged from early in the twenty-first century until 2007, when a UN force was dispatched to end fighting.

Sudan has always suffered from two basic problems that are exaggerated examples of dilemmas faced widely in Africa. The first is that the country (and now countries) lacks any sense of common national identity. As Williamson summarizes it, "No vision unites Sudan, no sense exists that various groups share a stake in the nation, no agreement pertains on what it is to be Sudanese." This multinationalism is reinforced by the second problem, which is a stark ethno-religious split between parts of the country. As noted, the north is dominated by people who consider themselves ethnic Arabs, who are adherents to a variant of the Islamic faith similar to Saudi Wahhabism, and who share an evangelism to spread their religious norms to nonbelievers, by the use of violence and coercion if necessary. The south, on the other hand, is composed of peoples who consider themselves to be African, generally practice either Christianity or traditional animism as their religion, and are resistant to conversion to Islamic religion and practices. These predilections are partly historic and linguistic: the north was influenced by the Egyptians and Turks, who brought Arabic with them, while the south was more influenced by a British presence that included adoption of English as the official language of South Sudan. These characteristics, it might be added, form part of the reason that Westerners are more drawn to South Sudan than they are to Sudan since the 2011 secession. That split has not, however, solved all the problems of either country.

Sudan and South Sudan: A Physical and Political Sketch

Before it split into two states, Sudan was one of the more physically formidable countries on the African continent. Located just south of Egypt and bordered by seven other east African states and the Red Sea, it was the largest country in Africa and the tenth-largest state in the world with a geographic mass roughly that of the United States east of the Mississippi River. With a Red Sea coastline just south of Egypt, its geopolitical position close to the Suez Canal was important to those heavily invested in that waterway (notably the British). The fact that the White and Blue Nile Rivers converge within its bounds and flow northward from Khartoum into Egypt makes it critical to the Egyptians.

The Sudan that attained independence in 1956 was always a politically unstable place. As noted, the bases of instability were partly ethnic and racial, pitting the self-styled Arabs of the north against the African population of the south, overlaid by strife within each part of the country. The major basis of political instability arose from the militant evangelism of the northern ruling tribes around Khartoum to impose their ascetic, fundamentalist interpretation of Islam both on less pious Muslims in the north and especially to impose their culture—including language and sharia law—on those who neither shared nor desired it.

The two Sudanese civil wars are the central political reality that comes from this clash and are the dominant political realities of Sudan's sixty-plus-years' existence. With a decade-long break between 1972 and 1983, when an interim ceasefire was in place, religiously motivated war was a constant until South Sudan overwhelmingly voted for and obtained the right to secede in a 2009 referendum that was implemented when an independent South Sudanese state was declared in Juba on July 9, 2011.

The two decades surrounding the movement to separation were the more spectacular. Distinctions included both the dynamics they demonstrated and the extent of opposition to the Khartoum regime. The second war followed the regime's institution of sharia law countrywide, which was a direct violation of the Addis Ababa agreement that had ended the first civil war. In January 1983, the government of Gaafar Muhammad Nimeiry abolished the southern region as an entity, declared Arabic the official language of the south, and transferred control of southern armed forces to the central government. Nimeiry was overthrown in 1986, and in 1989, a coup brought General Umar al Bashir to power. Bashir, who remains president, adopted a militant Islamist orientation (that included, among other things, offering sanctuary to Osama bin Laden) that further alienated southerners as well as less-committed Muslims within the northern part of the region.

The result was the two outbreaks of violence. The core of southern resistance was from southern units in the Sudanese army who rebelled against control by the northern government and coalesced under the banner of the Sudan People's Liberation Movement/Army (SPLM/A), led by Colonel John Garang, a Dinka southerner. This movement received support from surrounding Ethiopia, Eritrea, and Uganda. These countries and Kenya joined to try to moderate the slaughter of the war, which, after some predictable stops and starts, formed the basis for the CPA signed in 2005.

The other conflict, of course, has been in Darfur. This region, which has a long history of independence, became part of Sudan in 1956, but like the south, preferred autonomy, particularly in terms of the form of Islam they practiced. The Darfuris rebelled against Islamic fundamentalist initiatives by the government. Rebellions occurred from 1987 to 1989, from 1995 to 1999, and most infamously, from 2003 until 2007. During the latter phase, the fate of Darfur received international publicity. The government unleashed the *Janjaweed* on their murderous, genocidal campaign that killed many natives and sent millions of refugees across the border to Chad, where, in turn, their fate was publicized (strict, even draconian, censorship by the Sudanese government had limited information previously) and the UN and charitable organizations came to the aid of Darfur. As in South Sudan, that fighting officially stopped in 2007. African and UN peacekeepers have been in place since, but violence continues at a more irregular, reduced, and less publicized level. Darfur, and Khartoum's determination to subdue it and subject the population to their fundamentalist, even Salafist, style of Islam, remains a major barrier to improved U.S.-Sudanese relations.

The successful secession has left the former Sudan as two separate sovereign entities. Of these, the Republic of Sudan, which is the successor to the original country, is the larger and slightly less impoverished. Its physical territory is 718,723 square miles (slightly less than one-fifth the size of the United States), sixteenth-largest in the world, and almost three times the size of South Sudan. Notably given its population, only 6.76 percent of its land is arable. That population is 35.5 million, thirty-seventh largest in the world, and is three times that of the south. The population is 70 percent Muslim, mostly Sunni. The economy has a GDP of just under $90 billion (seventy-ninth in the world), and per capita GDP is $2,600 (182nd in the world).

South Sudan is both smaller and poorer. Its physical size, at 248,777 square miles, is slightly smaller than Texas and is forty-second-largest in the world. The dominant physical feature of the country is the Sudd, the world's largest wetlands, that covers 15 percent of the country. The population of the country is 11.6 million, and it consists of numerous African tribes in a similar manner to many sub-Saharan countries. The dominant tribes are the Dinka (36 percent of the population) and the Nuer (16 percent), and the two vie for political control. Most inhabitants are either Christian or animist, and the official language of the country is English, reflecting the British influence. At $14.7 billion, its GDP is 144th in the world, and its extreme poverty is illustrated by a per capita GDP of $1,400, 207th in the world. Over half the country's population lives below the poverty line of $1 a day in income.

The economic hope for Sudan arises from the discovery and exploitation of oil. Petroleum was originally discovered in parts of Sudan around where the current international boundary is located in 1974, and oil began to be produced in 1994, over half of which finds its way to market in China. Most of the oil is located in territory ceded to South Sudan, but that country is landlocked, and the only feasible way to get the oil to market is through Port Sudan, a part of Sudan on the Red Sea. Both countries see oil as a source of income to lift their populations out of extreme poverty, and so there have been and continue to be intense negotiations regarding the division of revenues to the source of the oil (South Sudan) and the route over which it must traverse to market (Sudan). Fighting in South Sudan has interrupted the flow since 2013, and an agreement was negotiated to resume production in August 2016. The fate of the agreement is problematical given the overall pattern of relations both between and internally in both countries, making a return to the mutually self-abnegating practice of shutting down oil production at least a possibility.

The major factor in Sudanese politics and in American relations with both countries has been the outcome of the second civil war between north and south. The root cause of rebellion that made separation the only sensible long-term solution arose from the fact that the two regions had been arbitrarily united in 1956 and never had any reason to form one country. As the second war dragged on, however, additional factors accumulated leading to its conclusion. Natsios lists three. First, the brutality of the regime's conduct of the war to end southern resistance became increasingly public despite Khartoum's efforts to hide it, especially since the underlying issue was portrayed in militant Islamic versus Christian terms, and its expense (along with Darfur) was draining regime coffers. Second, Africans in the south became increasingly alienated by the militant Islamism of Khartoum, which included the practice in the early 1990s of providing safe haven for militant Islamic terrorists, most notably bin Laden and his cohorts. The regime eventually backed away from this practice, and with American pressure, expelled Al Qaeda in 1996 (from which they migrated to Afghanistan). Third, and for some purposes most important, the discovery of oil in territories under contention in the war gave a strong economic incentive for both sides to reach a resolution favorable to them. These factors, and increasing international pressure on the Khartoum regime to cease its excesses in South Sudan and Darfur, helped lead to negotiations that eventually created the Republic of South Sudan.

The agreement that led to secession was completed in 2005 and was known as the Comprehensive Peace Agreement (CPA). It did several things. First, it created a "government of national unity" and established an autonomous "Government of South Sudan" (GOSS) with independent authority over most strictly southern concerns. This provision also guaranteed southern participation in governance in Khartoum. Second, it rescinded the most objectionable aspects of sharia law on non-Muslims, mandatory use of Arabic in the English-speaking south, and the attempted integration of southern military units (mostly affiliates of the Sudanese People's Liberation Army or SPLA) into the Sudanese Armed Forces (SAF). Third, it called for free and democratic elections throughout the country in 2009, which were later delayed until 2011. Fourth and most consequentially for the future, it set an interim period leading to a referendum on continued union for 2011. Finally, it called for establishing a special status for some contested areas along the frontier between the two states in places such as Abyei. The latter is still a matter of contention.

These were extraordinary concessions by the Khartoum government reflecting their growing image as a pariah state and their inability to subdue the revolutions against it, especially in the south. Its acquiescence was also reinforced by other dynamics, such as issuance of an arrest warrant by the International Criminal Court (ICC) against Sudanese president Bashir in 2009 on grounds of war crimes in Darfur (a charge Khartoum denies) and drops in the price of oil, revenue from which was the mainstay of the economy. In addition, the election of Barack Obama in 2008 was viewed by the Sudanese government as evidence that anti-African behavior might result in additional American displeasure with the regime in Khartoum.

In this setting, the CPA-mandated referendum was held in the south under international observation in January 2011. An overwhelming 98.6 percent of the 3.5 million registered southerners voted for secession, an outcome surprising only in its virtual unanimity. Given this mandate, the Sudanese government had little choice but to accept the results. The new Republic of South Sudan was born on July 9, 2011, in its capital of Juba. The U.S. delegation was led by Ambassador to the UN Susan Rice, and President Obama declared the event an "exercise in self-determination long in the making."

Basic U.S. Relations with Sudan/South Sudan

The United States has never had a significant relationship with Sudan; this condition is also largely true since South Sudanese secession. Much of the public attention has surrounded issues arising from human rights abuses and other excesses conducted by the Khartoum regime that reflect its fundamentalist Islamic orientation (which is similar to the faith practiced in Saudi Arabia); this has set the United States and Sudan at some odds and has strained relations between the two. The United States strongly objected to the regime providing refuge for bin Laden in the early 1990s, and its pressure helped cause the Sudanese government to expel Al Qaeda and its leader in 1996. The United States has also been among the loudest critics of the virtual genocide sponsored by Khartoum against the residents of Darfur. In addition, there has also been consistent, if low-visibility, opposition to the historic efforts of the Muslim north to suppress the residents of the south.

In the period leading to secession and since, the United States has "tilted" toward support of the south, a position made more difficult by complications, including tribal violence, that continue and center on the major tribes, the Dinka and the Nuer. The affinity for South Sudan arises from the fact that many of the South Sudanese are African, Christian, and English speakers, making them more apparently similar to Westerners than the Arab Muslims of the north. The south also has numerous adherents to traditional, animist beliefs that put them at some odds with the Christians, and this tribal/religious conflict makes both progress and stability in the new country more problematical than it might otherwise be.

Serious matters of contention between the two Sudans and within South Sudan make relations with the United States more difficult. Two issues divide the two states. The first is, as introduced earlier, the question of who receives what part of the revenue from the oil, and the second relates to the status of contested areas such as Abyei as part of one country or the other. The third issue, largely internal to South Sudan but partially manifested in the Abyei dispute, is the distribution of power in Juba along tribal lines. All of these questions are ongoing and are matters of at least some concern for the United States.

The question of Sudanese oil is the most important, high-stakes disagreement between the countries. The extreme poverty of the region meant that the discovery of petroleum in what is now South Sudan was a godsend in developmental possibilities. The estimated reserves are about 3.75 billion barrels, which is a modest twenty-ninth among national reserves worldwide, but in an area such as South Sudan, even a modest infusion of capital can make a sizable difference. When separation occurred, the areas containing oil were lost to the original Sudan, and the question was how Sudan could gain revenue from the resource they had lost.

As noted, South Sudan's landlocked condition provided an answer and a source of ongoing tension. Put simply, South Sudan has the oil but no way to get it to market except by shipment across some other country. Sudan, on the other hand, lacks oil but, according to Williamson, "there is no alternative route" for South Sudanese to the oceans to get its oil to market except across Sudan to Port Sudan. The source of South Sudan's leverage is the ability to withhold its product from distribution, and Sudan's is its ability to allow or forbid that product to cross its territory. The conflict is over how much Sudan can charge for transshipping availability, and the resulting issue is the division of oil revenues. Given their mutual history and need for capital, it is not an issue on which cooperation is likely. The leverage each has, of course, comes not only at the expense of their opponent but at their own as well. Unless they can agree on revenue division, South Sudan can withhold oil or Sudan can refuse to accept it: either side exercising its option creates an effective lose-lose situation in which both are deprived of the income.

That is exactly what has happened. In a dispute over income distribution in 2012, South Sudan suspended production, reducing to zero the revenues either side receives. Pre-secession figures indicate the dependence both governments had on oil revenue. Prendergast and Thomas-Jensen argue that "in 2008, oil sales accounted for 64 percent of revenues received by the government of national unity (the central government) a whopping 90 percent of revenue for the GOSS." More recent figures are unreliable, but since 2012, they have been reduced to nothing. The direness of the situation is made worse by the collapse of oil prices that began in 2013 and means that even should the two sides reach some kind of reconciliation on the issue, the revenues would be reduced. This collapse has left both states increasingly dysfunctional and incapable of performing basic services, which led Natsios to declare in 2012, "Sudan is becoming a failed state." The 2016 Fragile State Index prepared by the Fund for Peace places South Sudan second and Sudan fourth on its worldwide list. This situation demonstrates the dual liabilities of being highly economically dependent on a single commodity the value of which fluctuates greatly, and the vulnerability of having that resource as a key point of contention in an international dispute.

The second point of major contention is over the town of Abyei along the border between the two countries. Both claim sovereign rights over the municipality and surrounding area, and it has been a volatile symbol that Natsios describes as "the powderkeg of Sudan—the Kashmir of the north-south conflict." The city has a mixed Muslim and African population, although Africans of different tribes constitute a clear majority. It was an agenda item in the separation debate, but a crisis that is ongoing occurred when irregular members of the SAF invaded the city and sent roughly 100,000 citizens— mostly African—fleeing into the surrounding bush, from which many were unwilling to return out of fear for their lives. Because of this displacement, the disposition of Abyei was not included in the 2011 agreement, and it has remained a source of contention between the two states. The area remains a source of contention that impedes normalization of relations between them.

On October 31, 2013, a nonbinding referendum was held in Abyei to allow citizens to express their preferred future political status. The Muslim minority boycotted the voting, and over 99 percent of those who did vote said they preferred incorporation into South Sudan. A large part of the reason for this affinity is that, as Williamson points out, "The Abyei area . . . is home of the Ngok Dinka, the tribe to which many of the most prominent personalities in South Sudan belong." The Abyei area, of which the city is the major focal point, remains a point of major contention and sporadic violence, despite repeated attempts by outsiders, including Ethiopian peacekeepers sanctioned by the UN, to maintain order. As long as the issue remains unsettled, there seems to be little prospect of resolving other disputes between the two countries.

The basis of the third dispute is internal to South Sudan. At heart, it is a power struggle between the Dinka and the Nuer over power sharing. When South Sudanese independence was established, the presidency was awarded to a Dinka, Salva Kiir, who succeeded SPLA leader and presumptive political leader John Garang, who was killed in a 2005 helicopter accident. The vice presidency went to a Nuer, Riek Machar. In 2013, long-standing conflicts between the two tribes and their leaders erupted in violence, as Nuer units of the South Sudanese armed forces rebelled and widespread violence "with devastating implications for the South Sudanese" broke out, according to the U.S. State Department. With U.S. encouragement, negotiations to solve the dispute were commenced in Addis Ababa in December 2013 that resulted in an August 2015 Agreement to Resolve the Conflict in South Sudan (ARCSS) before scheduled 2018 elections. The situation is not much better in Sudan, where ongoing tensions in Darfur occur beside disputes over the South Kordofan and Blue Nile states.

The United States has adopted differential policies toward the chaos in both states. It has been especially critical of Sudan, largely because of its historic and episodic flirtation with Islamic extremism that, in 1997, caused the United States to include Khartoum on its list of terrorist states and to suspend relations with Sudan. Relations were reestablished in 2002 but were interrupted again with the outbreak of the alleged genocide in Darfur. Relations with Juba have been somewhat better but are restrained by the virtual anarchy and desperate plight of the residents of the country. As both countries plunge more deeply into failed-state status, the fate of the entire region comes into play, but especially the plight of South Sudan, a country whose birth was supported by the United States but which progressively resembles a lost cause. The question is what, if anything, the United States can and is willing, based in its own interests, to do about the situation on both sides of the Sudanese frontier.

U.S. Policy Options

The absence of important American interests in both Sudan and South Sudan severely limits the options the United States realistically has in terms of trying to influence the behavior of either country. Of the two sovereign states, American relations with Sudan are the more negative, dating back to Sudanese internal actions against both the South Sudanese and fellow Sudanese Muslims such as the citizens of Darfur. Similarly, American orientation toward that government has a negative focus on Khartoum because of its flirtation with extremist interpretations of Islam, up to and including support for terrorism that began American sanctions against the Sudanese regime; these continue to this day. As a result, American-Sudanese relations are distinctly cool and minimal, a situation with little impact on the United States and a small effect on Sudan. Symbolically, the United States did not have an ambassador to Khartoum as of mid-2016, although it does have a sitting ambassador in Juba.

Whenever Sudan has popped up on American policy radar, it has usually been for highly publicized negative actions by the Sudanese government. These are generally the result of some level of fundamentalist Islamic actions intended to bring non-Muslims in South Sudan or moderate Muslims in places such as Darfur into compliance with more fundamentalist, strict observance of Islam, such as the imposition of sharia law or mandatory use of Arabic on people uninterested in either requirement. These policies were applied periodically in relations toward the south that were prominent causes and manifestations in both civil wars between the regions. Very strict, threatening censorship kept most coverage of these events suppressed, but reports leaked out nonetheless. Americans and other Westerners were upset by the fact that many acts were against Christians (there were, for instance, periodic reports that the Sudanese were crucifying miscreants, a charge Khartoum denied). When Darfuris began to flood across the border into Chad, where the Sudanese could not censor reports of their plight, world public opinion was enraged and the world reacted with sanctions and international efforts to aid the victims once it became aware of them.

Lacking interests beyond humanitarian concerns, there was not a great deal the United States could do to bring about dramatic change in Sudanese behavior. The United States did declare Sudan a terrorist state in 1997 and imposed mandatory economic sanctions on the country, but the fact that the two countries never had significant economic interchange detracts from the effects these measures have. The United States provides humanitarian assistance to Darfuris. It provided $7.1 billion in humanitarian assistance to Darfur between fiscal years 2002 and 2015, none of which was filtered through the Sudanese government. It is also American policy to promote democratic development in the country, but this preference is more an admonition than anything else in these circumstances.

American relations with Juba are somewhat warmer but are limited by interest level and opportunity. The ability to provide meaningful assistance to the South Sudanese is made more difficult by ongoing chaos in the country, which has two sources. One is internal and represented by political infighting and violence between Dinka factions loyal to president Kiir and opponents who rally around Nuer deposed vice president Machar. The result of this fighting has been to displace large numbers of South Sudanese into internal displaced persons (IDP) status and further complicate running the country, including its basically failed economy. The other source of destabilization comes from the influx of Sudanese refugees of the fighting in South Kordo-fan and Blue Nile province into South Sudan. The United States provides humanitarian assistance to South Sudan and supports efforts to implement the Agreement to Resolve the Conflict in South Sudan (ARCSS) that was pro-posed by neighboring states in 2015. Until the internal situation stabilizes, there is very little the United States can reasonably do to improve materially the condition of beleaguered residents of the new republic.

The situation in the territory that was once Sudan and now contains two states, each of which has internal and international problems, is bleak. The secession was supposed to separate competing groups who were enemies on religious and ethnic grounds, but it has not succeeded in resolving the schisms that exist within the successor states. The result is a chaotic situa-tion where even well-intentioned aid can become a victim of the fighting, and the situation is made even worse by the stalemated dispute over oil rev-enues and the bottom falling out of the global petroleum market. Solving all these problems, assuming they are amenable to solution, will require concerted, dedicated, and probably firm action by the international com-munity, including the United States. It is not at all clear that the American government and people perceive enough interest in the outcome to invest meaningfully in the enterprise.

CASE: THE UNITED STATES AND NIGERIA

It is arguable that any country in Africa can be described as an enigma in one way or another, and Nigeria certainly fits that description. In many ways, it is one of the true bright spots of the continent. When African countries with the greatest economic potential are listed, Nigeria and South Africa are the two countries that often make international lists. Jim O'Neill of Goldman Sachs, for instance, has popularized two aspirant lists to major economic power positions: the MINT countries (Mexico, Indonesia, Nige-ria, and Turkey) and the BRICS (Brazil, Russia, India, China, and South Africa). Both lists were devised by analysts at Fidelity Investments, and they are the only compilations that contain any African members. At the same time, however, Nigeria has one of the world's shortest life expectancies (212th) at 52.6 years due to the continuing presence of AIDS, and a literacy rate of only about 62 percent. Great disparities in the quality of life among Nigerians are, in some ways, reminiscent of the demographics of India de-scribed in chapter 4.

Nigeria is also an incredibly diverse and politically fractious place. Largely thanks to its reserves of oil (discussed below), it has the potential to be a wealthy state, but the downturn in oil prices since 2013 has crippled the economy and relations with the United States, which used to be but no longer is the largest consumer of Nigerian petroleum. Politically, the country is less than sixty years old, but it has had seventeen heads of state, mostly military officers. It has had four separate "republics," including the present and longest-enduring structure, the Fourth Republic, which has been in effect since "democratization" in 1999. Its enigma is captured by Kendhammer, who suggests, "it is possible to see Nigeria as both a rapidly modernizing success story and a deeply troubled state." Dowden adds, "It has been described as a failed state that works."

Nigeria is a consequential state. The country has an estimated 177 million people, making it the most populous state on the continent (Nigerians constitute about one-quarter of the population of sub-Saharan Africa) and eighth in the world overall. Moreover, that population (like much of Africa) is growing rapidly. Epprecht, for instance, reports that "projections show it will surpass the United States within three decades, and by 2080 it will outnumber the whole of Europe, including Russia."

It also has an enormously diverse population, consisting of over 500 distinct tribes speaking over 500 languages. Dowden reports by means of comparison that "Africa has more than 2000 languages and cultures." Nigeria, like most of the African continent, is an incredibly variegated place, and understanding it and dealing with it should take into consideration the contrasts that exist within this country situated in the heart of the Niger River basin.

Nigeria: A Physical and Political Sketch

The study in contrasts that marks Nigeria begins with its geography and demographics. It is located at the elbow of western Africa, where the sub-Saharan coastline that runs from west to east turns southward. To its north are Saharan states, notably Niger and Chad, and the gradual desertification of those countries (the relentless southward incursion of the Sahara Desert) has been accompanied by the invasion of Nigerian territory over the centuries by Arabs and other Muslim people, to the point that Muslims now constitute about half the population. Benin separates Nigeria from more consequential west African states such as Ghana, the Ivory Coast (Côte D'Ivoire), and Liberia. Its southern border is with Cameroon, a country with which it shares demographic characteristics and tribal ties. Notably, nearly 40 percent of Nigeria is arable.

The dominant physical feature of Nigeria is the Niger River, and most notably the Niger Delta, where the river empties through its multiple mouths into the Gulf of Guinea and the Atlantic Ocean. The significance of the delta region, and especially its southeastern extremities, is that this is where Nigeria's petroleum reserves are located. The influence of oil is a ubiquitous factor in Nigeria. Petroleum revenues are the source of most of the economic base in the country and virtually all government funds. As a result, the resource is economically vital to the country and an intensely important internal matter that was the cause of a bloody civil war in the latter part of the 1960s. Petroleum is the basis for most of the corruption that defines most aspects of Nigerian life, especially in the political realm.

Oil is also Nigeria's lingua franca in international politics. The country has proven reserves, as of 2013, of about 37.2 billion barrels of oil, tenth largest in the world. That oil has been exploited very aggressively: at 2.5 million barrels a day, Nigeria's production is twelfth largest in the world. Virtually all this oil is exported to other countries: 2.3 million barrels a day, fifth in the world. Oil is virtually the only Nigerian export, and the leading customer of Nigerian exports has been the United States. When American energy experts talk about reduced dependency on Persian Gulf oil, substituting Nigerian crude is always part of the calculus. Historically, the result, as Dowden summarizes it, is that "Nigeria is one country that western countries, dependent on oil, cannot afford to bully. They shrug off Nigeria's all-pervasive corruption, happy to talk softly and never waving a big stick."

Oil has been both a virtue and a vice for Nigeria, as it is for most of the "petrolist" states (to borrow Thomas Friedman's term for states such as Nigeria, Venezuela, and Russia whose economies are based almost entirely on petroleum revenues). When oil prices are high and demand for oil is expanding, these countries are in the proverbial "catbird seat," with many suitors willing to fill their coffers and the ability to influence their citizens' support by payoffs from oil revenues. When, however, the demand for oil declines and prices fall, that dependency becomes a curse, because it means wealth dries up and government can no longer use great wealth to assuage a population that is otherwise potentially discontented. The period from the initial exploitation of oil until the early twenty-first century represented the upside of oil dependency; the experience since about 2013 has witnessed the negative consequences for all the petrolist states, including Nigeria.

The vicissitudes of oil dependency are exemplified by recent U.S.-Nigerian oil dealings. Prior to 2014, the United States was the leading importer of Nigerian oil, from whom it bought about 10 percent of import needs. The shale oil and gas boom in the United States has removed the need for Nigerian oil (at least for now), and the United States has not imported any Nigerian crude oil since then. India has largely replaced the United States as a purchaser of Nigerian oil, but it is a less desirable partner both because the Indian economy is weaker than that of the United States and because the oil must be shipped around the Cape of Good Hope, a more difficult journey.

Nigeria is clearly a consequential African state by virtue of its population size. As already noted, it is the most populous country on the continent, as well as among the most diverse. Among its roughly 500 tribes, three ethnic groups stand out and are distinguished along racial and religious lines that are manifested in competing political movements. The largest tribe is the Hausa-Fulani of the north, which is an amalgamation of the original inhabitants, the Hausa, and the Fulani, who migrated south from the Sahara. The Hausa-Fulani make up about 29 percent of the country's population, and are almost all Muslim. They have been the dominant political force in Nigeria, and since 1970, only one president of the country has not been a northerner. The Yoruba dominate the southwestern region of Nigeria; they comprise about 21 percent of the national population. The Yoruba tribe contains both Christians and practitioners of traditional, largely animist religions. The third major group are the Igbo (or Ibo) of southeastern Nigeria, including the oil-rich Niger Delta. The Igbo are the most Anglicized part of the population and comprise about 18 percent of the total population. Religiously, about half the Nigerian population is Muslim, 40 percent are Christian, and the rest practice some form of animism.

Since the civil war ended in 1970, the Nigerian economy has focused the most attention on the country both domestically and in the world. Oil production and the ensuing wealth it creates is the major political reality of the country, and pursuing it is both the major political obsession and the source of what Dowden describes as "Nigeria's hilariously brazen corruption" that "puts it in another league" among states. Internationally, Nigeria would scarcely register on the agenda of most foreign offices (including those of the United States) for reasons other than humanitarian disasters. Oil, however, makes Nigeria a place with which one must reckon, even if it is not clear how.

Nigerian political history has been particularly tumultuous. The country was granted its independence in 1960 from Great Britain. In 1967, oil reared its consequential head, and the result was a bloody attempted secession. After that event ended in 1970, the military stepped into the picture and ruled the country until 1999, when civilian rule was reinstituted. The country has remained in civilian hands since. As with all things in Nigeria, none of these periods has been without excitement.

The territory that is now Nigeria has a long history that dates back to at least 700 BCE. In the period of the European Middle Ages, an advanced form of civilization arose in the Yoruba areas of southwest Nigeria, and Muslims from the Saharan north began to arrive and push southward in the last thousand years. European incursion began in the fifteenth and sixteenth centuries with the arrival of Portuguese and British slave traders, who enlisted alliances with coastal tribes to raid the interior for slaves and who shifted the traditional balance of tribal powers by paying those who did their bidding with, among other things, weaponry that was used for additional chattel procurement. The British, operating from a base in Lagos, gradually extended their sway inward and established a colony that became the physical basis for modern Nigeria.

British colonial rule ended on October 1, 1960, when Nigerian independence was established. Three years later, Nigeria declared the First Republic, which lasted until 1967. The republic collapsed when the Igbo eastern region of the country—where virtually all the petroleum is located—declared its independence as the Republic of Biafra. The attempted secession was economic, racial, and religious. Part of the rationale was that the revenues being generated by oil in Biafra were not being distributed fairly to the region but were instead being confiscated to support the Muslim northern regions, which also largely controlled the military and government. It was racial, because the rebels were almost all Igbo, and during the bloody conduct of hostilities, as many as one to three million, mostly Igbo, died, often from starvation because international relief efforts (including the receipts from a Biafra relief concert by the Beatles in Shea Stadium, then home of the New York Mets) could not get to refugees. It was also religious, because, as already noted, the Igbo were almost all Christian, a major reason for the international outpouring of support for them, and the Nigerian forces that opposed the secession were mostly Muslim. The Biafra War ended when the secessionists formally surrendered on January 12, 1970.

Nigerian politics remained volatile for the rest of the century. For most of the period between 1970 and 1999, the country experienced military rule, as a series of generals, predominantly Muslims from the north, overthrew one another to control the country. The Second and Third Republics were brief interludes in this pattern, which was finally broken when democratization was declared and leaders were chosen electorally. The Fourth Republic, which remains in force, "has lasted far longer than any previous attempt at civilian rule," as Kendhammer points out. In the early years, it was not clear that things had changed much, and Dowden, writing in 2009, still declared, "The coming of democracy in 1999, did not change the Nigerian system: the king is dead, long-live-whoever-has-got-the-oil-money."

The political equation changed after 2013. One major factor was the change in the role of oil. One cause was violent unrest, which Meagher describes: "The oil producing region of the Niger Delta spent the first decade of democratic rule engulfed in an insurgency that cut oil production by more than 25 percent and spilled insecurity into neighboring states." This unrest remains part of the political fabric in the country and is intensified by the fall of the price of oil and the American withdrawal from the Nigerian market. At the same time, the Boko Haram emergence in the north has added to instability.

The effect of this change has been to break the stranglehold that the military enjoyed between 1970 and 1999. In the early 1970s, Nigeria became an oil-producing power. The abundance and the comparative ease of transporting Nigerian oil to Europe or North America are particularly attractive as an alternative to Middle East oil. It does not have to round the Cape of Good Hope at the southern tip of Africa (a cost factor) or the Suez Canal (a geopolitical factor since the 1956 Suez War interrupted access and ongoing Egyptian-Israeli conflict made its reliable use problematical), to increase its attractiveness to oil consumers. These factors, combined with a general desire of many Western countries to reduce their dependence on Persian Gulf oil, have continued to form the basis for an attraction toward Nigeria and its petroleum.

In the period of military rule, oil also provided the underpinning of military coups and countercoups to gain control of oil revenues, often for the personal benefit of particular generals and their entourages. The devil's combination of gaudy oil revenues and the culturally enhanced proclivity for corruption for individual enrichment affected both the civilian and military communities, reinforced by tribal and regional differences and the desire to be certain one's own ethno-geographic region was not deprived of its perceived share of the resource pie. The result was that the quality of governance did not improve markedly when the generals ruled and that the growing pot of oil revenues increased and made the stakes even higher than they were before.

Civilians have ruled the country since. This distinction would be more dramatic were it not for the fact that many of the leading politicians in the country—including those at the top—are military figures who have changed into civilian attire rather than being true nonmilitary figures, and that most of the political alignments within the country reflect the same basic political cleavages as before. What has changed more than anything else in the period since 1999 is that centrifugal forces along ethnic, regional, and religious lines have sharpened at the same time that Nigeria's oil-driven wealth (and hence government resources) has shriveled with the worldwide decline in the price of oil. The result has been a possibly temporary diminution of Nigeria's place in the world and its relative standing in American foreign policy.

Elections in 2015 may have signaled a political turning point. A new political party, the All Progressives' Congress (APC), won the election, which, as Kendhammer points out, "marks the first electoral turnover from one party to another in Nigeria's history." The APC represents a coalition of regions and religions. The president, Muhammadu Buhari, is a northerner and Muslim who retired as a major general and led the country from 1983 to 1985—nothing unusual in Nigerian politics. His vice president, however, is retired General Olusegun Obasanjo, who ruled from 1976 to 1979 but is a southerner and a Christian. He is the only non-northerner ever to be president of the country, under the Fourth Republic (from 1999 to 2007). The new regime thus crosses the traditional divide between religions and regions that, as Kendhammer adds, set the stage for reconciliation: "the most important thing Buhari must do is to reach out to citizens of all religious, ethnic, and regional backgrounds." In testament to the start the new regime promised, President Buhari paid a state visit to Washington at the invitation of President Obama in 2015.

Basic U.S.-Nigerian Relations

The United States and Nigeria have maintained close and cordial relations for most of the time that Nigeria has been an independent state. There have been times, usually associated with political repression or the violent suppression of uprisings (e.g., the Biafra War of 1967–1970), when those relations have been strained, but these periods have been the exceptions rather than the rule. There is a basic synergism between the two countries at the interpersonal level that undergirds their relations. Poll data from 2012 revealed that 77 percent of Nigerians approved of American leadership, and in 2013, a BBC World Service poll reported that 59 percent view America's influence positively. Over a million Nigerians and Nigerian Americans live in the United States. Nigeria is America's largest trading partner in Africa.

There are policy concerns that enliven and sometimes complicate relations between the two countries. Three overlapping categories of concern stand out. The first is curbing and reconciling internal violence and instability in the country, a problem that is most dramatically associated with the government's struggle against Boko Haram. The second is economic development and is most closely associated with the related problems of oil and its revenues, enormous income disparities, and corruption. The third is political stabilization and democratization, a long-term goal that requires some settlement of the other two problems.

Internal Violence and Instability: Boko Haram

Regionally and religiously based sources of conflict, often overlapping and interconnected, have long been a primary characteristic of the mosaic of Nigerian life. Since 2002, much of that violence has centered on the emergence of the Islamic fundamentalist group Boko Haram, but the problem is more diverse than that.

Potentially, instability affects virtually all of Nigeria. As Lavinder points out, "Nigeria faces three distinct crises, with one common thread: the failure of governance." The ongoing military campaign against Boko Haram in the Muslim north is the most publicized and dangerous of the current galaxy of violent or potentially violent situations. In addition, she lists "a conflict between farmers and herdsmen in the middle" of the country over control of territory and a "renewed insurgency in the south—in the Niger

Delta region—[that] threatens to deplete oil production and government revenue." The roots of the southern difficulties have eerily similar grounds to those of the 1967–1970 civil war. Lavinder suggests that "the threat of a southern secession from Nigeria could be on the horizon," led by "Biafran activists" who are "campaigning for an independent state." This aspect of instability is not currently at a very active stage, but given the prospects of something like the attempted Biafra secession in 1967 on oil, it could be a very consequential and bloody event. As Meagher notes, the government's responses have generally been violent: "From the Niger Delta to Boko Haram, legitimate expressions of discontent have been radicalized by brutal repression."

The Boko Haram insurrection overshadows all other violent problems. The organization's name is derived from the Hausa language and is generally translated as "Western education is sinful." It came into being in 2002 under the leadership of a Muslim cleric named Mohammed Yusef, a Sunni fundamentalist preaching the need for a Wahhabi-styled government based in sharia law on religious and political grounds. Its early appeals included the dismantling of the secular Nigerian state and its replacement with a sharia-based religious regime. The group also refers to itself as Jama'atu Ahlis Sunna Lidda'awati Wal-Jihad, which translates as "People Committed to the Propagation of the Prophet's Teachings and Jihad." Among its more secular goals was to root out rampant government corruption and to guarantee that more oil revenue went to the Muslim north. It was not specifically violent. As Meagher points out, "It started out in the northeastern city of Maiduguri, in Borno State, as a religious community offering education, basic services, and informal livelihoods to the disaffected." Many of these goals, which are not inherently violent, are widely accepted among northern Muslims, making it more difficult for Nigerian forces to operate successfully in the northern regions where Boko Haram has control or influence.

In its early days, Boko Haram was more an annoyance than a threat, but that changed in 2009. In 2003, the army moved to destroy its base, and it went essentially dormant until July 2009. In that month, a Boko Haram uprising broke out and spread to other northern states, including Kana and Yobe. Government security forces retaliated by killing more than 800 members of the group and imprisoning others. Most notably, Yusef was captured and subsequently died in a government prison. Depending on whether Boko Haram or the government is doing the accounting, he was shot while attempting to escape or was the victim of an "extrajudicial execution." His death was recorded on YouTube, and in reaction, "tipped what started as a religious protest movement among the marginalized into a full-blown insurgency," again according to Meagher.

Boko Haram reemerged in July 2010 under the leadership of a more radical successor, Abubaker Shekau. The new leader is far more radical than

Yusef, and almost immediately added to both the violence of the movement and its international character. During the next four years, attacks by Boko Haram fighters against government forces and installations increased, as did the militancy of its demands and international recognition. The organization achieved international notoriety on April 14, 2014, when Boko Haram militants attacked a school in Chibok, Borno, and kidnapped 276 schoolgirls, who were taken into the bush where they became the subject of global concern and focus on the problems of Nigeria. The stated goals of the insurgents were to restore the Islamic purity to the girls, generally in their early teens, although many of them reportedly were forced to "marry" and bear children by their captors. As of late summer 2016, most remained unaccounted for despite highly publicized but ineffective actions by government forces to rescue them.

Boko Haram entered the international terrorist orbit in 2015. On March 7, the organization pledged allegiance to the Islamic State, which had already become active in Saharan countries such as Libya and had declared the expansion of the Caliphate to African Muslim countries. By its pledge, Boko Haram added itself to the caliphate movement headed by al-Baghdadi in Syria, where the parent organization had been experiencing territorial setbacks that had shrunk the size and population of IS. This merger has not been entirely successful and remains in a state of flux.

Part of the division seems to be a tactical clash about how to expand the caliphate. Although IS has been notorious for its brutality and treatment of those it considers apostates, Boko Haram's attacks against other tribesmen in the northern region have been even bloodier to the point of alienating even the leadership of IS. Some of the basis for the disagreement is undoubtedly attributable to a personality clash between the leaders, al-Baghdadi and Abubaker Shekau, and indeed, on August 3, 2016, IS announced that the true leader of Boko Haram was Abu Musab Al-Barnawi, the son of martyred leader Yusef, a claim denied by Shekau's supporters. As of late 2016, the outcome of this disagreement and its ultimate effect remains unknown. What is certain, however, is that Boko Haram remains a viable insurgent group that appeals to more Nigerians than the government may want to admit, and that much of northern, Muslim Nigeria is effectively a Boko Haram sanctuary, if not a de facto liberated region.

The effort to defeat Boko Haram has been notably unsuccessful. The government's efforts have been described as inept and half-hearted, and there is clearly support for at least some of the organization's aspirations among many Nigerian Muslims. Former U.S. ambassador to Nigeria John Campbell summarizes the appeal of the insurgents: "Many Northern Nigerian Muslims are deeply hostile to the sectarian state . . . as a continuation of British colonialism, with indigenous masters merely replacing the British and with values and behavior antithetical to Islam." To many of

these Nigerians, there is support for the goals of the insurgent organization, as Campbell (2016) describes them: "the destruction of the Nigerian
secular state, the end of Western influence, the creation of a 'pure' Islamic
state, and 'justice for the poor' through sharia law." Since half of the Nigerian population is Muslim, there is a very large potential support base
for these positions, the resolution of which will prove difficult at best and
may be impossible.

Oil, Economic Development, and Corruption

At least some of the support for Boko Haram has its roots in the venal-
ity of the secular government and especially its handling of the Nigerian
economy. As already described, Nigeria is one of the most corrupt countries
in the world, with a government that has routinely led the looting of that
economy for the benefit of the political elite. In macroeconomic terms,
Nigeria is one of the shining beacons of the African continent, but that
development is by no means equitably enjoyed by the population: the over
60 percent of Nigerians who live on $1 a day or less comprise almost 110
million desperately deprived citizens. This disparity is why Nigeria has the
third most impoverished population in the world after China and India.

As the section heading suggests, there are three basic variables in the
Nigerian developmental equation. Since its discovery, petroleum exploitation and the revenues it produces have been the major element in the
Nigerian economy. As in most petrolist states, however, its influence has
been a mixed blessing. In macroeconomic terms, oil revenues have inflated
national GDP to the point that, on the eve of the crash in global oil prices,
Nigeria had passed the Republic of South Africa as the continent's biggest
economy. That growth at the macro level, however, has had decidedly
different effects at the micro level. In essence, oil revenues have not only
fueled growth; they have also stimulated the acquisitive instinct among in-
fluential and powerful Nigerians. Epprecht's citation of the 44 percent rise
in the number of millionaires between 2008 and 2014 is a testimony to the
victory of greed at a time of strangling levels of utter poverty for most Nigerians. These disparities and the levels of corruption that accompany them
are part of the antipathy that many Nigerians—especially in the Muslim
north—hold toward the government and Abuja. The collapse of oil prices
has burst some individual bubbles, and like other countries so dependent
on oil for national wealth, its continuation will continue to trickle down
and affect the Nigerian economy and political system.

The United States is part of this problem. As the U.S. State Department
proudly announces in "U.S. Relations with Nigeria," the United States is
the largest foreign investor in Nigeria, "with U.S. direct foreign investment largely concentrated in the petroleum/mining and wholesale trade

sectors." The United States does view Nigerian oil as an alternative to Persian Gulf oil in its energy and national security strategies, because that oil contributes to American energy independence—especially from Gulf states. At the same time, the United States has quit buying that oil as abundant supplies of petroleum are becoming available from sources such as North American shale and natural gas, relegating Nigeria to a backup role in American strategy. This shift may make excellent sense for the United States, but it does nothing to improve conditions in Nigeria. It also probably weakens American leverage to induce other change within Nigeria in both the economic and political arenas.

The need for developmental efforts to stabilize the country is tied to Nigeria's future evolution and to its rampant corruption. The problem for the Nigerians is how to nurture development that is acceptable and equitable for the large and incredibly diverse population in the country. It is a simple fact that efforts in any ethno-religious region will be interpreted negatively in others. Efforts to strengthen the economy and polity in the north, for instance, will be greeted with derision among Boko Haram supporters as bribes to weaken the movement toward a religious, sharia-based political system, and cries from the south that northern politicians are stealing oil revenues generated in the south for their own benefit. Attempts to assist southerners to lessen their secessionist proclivities will be greeted with derision in the north and southwest. It is a difficult, and in the short run, a negative-sum game made worse by dwindling oil revenues.

The Need for Political Stabilization

As noted, there are insurrectionists and separatists in all parts of the country who form the tip of the iceberg of the lack of national unity and nationalist sentiment. As so much of Africa, Nigeria was born with a nationalist deficit where most Nigerians considered themselves as Hausa or Igbo or Yoruba before they thought of themselves as Nigerians. Little has occurred since to cause a transfer of primary loyalty to the country itself, and until that occurs, Nigerian politics will remain fractious and parochial. The 2015 formation of the Buhari government, including the inclusion of Obasanjo, represents an attempt to broaden the constituent base for the central government, and the gradual transfer of loyalty from more parochial ethno-religious and geographical bases to a true sense of Nigerian identity is clearly a necessary priority. As Kendhammer points out, "Nigerians have long ranked near the bottom among Africans in their prioritization of national over ethnic or religious identities."

Current conditions reinforce the divisiveness of Nigerian politics. It may be true, as Dowden maintains, that "religion reinforces some of Nigeria's political divisions but is not a cause of the division," but the north-south split is largely a religious divide, and the most spectacular manifestation of that division, the Boko Haram insurrection, has its bases in the Islamic fundamentalist rejection of secular rule. The volatile condition of the petroleum industry, manifested both in terms of the economic squeeze created by the decline in oil prices and the battle over which individuals and groups get most of those revenues, also has politically divisive connotations. The possibility of another attempt by Biafran nationalists to secede would certainly create a violent government response.

U.S. Policy Options

The problems of Nigeria are enormous, and most of them represent difficulties that outsiders, including Americans, do not understand or have much ability to influence in any decisive way. Most of the root problems are internal, the reflections of the artificiality of the Nigerian state and what is now moving toward a sixty-year inability to reconcile and overcome the divisions that existed at statehood. The structure of ethnicity, geography, and religion reinforces these divisions, and especially as militant Islam has spread southward into the region, it has exacerbated the considerable divisions that would exist anyway. Layered upon these sources of division is a structurally misaligned national society where a very few are rewarded lavishly and the majority toil in extreme grinding poverty. The ubiquitous influence of corruption underlies this structure and helps perpetuate it. These are all problems that everyone knows and understands, but there is very little anybody but the Nigerians can do about it. Those who benefit most luxuriantly are unlikely to voluntarily surrender their advantages and perquisites. The situation forms a vicious circle that has been playing out for over a half century.

There is very little the United States can do to change these conditions. When Nigerian politics become violent or elections are clearly fraudulent, the United States roundly condemns the misdeed and exacts small penalties, but as Dowden reminds us, Nigeria's possession of large and available oil reserves means that punitive threats are relatively hollow. Nigeria cannot be bullied into better behavior because they might retaliate by turning off the spigot. The United States has not bought Nigerian oil since 2014, but it might have to sometime in the future as an alternative to going hat in hand to the Saudis. The U.S. government knows this, and so do the Nigerians. This dynamic severely limits the leverage the United States has. If there is a basic, underlying desire that the United States has for Nigeria and U.S.-Nigerian relations, it is premised on peace and stability in Africa's most populous country. Political reform and democratization are the goals, but it is not clear how they can be pursued effectively if the Nigerians themselves will not or cannot pursue them as well.

The one concrete and pressing matter is Boko Haram, for two reasons. One is that the revolt is growing, both within Nigeria and into surrounding countries. The formation of joint efforts between Nigeria and neighbors such as Niger has simply caused the insurrectionists to widen their operations into the surrounding states. The affiliation with other radical Islamist movements and the declaration of an African caliphate with Boko Haram at its center is geopolitically disturbing, and it elevates the problem from a local threat to one that is part of the wider American concern with global terrorism and Islamic extremism. The other part of the problem is that the local parties have not been particularly effective in dealing with the Boko Haram threat on their own. Largely ineffective efforts to locate and free the Chibok schoolgirls remain a vivid reminder of the ineffectiveness of Nigerian military efforts in a hostile part of the country where many of the insurgents' goals have widespread support. The United States has tried to provide aid to the Nigerian military through the U.S. African Command's provision of supplies and Special Operations Forces (SOFs) to help train the Nigerians and forces from neighboring countries, but these efforts remain mired in controversy as well. Nigerian complaints that the United States is not giving them access to U.S. helicopters is a recent example.

The most basic source of American inability to influence Nigeria, however, arises from the place of Nigeria in the hierarchy of American foreign policy priorities. Africa is indeed at or near the bottom of U.S. foreign policy priorities and always has been. Nigerian petroleum and sheer size make it one of the most important places on the continent for America, but as long as the oil is kept flowing (or the spigot can be turned on again), Nigeria is not at the center of attention. When it is, it is for negative reasons: a program to apply President Bush's anti-AIDS campaign to the country a decade ago or a response to the potential spread of Boko Haram more generally. Unless such disasters arise, Nigeria remains at a low level in the American national and foreign policy consciousness.

CONCLUSION

African countries and the continent as a whole remain at the periphery of mainstream international relations and thus the concentrated foreign policy concerns of the major powers, including the United States. The European countries that colonized the continent and produced the crazy-quilt political map that defines the states of the continent have a greater interest, but they also bear the greater responsibility for the African condition, since they produced the "concocted countries" (Dowden's term) that are the rule rather than the exception there.

Africa has been ignored because it has been ignorable. Hardly any of the states on the continent are major players in world affairs. They have been isolated primarily because of their backwardness and lack of development. No African states pose a military threat to anyone beyond the continent's shores, with small exceptions such as the Somali pirates of the last decade. No African economic powers imperil the world economic order. Any economic clout possessed tends to be because Africans possess natural resources—Nigerian oil, diamonds and gold from Zimbabwe, some South African manufactures—but that is about all. When economically rising states in the developing world are mentioned, Nigeria and South Africa are the only states that generally make the lists. For the most part, African states are very poor, very divided, and very short of prospects to change their situations in the short to medium terms. The desperate plights of Sudan and South Sudan are close to the African norm.

Africa is, in other words, geopolitically marginal. Boko Haram, as a manifestation of the spread of Islamic extremism, represents a partial exception if it manages to spread more widely toward non-Muslim central Africa. If it remains confined to the Muslim hinterlands of Saharan countries or the countries of the Sahel, containing it and hoping for it to shrivel and blow away is probably as much as the international community will do. Otherwise, the interest of the United States and other developed countries will remain marginal. There will be continued hortatory pleas and token monetary contributions to efforts to stabilize and democratize African states. When humanitarian disasters occur such as Ebola or AIDS breakouts (and especially if they might spread untreated to the developed world), there will be major efforts at containment. There will not be massive economic development transfers to Africa from the West because those actions are unpopular in countries that feel they have important domestic priorities that require attention. Should the United States invest billions of dollars in developmental assistance to South Sudan, or should it use the money to cut taxes or rebuild the American infrastructure? Unfortunately for Africans, the answer is easy and not to their advantage.

The problem is that Africa and its problems are not going away. If anything, they will get worse. African populations are exploding, and the demographics show that in the reasonably near future, Africa and Asia will have over half the world's population. At the same time, populations in most of the developed countries are stagnant or declining, with negative implications for the work force, productivity, and hence prosperity. Europe is already experiencing this problem, and the only solution is to import workers to replenish diminishing domestic supplies. Until now, many of these foreign immigrants have come from the Middle East and have created problems with which European governments have struggled. The United

States has replenished its manpower supply from south of the border, but that has created a different set of problems, discussed in chapter 6. The great—and growing—pool of humanity is African, and that pool will have to be tapped in coming years. When that occurs, then maybe Africa will rise on the foreign policy agenda.

STUDY QUESTIONS

1. What are the general characteristics of Africa that help shape its contemporary politics? Relate these to the colonial experience, including the process of decolonization and the nature of the states created at the time of independence. Include a discussion of multinationalism and artificial states in your answer.
2. Trace the history of Sudan up to and including the secession of South Sudan. Was there ever a compelling reason for a state of Sudan to exist? What are the bases of cleavage both within the original country and since secession, including ongoing internal disputes and relations with newly independent South Sudan?
3. Has its secession from Sudan resulted in stability for South Sudan? Why not? Discuss in terms of the intertribal politics of the country and variables such as oil and the status of Abyei.
4. What is U.S. policy toward the two Sudans? Why is it different, and how? Why does the United States get along better with South Sudan than Sudan itself? What limits the degree to which the United States gets involved in the two countries?
5. Discuss the role of oil in Nigeria. What does it mean to describe Nigeria as a "petrolist" state? How does oil ultimately contribute to Nigeria's internal difficulties? How is oil wealth simultaneously a blessing and a curse for Nigeria?
6. Discuss Nigerian demographics. What are the basic regional differences in ethnic and religious terms, and how do they make governance more difficult than it might otherwise be?
7. What is the geopolitical attractiveness of Nigerian oil for the United States in its contemplation of energy futures? How does this calculation increase the leverage Nigeria has in its relations with the United States and other developed countries?
8. What are the basic interests of the United States in Nigeria? How do they compare in importance with American interests in other parts of the world discussed in this volume? Are Nigeria and Sudan/South Sudan symbols of the marginality of Africa in American foreign policy? What must happen for this perception to change?

BIBLIOGRAPHY

Achebe, Chinua. *The Trouble with Nigeria*. Rev. ed. Enugu, Nigeria: Fourth Dimension, 2000.

Arnold, Matthew, and Matthew LeRiche. *South Sudan: From Revolution to Independence*. New York: Oxford University Press, 2012.

Bourne, Richard. *A New History of a Turbulent Century*. London: Zed, 2015.

Campbell, John. "Civil War within Nigerian Islam." *The Cipher Brief* (Council on Foreign Affairs online), August 25, 2016.

———. *Nigeria: Dancing on the Brink*. Updated ed. Lanham, MD: Rowman & Littlefield, 2013.

Collins, Robert O. *A History of Modern Sudan*. Cambridge, UK: Cambridge University Press, 2008.

Copnall, James. *A Poisonous Thorn in Our Hearts: Sudan and South Sudan's Bitter and Incomplete Divorce*. London: Hurst, 2014.

Dagne, Ted. *The Republic of South Sudan: Opportunities and Challenges for Africa's Newest Country*. Washington, DC: Congressional Research Service, 2011.

DeWaal, Alexander, and Julie Flint. *Darfur: A New History of a Long War*. London: Zed, 2008.

Dowden, Richard. *Africa: Altered States, Ordinary Miracles*. New York: PublicAffairs, 2009.

Epprecht, Marc. "Africa's New Political Homophobia." *Current History* 113, no. 763 (May 2014): 203–4.

Falola, Toyin, and Matthew M. Heaton. *A History of Nigeria*. Cambridge, UK: Cambridge University Press, 2008.

Feinstein, Lee. *Darfur and Beyond: What Is Needed to Prevent Mass Atrocities*. New York: Council on Foreign Relations Books, 2007.

Finian, William W., Jr. "Darfur and the Politics of Altruism." *Current History* 106, no. 700 (May 2007): 235–36.

Friedman, Thomas L. "The First Law of Petropolitics." *Foreign Policy*, May/June 2006, 36–44.

Fund for Peace. "Fragile State Index, 2016." Washington, DC: Fund for Peace, 2016.

Jok, Jok Madut. *Sudan: Race, Religion, and Violence*. London: Oneworld, 2015.

Kendhammer, Brandon. "Nigeria's New Democratic Dawn?" *Current History* 114, no. 772 (May 2015): 170–76.

Lavinder, Kaitlin. "Niger Delta Militants Compound Nigeria's Security Crisis." *The Cipher Brief* (Council on Foreign Relations online), August 4, 2016.

Levi, Patricia, and Zawaiah Abdul Latif. *Sudan*. 2nd ed. New York: Marshall Cavendish, 2008.

Meagher, Kate. "The Jobs Crisis Behind Nigeria's Unrest." *Current History* 112, no. 754 (May 2013): 169–74.

Natsios, Andrew S. *Sudan, South Sudan, and Darfur: What Everyone Needs to Know*. New York: Oxford University Press, 2012.

Page, Matthew. "Instead of Cutting Waste, Nigeria Racks Up Debt to Replace Oil Revenues." *The Cipher Brief* (Council on Foreign Relations online), March 28, 2016.

Piombo, Jessica. "US Africa Policy: Rhetoric Versus Reality." *Current History* 111, no. 745 (May 2012): 194–97.

Prendergast, John, and Colin Thomas-Jensen. "Sudan: A State on the Brink." *Current History* 108, no. 718 (May 2009): 208–13.

Smith, Mike. *Boko Haram: Inside Nigeria's Unholy War*. London: Tauris, 2016.

Snow, Donald M. *National Security*. 6th ed. New York: Routledge, 2017.

Straus, Scott. "Darfur and the Genocide Debate." *Foreign Affairs* 84, no. 1 (January/February 2005): 125–33.

Teny-Dhurgon, Riek Machar. *South Sudan: A History of Political Domination*. Philadelphia: University of Pennsylvania African Studies Center, 1995.

Turse, Nick. *Next Time They'll Come to Count the Dead: War and Survival in South Sudan*. Chicago: Haymarket, 2016.

U.S. Department of State. *Country Note: South Sudan*. Washington, DC: U.S. Department of State, 2016.

———. "U.S. Relations with Nigeria." U.S. Department of State Bureau of African Affairs, June 20, 2016.

———. "U.S. Relations with South Sudan." U.S. Department of State Bureau of African Affairs, September 16, 2015.

———. "U.S. Relations with Sudan." U.S. Department of State Bureau of African Affairs, November 3, 2015.

Williamson, Richard S. "Sudan on the Cusp." *Current History* 110, no. 736 (May 2011): 171–76.

Index